Quilts in Modern Color

CREATING OMBRÉ PALETTES

14 PROJECTS

Amber Elliot

stashBOOKS®

an imprint of C&T Publishing

Publisher: Amy Barrett-Daffin

Creative Director: Gailen Runge

Senior Editor: Roxane Cerda

Editor: Madison Moore

Technical Editor: Helen Frost

Cover/Book Designer: April Mostek

Production Coordinator: Tim Manibusan

Illustrators: Amber Elliot, Kirstie Pettersen

Photography Coordinator: Rachel Ackley

Front cover photography by Amy Wennerlind

Photography by Amy Wennerlind, unless otherwise noted

Published by Stash Books, an imprint of C&T Publishing, Inc.,

P.O. Box 1456, Lafayette, CA 94549

Library of Congress Cataloging-in-Publication Data

Names: Elliot, Amber, 1988- author.

Title: Quilts in modern color, creating ombré palettes : 14 projects / Amber Elliot.

Description: Lafayette, CA : Stash Books, an imprint of C&T publishing, [2025] | Summary: "Learn to craft stunning contemporary color palettes to elevate your gorgeous modern quilts! This stunning collection includes ten full size quilts and four smaller quilt projects that all fit together in a beautiful gradient suite. The quilts offer a variety of design elements and skill levels, from simple and classic design elements to hypnotic medallion projects"-- Provided by publisher.

Identifiers: LCCN 2024040254 | ISBN 9781644035290 (trade paperback) | ISBN 9781644035306 (ebook)

Subjects: LCSH: Quilting--Patterns.

Classification: LCC TT835 .E4653 2025 | DDC 746.46/041--dc23/eng/20241101

LC record available at https://lccn.loc.gov/2024040254

Printed in China

10 9 8 7 6 5 4 3 2 1

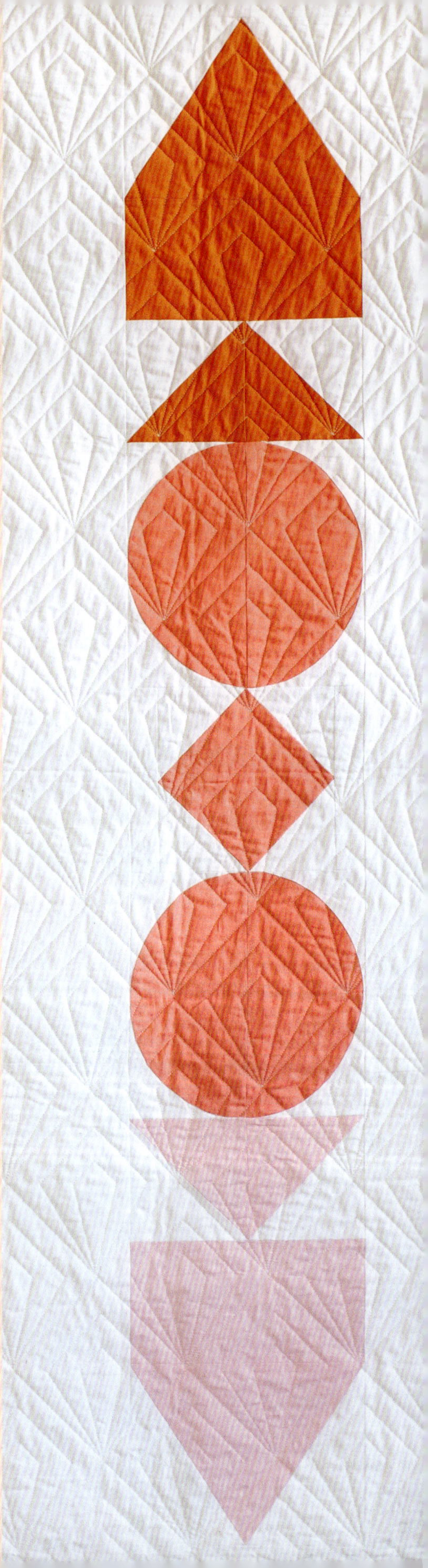

Dedication

For Thomas, Alder, and Lily.

Acknowledgments

First and foremost, I'd like to thank my husband and family. Without their support, this book could not have been written, and I am so grateful for how generous they are with their time and energy. My dear friend Justine, who has always been there for me on this journey and supported my work: you're the best!

Next, I want to extend a huge thank you to everyone in my quilting community. I've been so happy to find such an unbelievably talented and welcoming group of people, and am eternally grateful for their support and kindness. To my quilty colleagues (you know who you are)—you keep me sane through the insanity of running a business. To anyone who has supported my business in any way, whether sending me a kind social media message or making my patterns— you are the reason this book exists and why I am able to live my dream. Thank you, thank you, thank you.

Additionally, I'd like to thank Kacey Crutchfield for her excellent technical editing skills, Riley Blake Designs for providing the most gorgeous fabric for this book, Amy Wennerlind for her fantastic photography, and Jennifer Smith of Jenn B Quilts and Lilo Whitener—Fey of Trace Creek Quilting for their gorgeous long—arm quilting skills. Finally, my team of testers and production assistants: Christina West, Katie Dean, Heather Heck, Breanna Gaudaur, and Beth Pacyk.

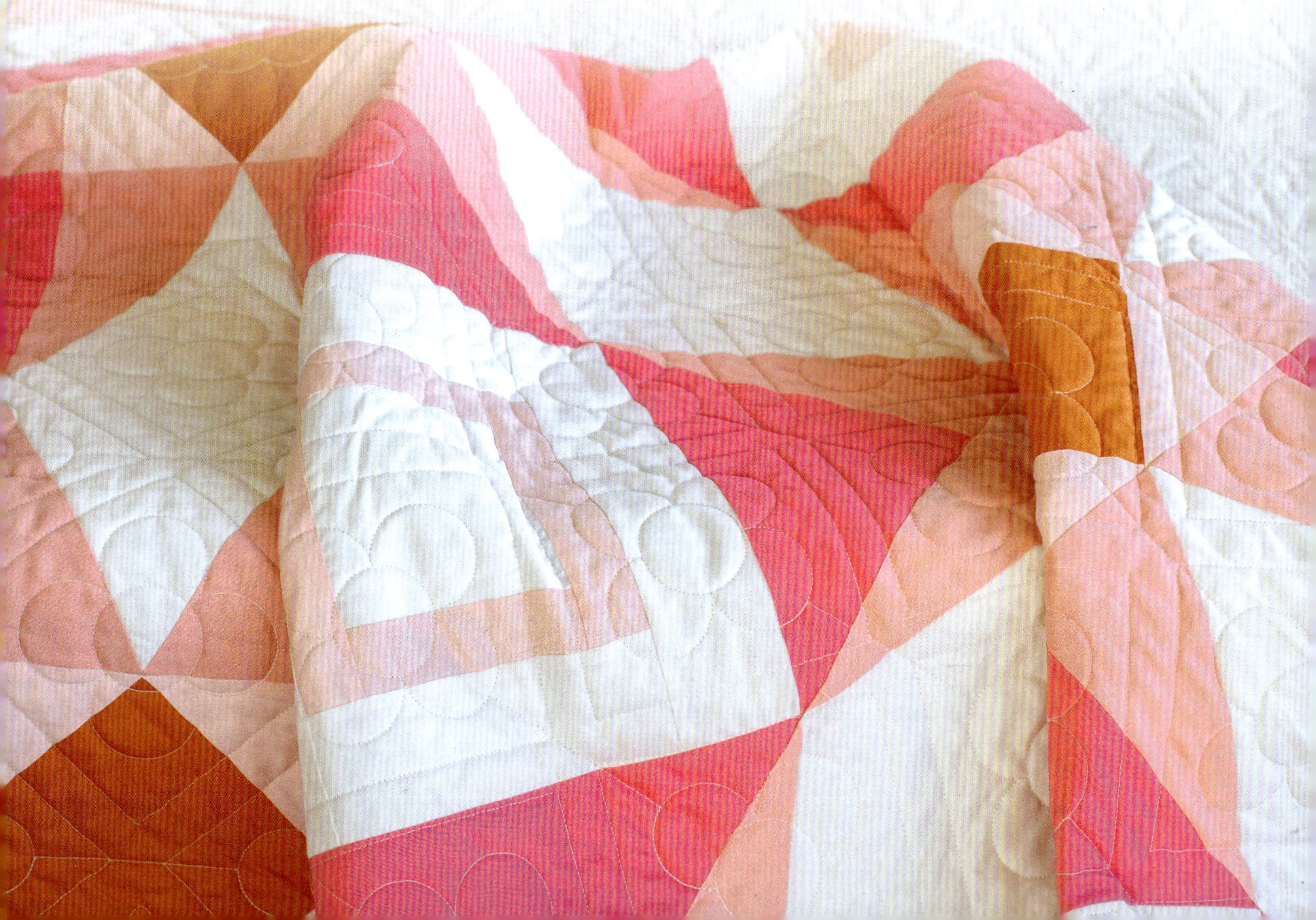

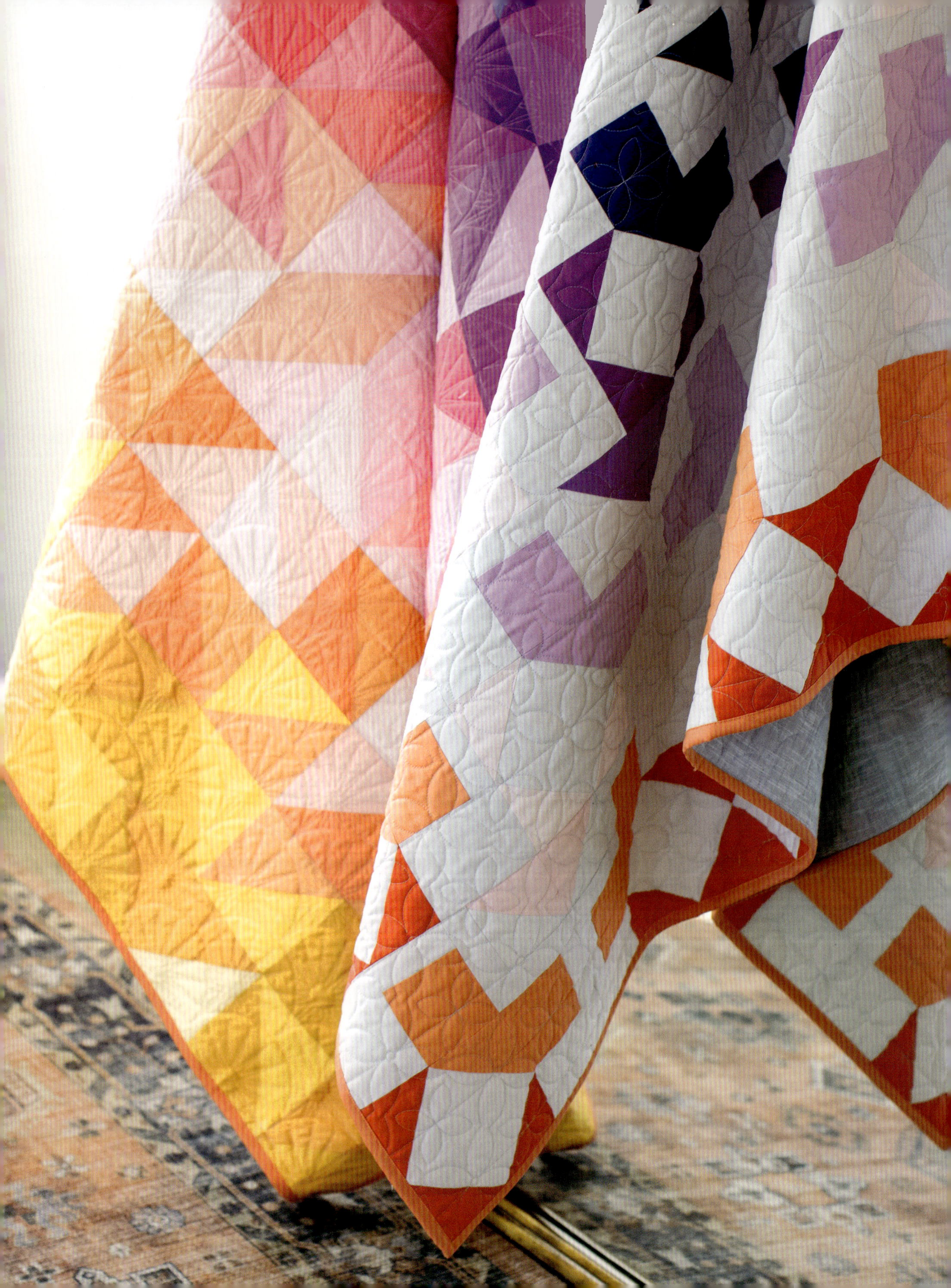

Contents

Introduction

I have a confession; I've often struggled with putting together fabric pulls for my quilts. While I have an art background and a solid understanding of color theory, coming up with fabric pulls that just felt *right* was a skill that seemed to elude me.

But, once I started basing fabric pulls on gradients, everything changed. Looking at fabric through the lens of gradients—both in hue and value—completely altered how I approached the process of creating color palettes. My love of ombré quilts was born. Many of my quilts utilize an ombré color scheme to some degree, even if it's subtle. I find that whenever I'm struggling with a color palette, going back to a gradient scheme never fails me.

In this book, you will learn how to construct your own color palettes for gorgeous gradient quilts. We will talk about different types of gradients, using the color wheel to find the perfect color combinations, and more. Most of the patterns fall within the confident beginner to intermediate range, and assume you have basic quilting knowledge and skills. If you've been looking for a project to try curves for the first time, there are some great options for you in this book! Several of the patterns use templates (either for curves or for more interesting shapes), so you'll have some opportunities to sharpen your template skills.

I hope that after reading this book, you will have the confidence and skills to create perfect ombré palettes for all of your quilt—making adventures!

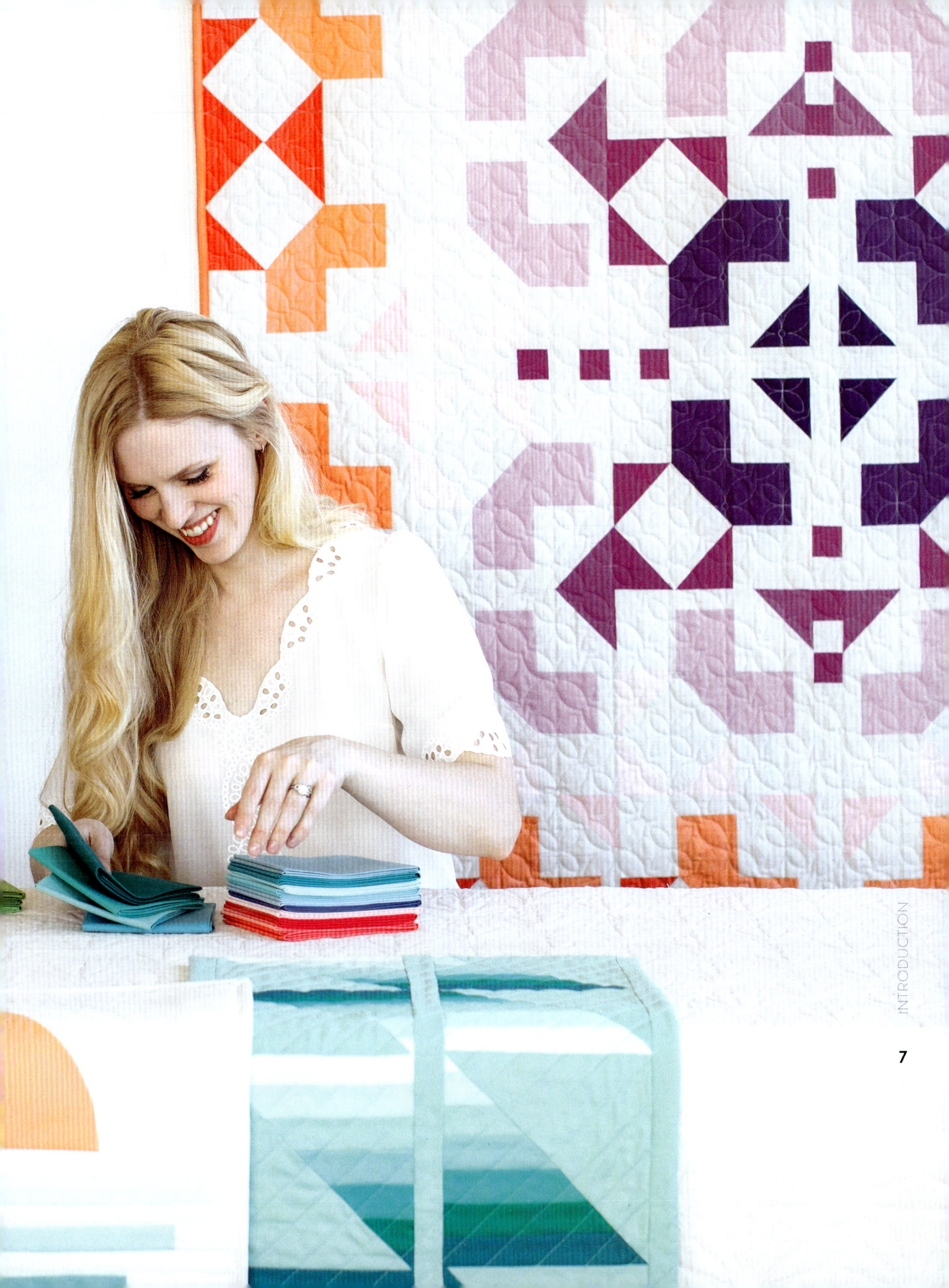

Tools and Materials

Tools

This book assumes a basic knowledge of quilting and that you have the required basic tools: a cutting mat, sewing machine, rotary cutter, and basic ruler. There are a few extra tools that I recommend as well to make your quilting experience safer, more efficient, or just more enjoyable!

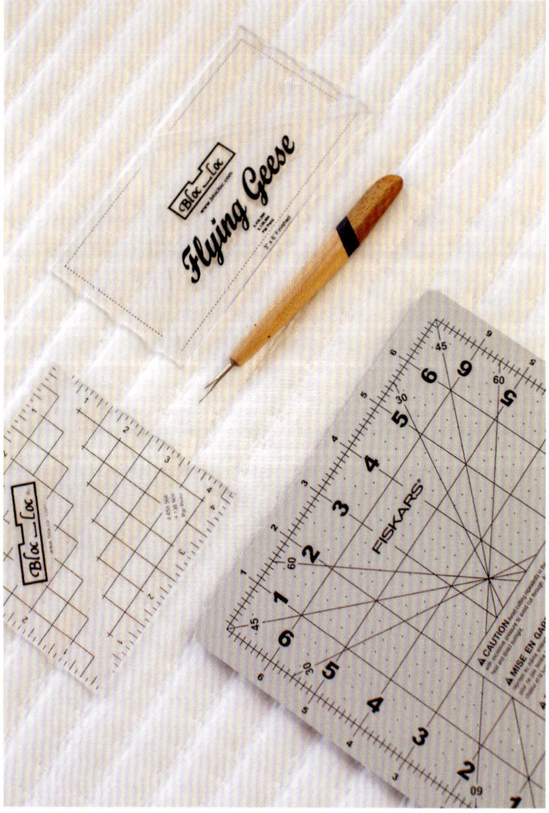

BLOC LOC RULER

Bloc Loc rulers have a special slot that holds them in place as you trim completed blocks. They are a bit expensive, but I use them constantly, and they have saved me so much time (and a few fingertip close—calls as well). I have a set of the Half-Square triangle rulers as well as the Flying Geese set, and they make trimming a snap.

ROTATING CUTTING MAT

Pair a rotating cutting mat with the Bloc Loc rulers, and your trimming time will be cut in half. Rotating mats don't need to be expensive or fancy; I have an 8″ one that works just fine for the majority of my blocks.

RULER HANDLE

In my line of work, I've seen a lot of really nasty rotary cutter injuries. Please do yourself a favor and pick up a ruler handle to lift your hand up and out of the danger zone! Mine has saved me from several hospital trips when my blade has jumped up onto my ruler, and it's more ergonomic for your joints as well.

WOOD SEAM RIPPER

I have many seam rippers, and most of them enjoy hiding when I need them most. But my gorgeous wood seam ripper from Modern American Vintage not only feels great in my hand, but is always easy to find because of its large size.

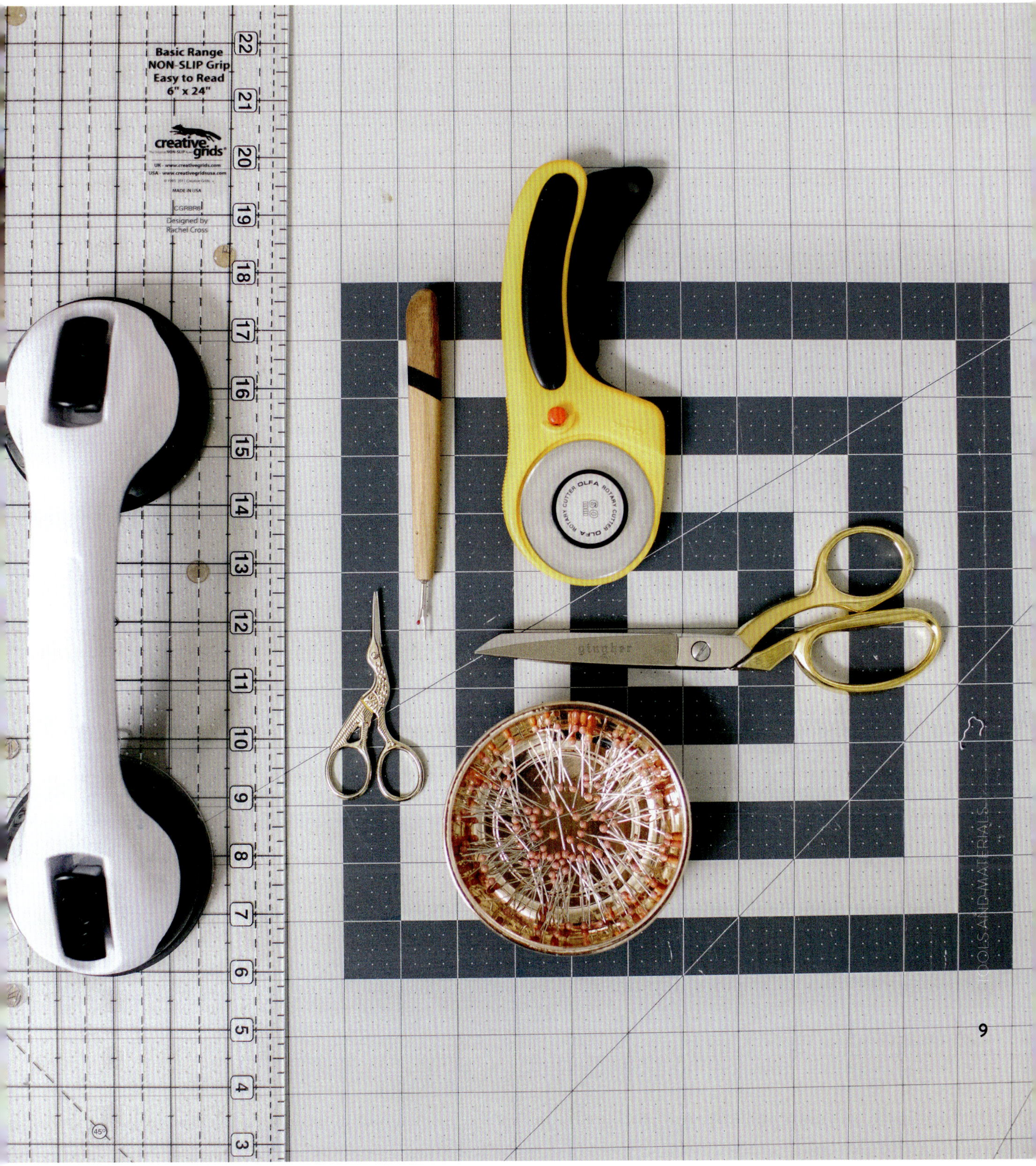
Basic Range
NON-SLIP Grip
Easy to Read
6" x 24"
creative grids
Designed by
Rachel Cross
OLFA ROTARY CUTTER
gingher

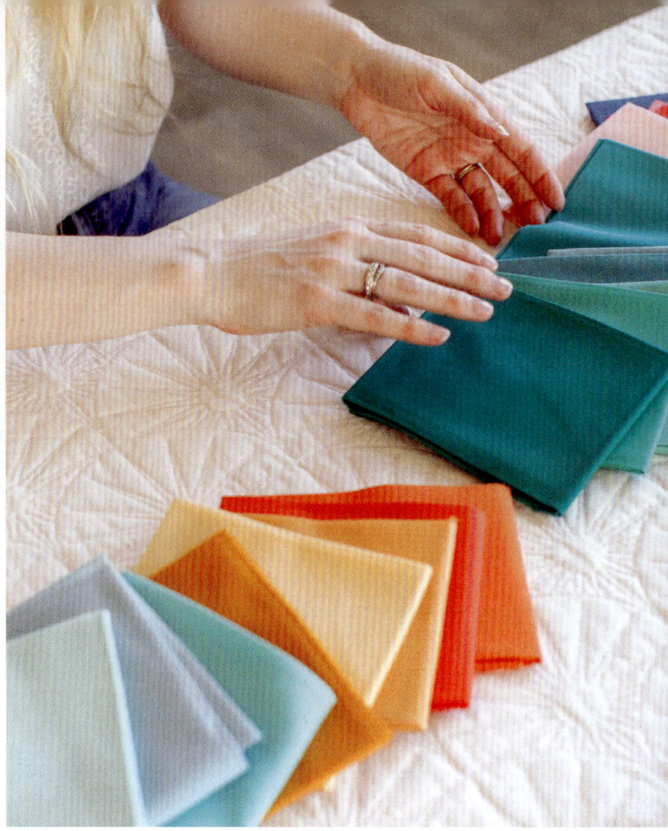

Fabric

RECOMMENDED FABRIC

I suggest using a high–quality quilting cotton, chambray, or a linen–cotton blend for creating ombré quilts. While chambray and linen have a looser weave and therefore require a bit of extra handling care and expertise, they create quilts with a lovely drape and softness!

In this book, I use Riley Blake Confetti Cotton Solids. These fabrics are very soft, and I love working with them. Any solid brand will do, though I do suggest buying fabric made by a well–known and high–quality manufacturer to avoid color bleeding and ensure your quilts will last through the years. I've also used Robert Kaufman Kona Cotton, Moda Bella Solids, and Art Gallery Fabrics Pure Solids many times with good results.

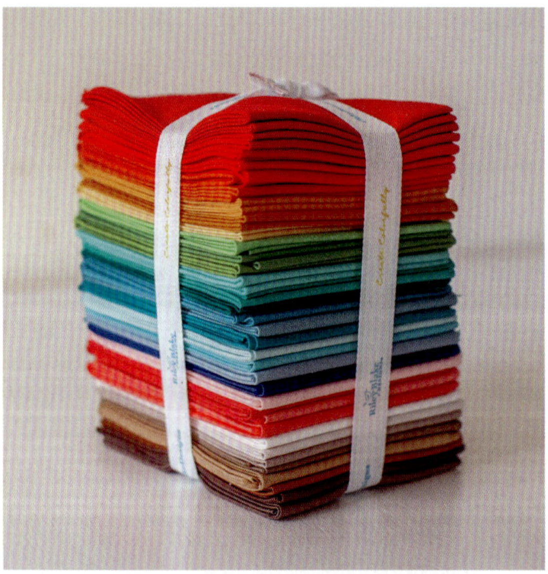

SOLIDS VS. PRINTS

It is easiest to create ombré and gradient color palettes using solid fabrics, but that doesn't mean it can't be done with prints! We will discuss some tips later in this chapter for using printed fabrics in ombré quilts.

OMBRE FABRICS

This book focuses on creating ombré quilts from standard fabrics. However, there are a few lines of actual ombré fabrics out there that are absolutely gorgeous and lots of fun to use! You can experiment with using these fabrics if you'd like to up your ombré game.

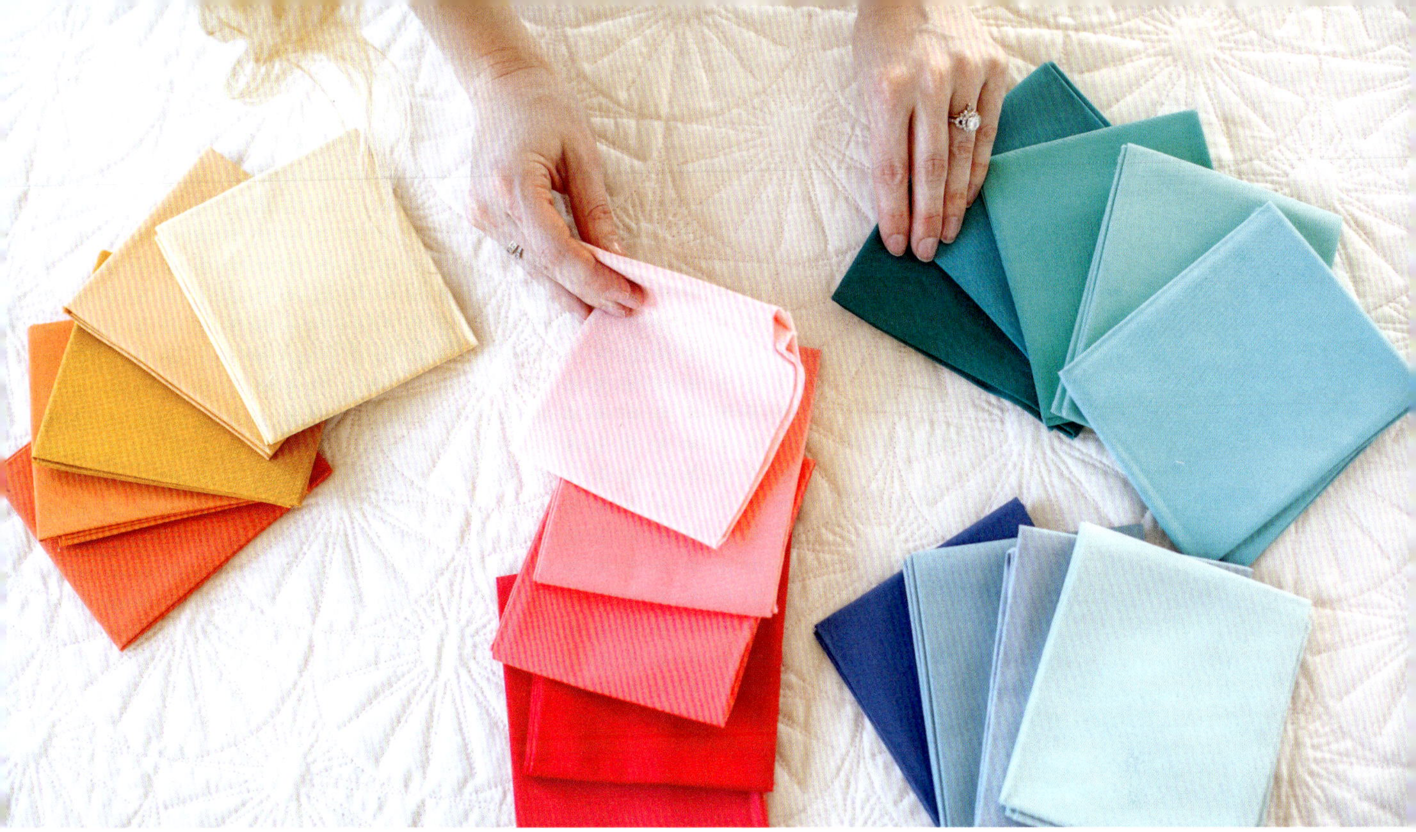

Color Tools

COLOR WHEEL

Many art and craft supply stores carry color wheel tools that are very helpful when putting together color palettes. They offer a quick reference to color mixing, complementary colors, and more and are so fun to use. I used my C&T Publishing Palette–Builder Color Tool and Color Wheels by Joen Wolfrem often when writing this book!

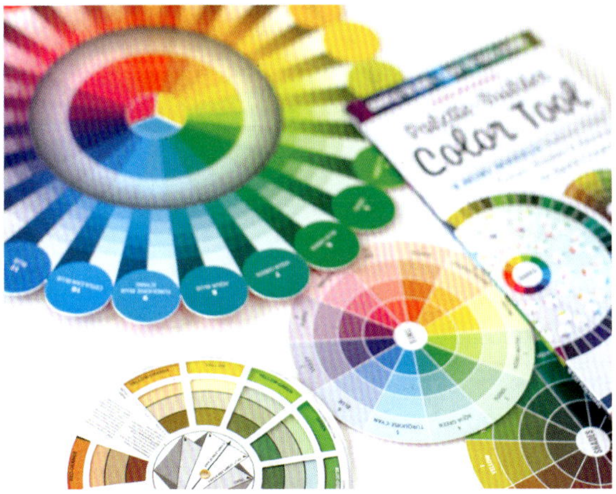

SWATCH CARDS

Most major fabric brands offer swatch cards or booklets so you can see their fabric colors in real life. I've always found relying on website representation of colors to be a risky option, as they're subject to photography and screen color differences. So, swatch cards are a must—have tool in my opinion. I personally have swatch cards of most major brands that allow me to compare colors and create color palettes.

I also love to create individual magnet tiles with my fabric swatches. This allows me to compare colors easily and to audition color palettes together with ease. There are many blog tutorials online that show how to do this, and there are also makers on Etsy that sell magnetic swatches.

Quilting Techniques

Basic Skills

READING CUTTING CHARTS

Let's walk through a sample cutting chart.

Sample Cutting Instructions

Fabric	Quilt Size (e.g. Twin)
Fabric A	*Cut 2 – 5″ × WOF strips; subcut into* 12 – 5″ × 5″ squares (**A1**) 5 – 4″ × 4″ squares (**A2**) *Cut 1 – 4″ × WOF strips; subcut into* 10 – 4″ × 4″ squares (**A2**)*
Fabric B	*Cut 3 – 3½″ × WOF strips, and sew them together; subcut into* 2 – 3½″ × 44½″ strips (**B1**) 4 – 3½″ × 3½″ squares (**B2**)

** You will cut 15 total A2 pieces*

In this example, cut two 5″ × WOF strips from Fabric A yardage. Then, cut twelve 5″ × 5″ squares and five 4″ × 4″ squares from these strips. We will call these respectively A1 and A2 moving forward. It can help to stack fabric pieces as you cut them and label the top piece with the label listed in the cutting chart to stay organized.

Next, cut one 4″ × WOF strip from Fabric A yardage and cut this strip into ten 4″ × 4″ squares. You will now have fifteen total 4″ × 4″ squares, all labeled A2.

Then, cut three 3½″ × WOF strips from Fabric B yardage. Sew them together, end to end to make a long strip. Finally, subcut the strip into two 3½″ × 44½″ strips and four 3½″ × 3½″ squares.

PRESSING INSTRUCTIONS

As with any quilting project, you will need to press after every seam. Pressing instructions are given in this book when a specific method will give the best results; if no pressing instructions are given, press with your preferred method.

SEAM ALLOWANCES

I use a standard ¼″ seam allowance for most of the projects in this book. But, as with many patterns, a scant ¼″ seam allowance will give you the best results. A scant ¼″ seam allowance is just a tiny bit smaller than a standard ¼″ seam allowance, accounting for the space taken up by the thread and the folding of fabric. This may seem like splitting hairs, but if a block has several seams it adds up quite a bit!

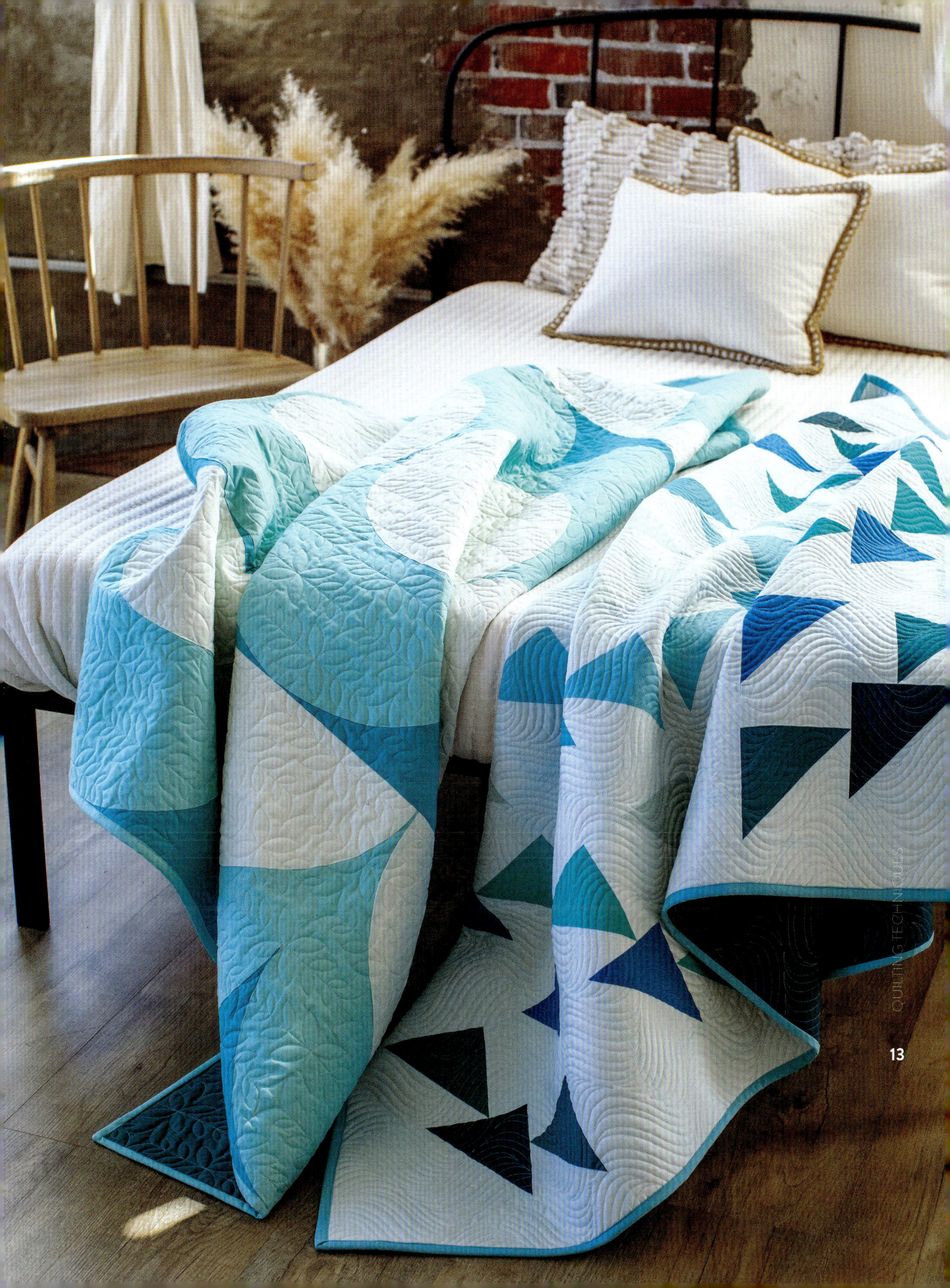

To determine if your scant seam allowance is correct, cut six 1½″ × 5″ strips. Sew them together along the long sides with a scant ¼″ seam allowance. Then, measure the width of the unit. If it measures less or more than 6½″, then you need to experiment a bit to achieve an accurate seam allowance. I do this by moving my sewing machine's needle until it's just right, or you may need to change the way you're lining up the fabric.

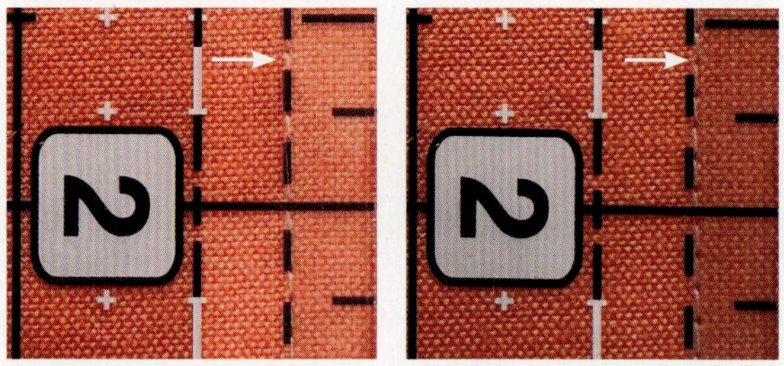

Standard ¼″ seam   Scant ¼″ seam

Curves

This book has several patterns that utilize curves. Some of them are a beginner—friendly option if you've never sewn curves (see *Resonance*, page 54), and some are better suited for someone comfortable with curves (see *Starfall*, page 98). All the needed templates for sewing curves can be found as a PDF download (see below).

Using Templates

To download and see all templates used in this book, see Templates (page 126).

Print or transfer the templates onto cardstock, tape the pieces together (if necessary), and cut them out. Make sure that the templates are printed at 100%, and check by measuring the test square. When the templates are taped together correctly, the curves will line up perfectly and smoothly.

tip *If your curved units aren't measuring the proper size, it's most likely because the templates weren't printed correctly or your seam allowance is too large—make sure to check!*

Once your templates are prepared, lay them out on the fabric. Be sure to stagger them as shown in the diagram below. Cutting instructions and fabric requirements assume that templates are staggered to reduce waste.

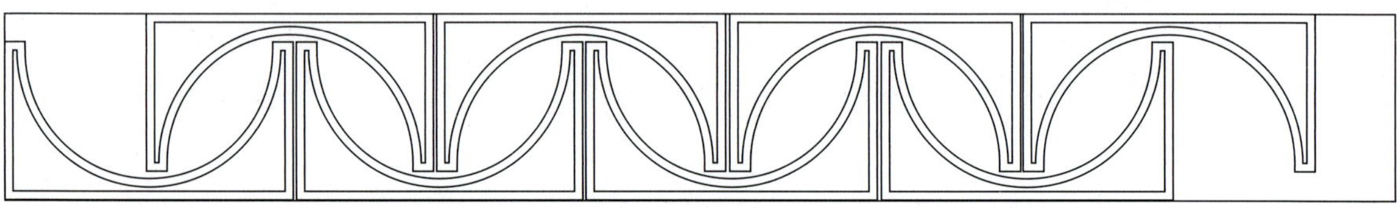

When staggered, 8 of these templates can fit on a single width of fabric.

SEWING CURVES

If you haven't sewn curves before, try creating some test units using scrap fabric before jumping into a project. It's rare for a first attempt at curves to look great; rest assured that with a little bit of practice you'll be zipping through them in no time!

Curved units will have two templates: An outer concave template and an inner convex template. The following example and instructions show a half–circle curved unit, but a quarter–circle curved unit follows the same construction steps.

tip *Even experienced quilters often wind up with slightly wonky curved units. After years of pattern writing, I began adding extra buffer room in my templates that allows for the final unit to be trimmed to size. This makes both the sewing experience and end result much better!*

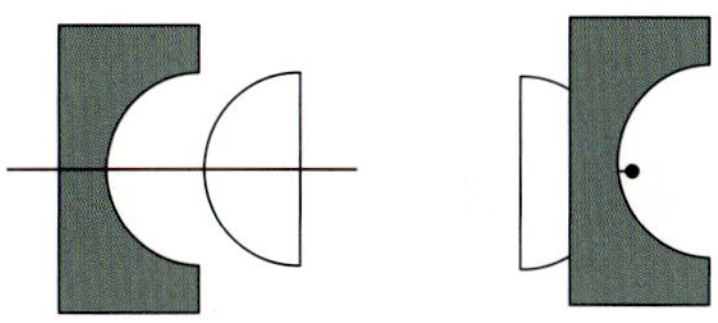

1. Pair the outer and inner pieces together. Mark the center of each piece (folding them in half can help you find the center quickly). Place the outer piece on top of the inner piece, right sides together and matching centers, and pin as shown.

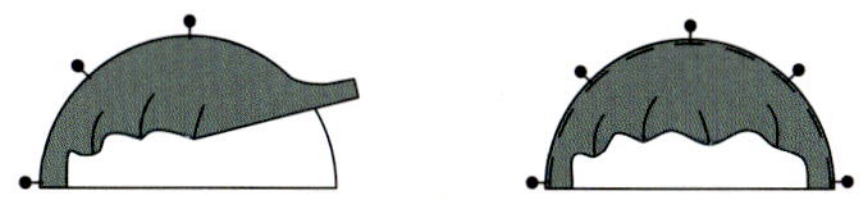

2. Curve the outer piece around the inner piece, pinning them together along the curved edge. It's always better to use more pins if you're new to curves.

3. Slowly sew around the curve, pausing and lifting the machine foot if needed to ease the fabric through and avoid puckering.

4. Press the unit toward the inner piece, unless the pattern recommends otherwise. Then, trim the block to the final size indicated by the pattern.

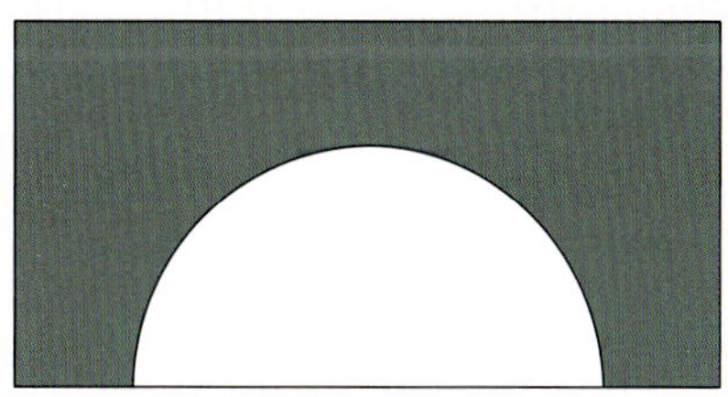

TRIMMING CURVES

To trim any block with curves, first lay the ruler along the bottom edge of the convex template piece. Trim as close to this bottom edge as possible, trimming the edge to be flat without removing much length. Then, trim the top edge to the required length. Finally, trim an even amount from the center on each side of the block to reach the required width.

If the curved unit you are trimming has curves that extend to the very edge of the finished unit, follow the same trimming order as above, but you'll need to pay extra attention to the seam allowance. Make sure to trim precisely to allow exact ¼" seam allowances on each side of the curves.

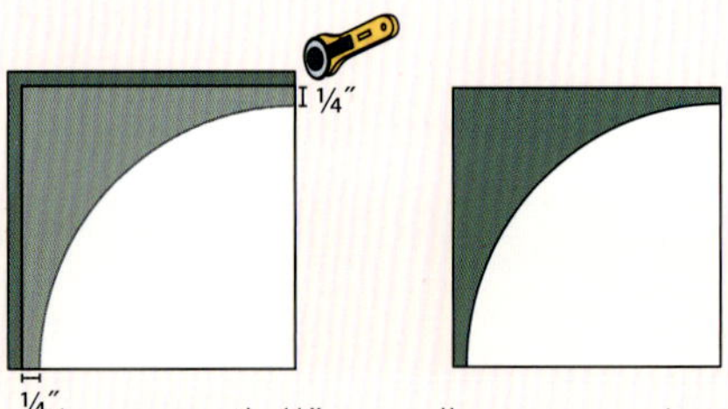

Trimming so exactly ¼" seam allowance remains and curve will extend to the edge of the final block

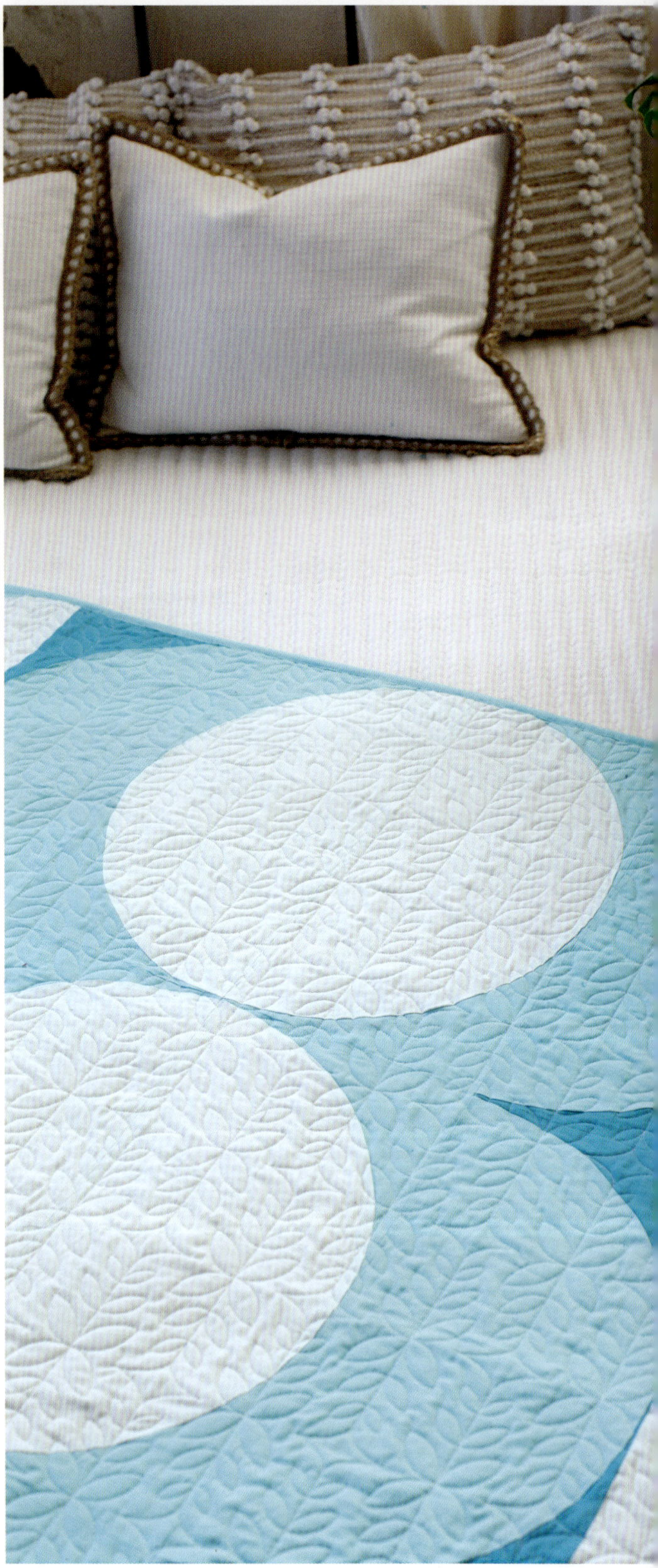

In this block, the curve butts against the edge in the finished block. Trimming must be done with care so that there is an exact ¼" seam allowance left around the curve.

Basic Blocks

This section provides the techniques you need to make a few basic blocks. Refer to specific projects for piece measurements and block dimensions.

HALF-SQUARE TRIANGLES

I use three different methods for creating half–square triangles (HSTs) in this book.

Two-at-a-Time

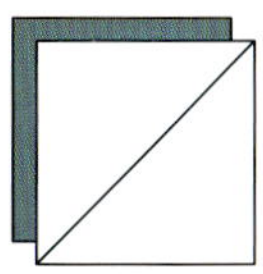

1. Cut 2 squares. Draw a diagonal line across the wrong side of the lighter fabric, corner to corner, then place the squares right–side together.

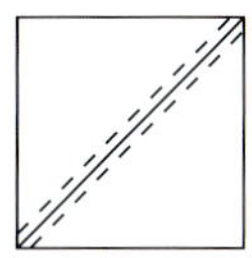

2. Sew a ¼″ seam on each side of the diagonal line.

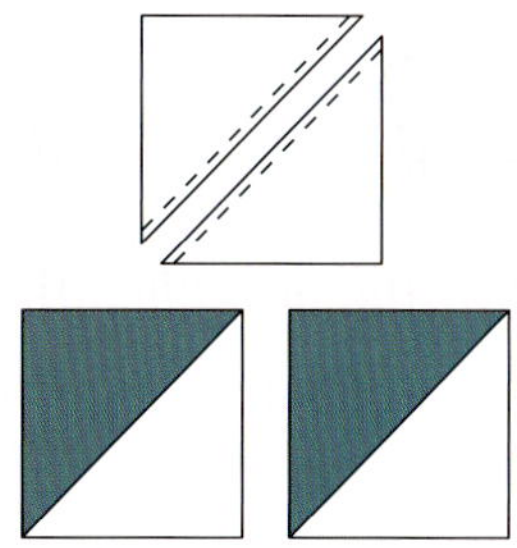

3. Cut on the line to create 2 HSTs. Open the HSTs and press them. Trim to the size listed in the project.

tip *It can be tempting to skip trimming, but resist the urge! Your units and final quilt will not come together correctly if you do not trim as instructed.*

Four-at-a-Time

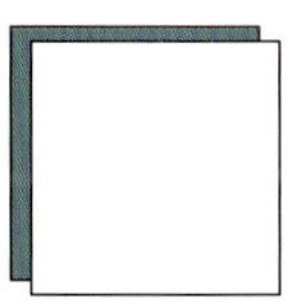

1. Cut 2 squares, then place the squares right sides together. Pin together at the corners and center.

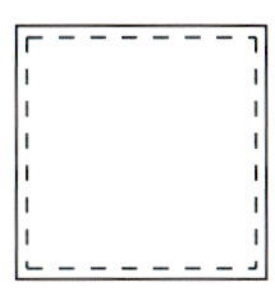

2. Sew a ¼″ seam all along the edge of the squares.

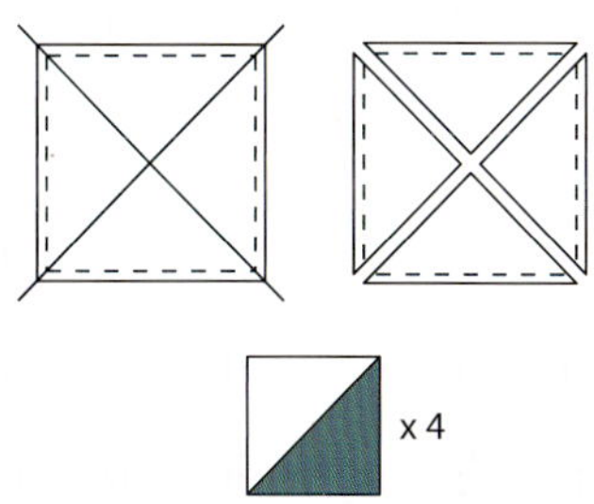

3. Cut the unit into quarters on the diagonal to create four HSTs. Open the HSTs and press, then trim each HST to the size listed in the pattern. Handle these units very carefully, as they have bias edges.

Eight-at-a-Time

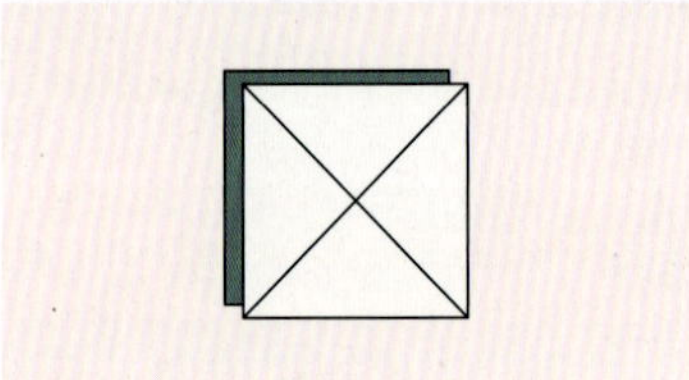

1. Cut 2 squares. Draw diagonal lines corner to corner in both directions across the wrong side of the lighter fabric square, then place the squares right sides together. Pin together at the corners and center.

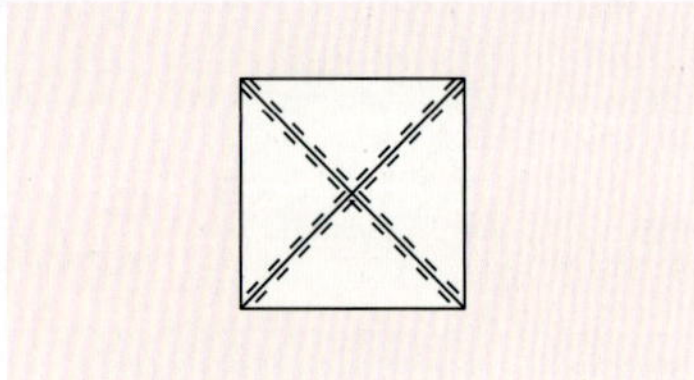

2. Sew a ¼″ seam on each side of each diagonal line.

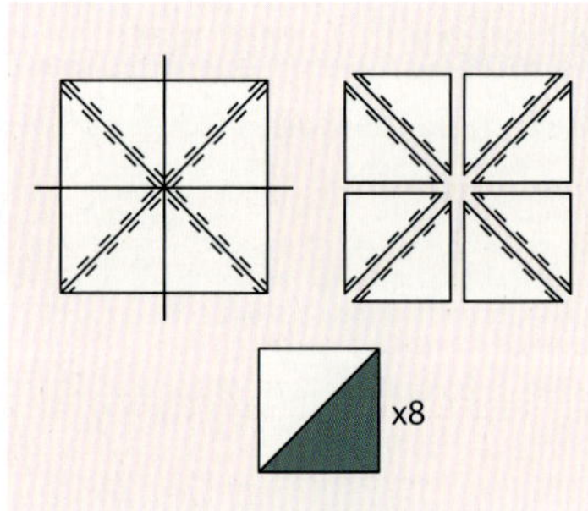

3. Cut the unit in half both vertically and horizontally, then cut along the drawn lines to create eight HSTs. Open the HSTs and press, then trim each HST to the size listed in the pattern.

FLYING GEESE

I use two different methods for creating flying geese units in this book.

One-at-a-Time

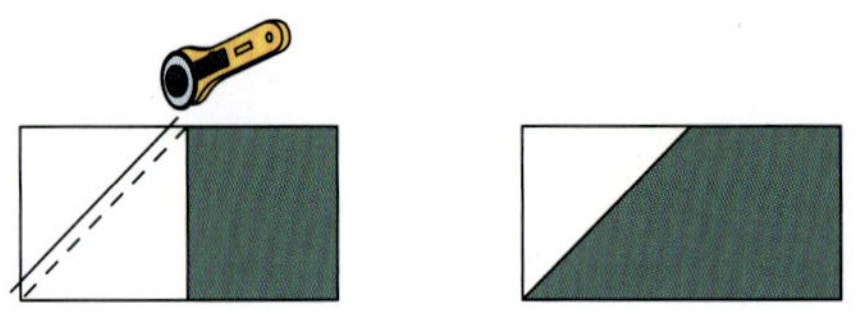

1. Cut 2 squares and a rectangle. Draw a diagonal line, corner to corner, across the wrong side of each square. Place a square on the left side of the rectangle, line facing up. Sew along the line, then trim ¼″ away from the line. Press toward the darker fabric.

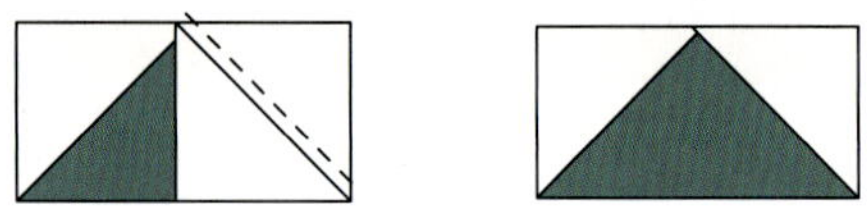

2. Place a square on the right side of the rectangle, line facing up. Sew along the line, then trim ¼″ away from the line. Press toward the darker fabric.

Four-at-a-Time

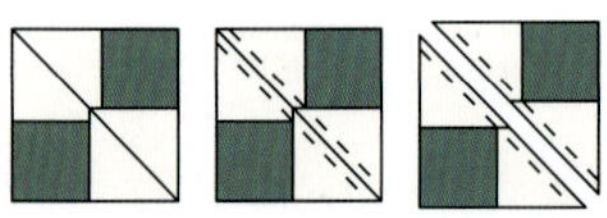

1. Cut 4 small squares and 1 large square. Draw a diagonal line, corner to corner across the wrong side of each small square. Place 2 small squares in opposite corners of the larger square, overlapping, then sew a ¼″ seam on each side of the line. Cut on the line.

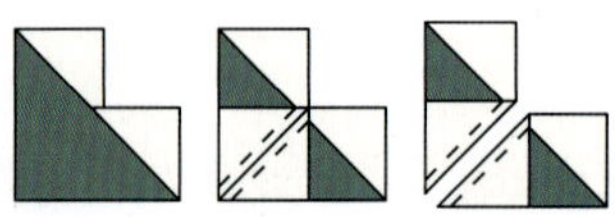

2. Press both units toward the darker fabric. Place a small square in the corner of each unit as shown. Sew a ¼″ seam along each side of the lines, then cut on the lines to make four flying geese.

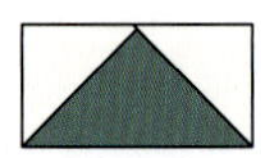

3. Press toward the darker fabric, and trim each flying geese to the size listed in the pattern.

Pillow Covers

Adding a pillow cover to a mini quilt is a quick and easy way to create something beautiful and functional for your home. They also make great gifts! There are many ways to create pillow covers, but I prefer a simple envelope enclosure.

Before creating the pillow cover, quilt the mini quilt top, but do not bind it. You can quilt it using only batting for less bulk, or quilt it as normal with a backing fabric to avoid exposed batting inside of the pillow cover.

1. Cut 2 pieces of fabric for the back of the pillow using the following equation:

   Length = Length of mini quilt

   Width = (Width of mini quilt / 2) + 5

For example, if your mini quilt's finished measurements are 16″ × 20″, you will need two pieces of fabric that measure 16″ × 15″.

tip *Make sure that you are considering the desired pillow orientation when cutting the fabric for the pillow back. The longer side may not always be the length, depending on how you want the design to be displayed on the pillow.*

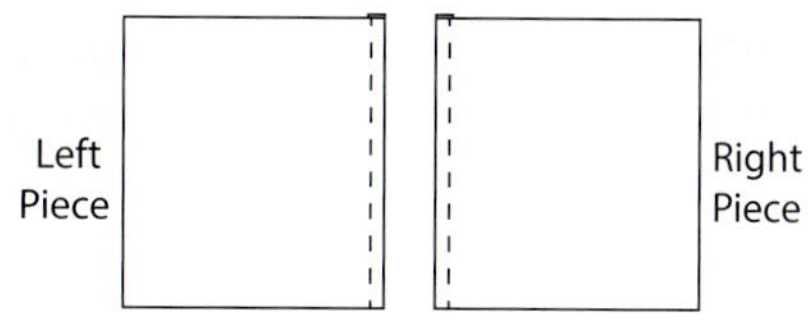

2. On each piece of pillow backing fabric, fold one length edge ½″ to the wrong side. Press. Fold over again, enclosing the raw edge, and press. Stitch along the edge. Repeat with the second backing piece. These are now envelope pieces.

If you are using a solid fabric, you do not need to pay attention to which length you are finishing. However, if you are using a non-reversible print, mirror the edges you finish.

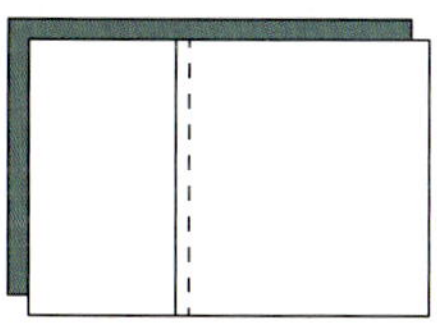

3. Place the finished mini quilt right side down, then place the envelope pieces on top, right sides up (wrong sides together). Line up the raw edges of the envelope pieces with the edges of the mini quilt, with the finished edges of the envelope pieces overlapping in the middle. Either envelope piece can be on top.

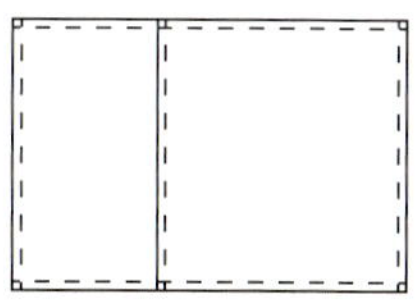

Edges not yet bound

5. Carefully pin the pieces in place, then sew along the perimeter. Bind the raw edges to create a finished exterior edge.

tip *If you'd prefer to not have binding on your pillow cover, you can instead sew the mini quilt and envelope pieces right sides together, then turn the pillow cover right side out after sewing.*

Color Theory

The Basics

In order to create beautiful gradient color palettes for quilts, we need to understand the basics of color theory.

THE COLOR WHEEL

The color wheel is a fantastic tool you will refer to again and again when creating color palettes. It shows how colors relate to one another and is a wonderful guide to help us understand how to build ombré and gradient palettes.

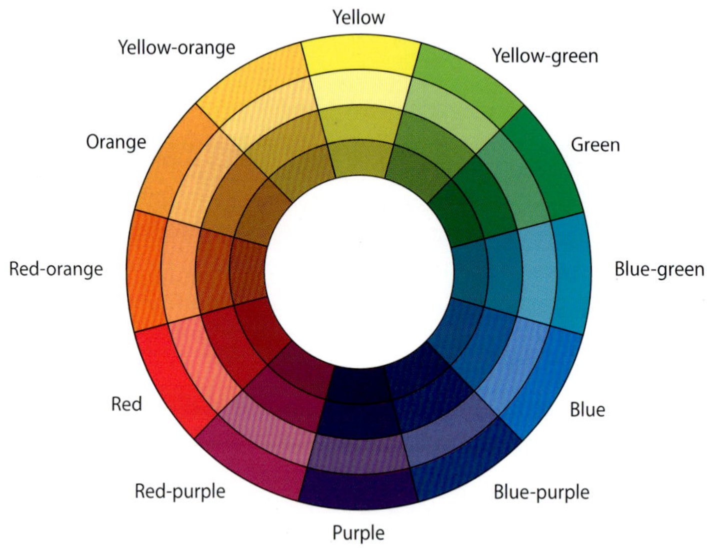

Primary Colors

Primary colors seem simple—they're primary, after all!—but understanding them completely can be like opening a can of worms. In theory, primary colors can be mixed in different amounts to create any other color. In this book, we're sticking to the basic and traditional primary colors: red, yellow, and blue.

Secondary Colors

Secondary colors are created by mixing together the primary colors. When I refer to secondary colors, I mean orange (red and yellow), green (yellow and blue), and purple (red and blue).

Tertiary Colors

Tertiary colors are created by mixing together primary and secondary colors. When I refer to tertiary colors, I mean red-orange (vermillion), yellow-orange (amber), yellow-green (chartreuse), blue-green (teal), blue-purple (violet), and red-purple (magenta).

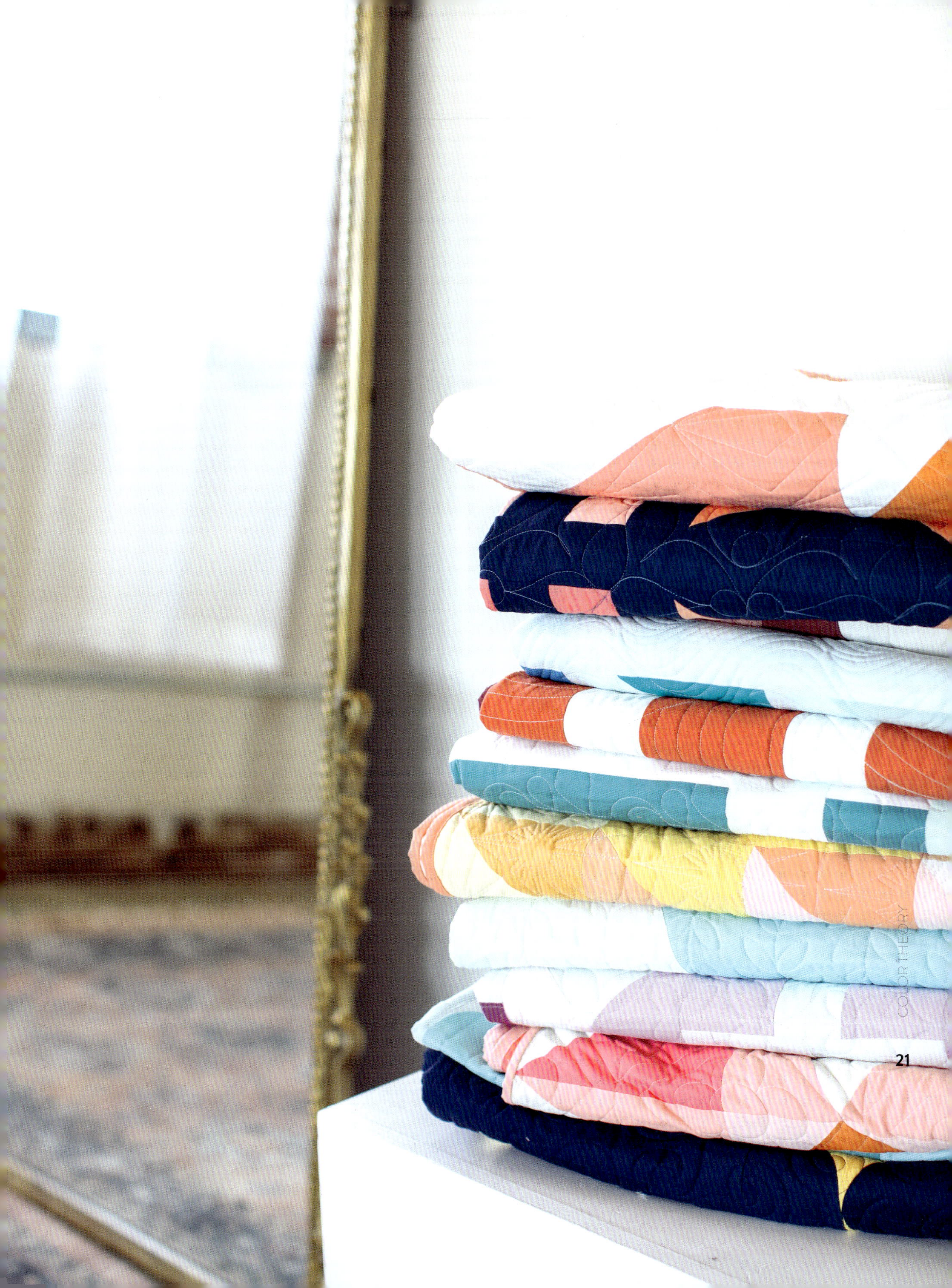

Color Temperature

A good understanding of color temperature helps with constructing color palettes. Half of the color wheel can be thought of as *warm* colors, while the other half can be thought of as *cool* colors. Red, orange, and yellow are warm colors while green, blue, and purple are cool colors. Using only warm or only cool colors in a project will create a uniform and soothing feel, while mixing warm and cool colors will create a sense of contrast and interest.

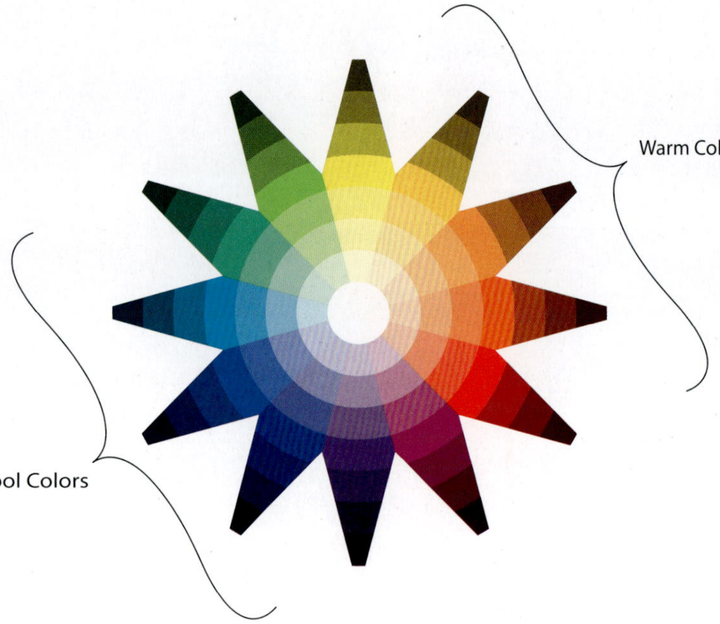

Describing Colors

There are six terms that are commonly used to describe colors. These may seem confusing at first, but once you understand them, you will unlock a whole new way of thinking about color and evaluating color palettes. *Hue*, *value*, and *saturation* are attributes used to define and describe a color. *Tint*, *tone*, and *shade* describe how hues change when they are mixed with white, black, or gray.

HUE

Hue refers to the actual color. Red, orange, blue—these are all hues. *Hue* and *color* are often used interchangeably.

VALUE

Value describes the lightness or darkness of a color. The circle on the left is darker value than the circle on the right. Value can be easier to think about in grayscale. If you imagined putting a grayscale filter over the circles, which would be lighter? The circle on the right, meaning it is lighter value.

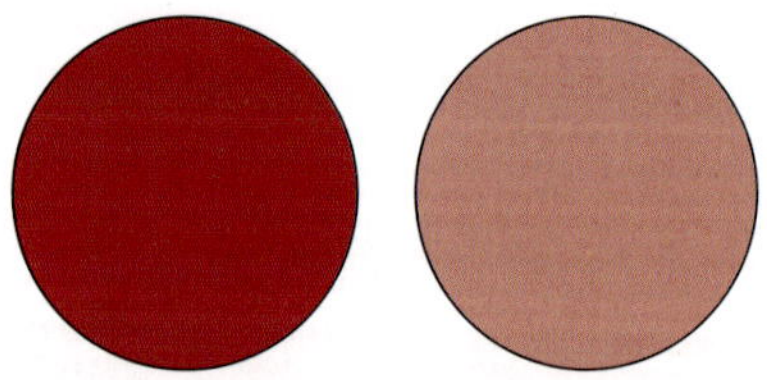

tip *A well–balanced color palette will usually have a mix of values. Use the grayscale trick above to check a fabric pull or color palette to see if there is a good variety of values. Take a photo, then edit it to be black and white/grayscale. Removing the hues from the photo will show you the value of each color more clearly!*

SATURATION

Saturation refers to a color's intensity, meaning how close it is to a pure hue. A pure color with no white, black, or gray mixed in is very saturated. As you add these elements to the pure color, it becomes less saturated.

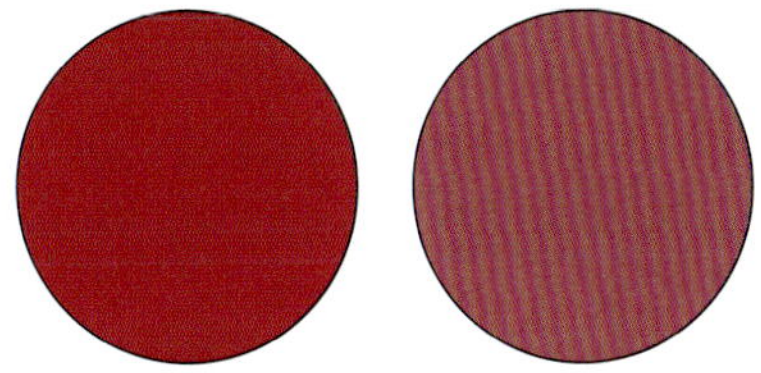

Left: highly saturated hue
Right: same hue with gray added, making it less saturated

TINT

To create a tint, add white to a pure hue. Tinting a color will lighten the value of the hue.

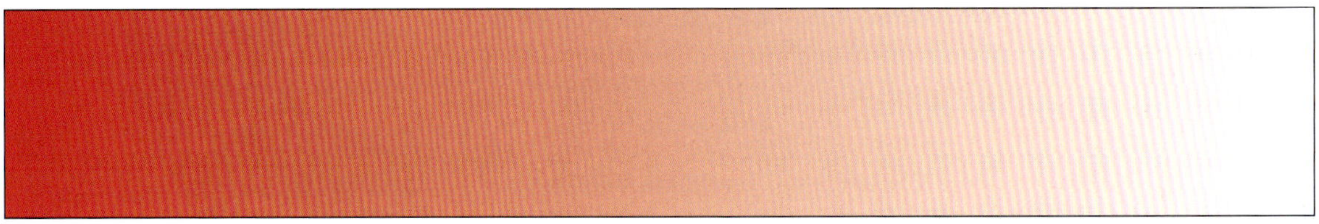

Scale from pure hue to white, with tints in between the two extremes

TONE

To create a tone, add gray to a pure hue.

Scale from pure hue to gray, with tones between the two extremes

SHADE

To create a shade, add black to a pure hue. Shades will have a darker value than the pure hue.

Scale from pure hue to black, with shades between the two extremes

Color Palettes

There are four basic types of color palettes we will discuss here, but playing with color should be just that—play! It should be fun. Practice mixing and matching different colors to create go—to palettes you enjoy.

MONOCHROMATIC PALETTES

A monochromatic palette uses the same hue in different tints, shades, and tones. Monochromatic color schemes are the key to many ombré palettes! Monochromatic color palettes really let an ombré effect shine, and can be very soothing and meditative.

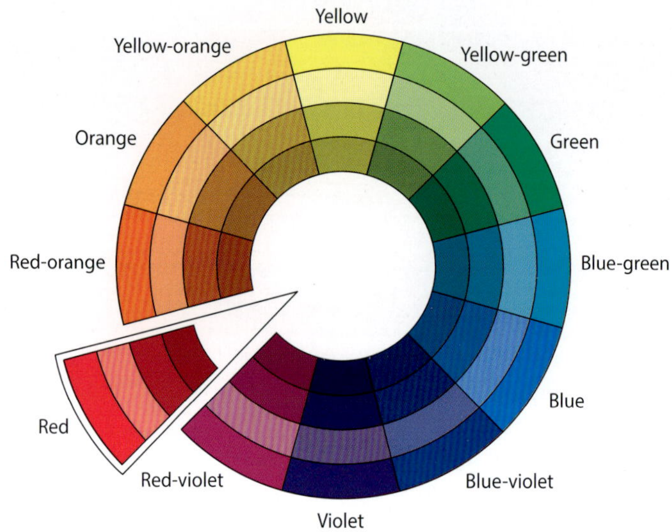

ANALOGOUS PALETTES

I like to think of analogous color palettes as the quirky sister of a monochromatic color palette. These palettes use colors that are neighbors on the color wheel. An example of an analogous color scheme would be a variety of values in the hues yellow, chartreuse, and green.

These types of color palettes can create ombré effects that have a similar feel to a monochromatic palette, but with a bit more visual interest.

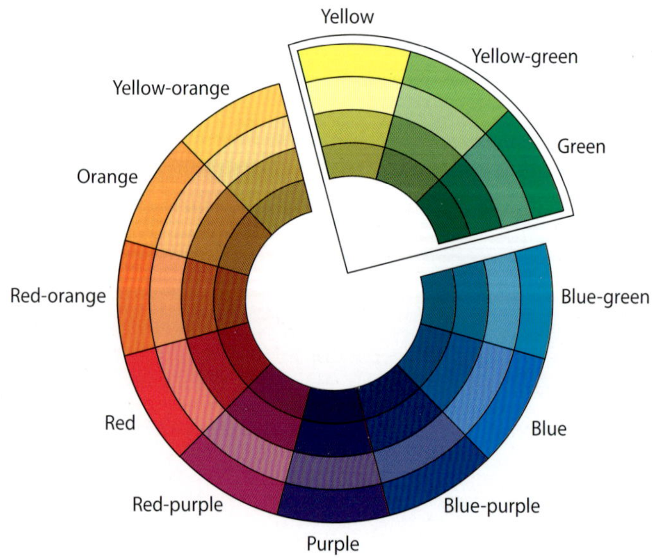

COMPLEMENTARY PALETTES

Complementary color palettes use hues on opposite sides of the color wheel. They are a great way to introduce hue contrast within your color selections. Complementary color palettes lead me to using color combinations that I wouldn't normally use.

One of my current favorite ombré palettes uses a complementary scheme of purple and yellow—two hues that I don't love by themselves, but that together make a fascinating palette!

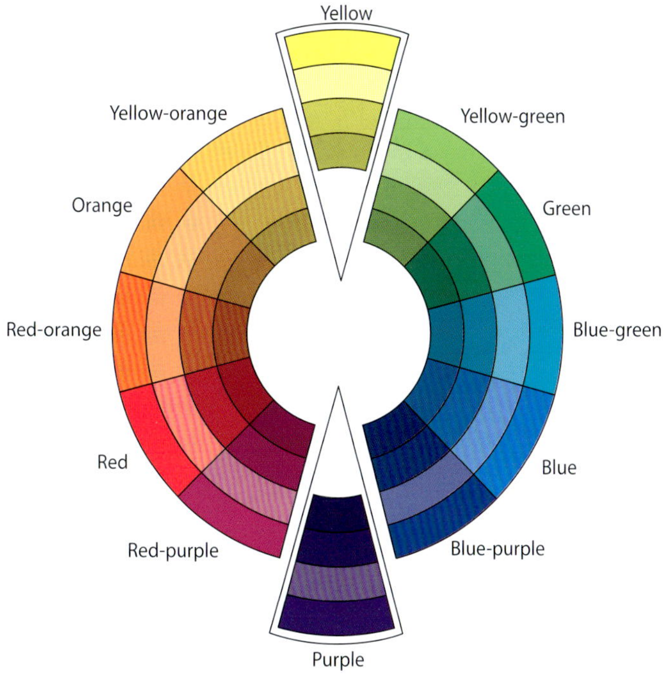

Complementary pair

TRIADIC PALETTES

Triadic color palettes are similar to complementary color palettes, but they use three colors equidistant from one another on the color wheel. For example, the primary colors of red, yellow, and blue are actually a triadic color palette.

Triadic color palettes can sometimes be a bit tricky to fit into an ombré color scheme, but when a project features many different fabrics, this scheme can have a big impact!

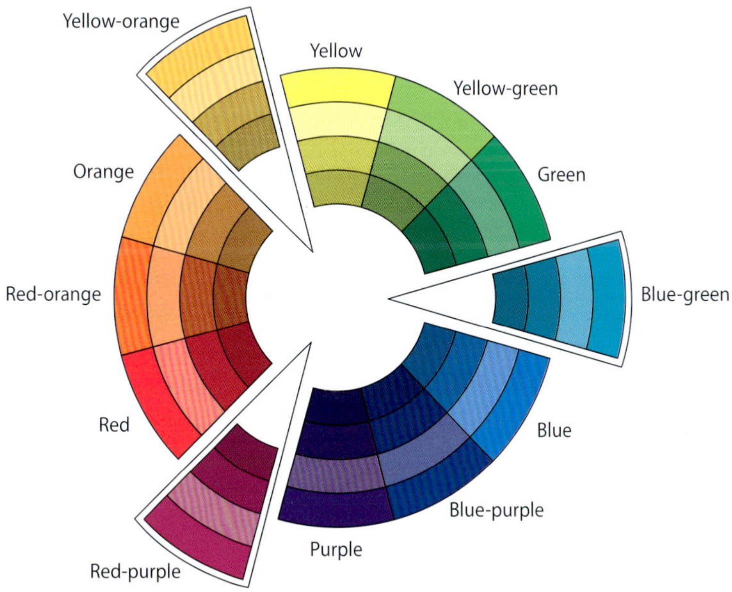

Triadic grouping

Gradients in Quilts

Gradient vs Ombré

The terms *ombré* and *gradient* can be a bit confusing, as they are often used interchangeably. They can even have different, overlapping, or conflicting definitions across different industries! I personally think of ombré palettes as using a single hue with different values, and gradient palettes as using more than one hue (in addition to different values). However, because they are used in so many different ways, for the purposes of this book we will use them interchangeably to avoid confusion.

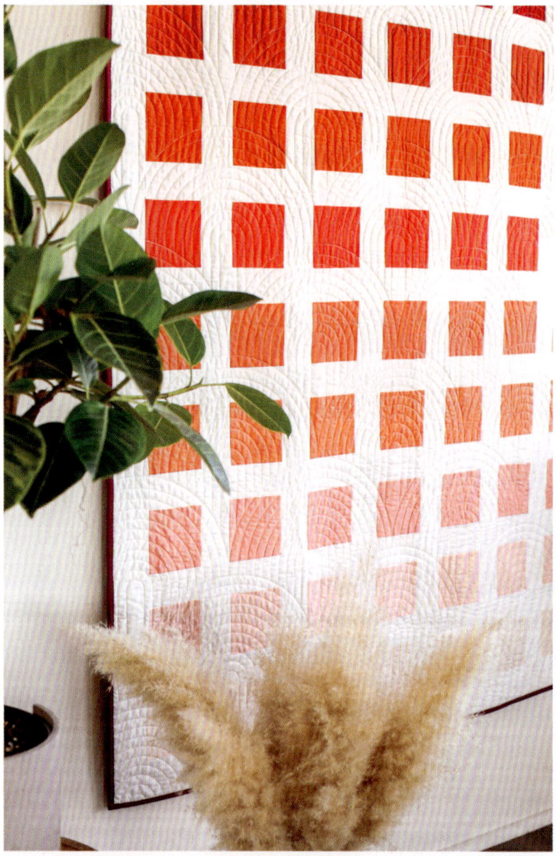

Gradient and Ombré Layouts

There are different ways of laying out a gradient or ombré palette. Each of these types of layouts can progress in either hue or value, or in both.

LINEAR GRADIENTS

Linear gradients are designed to move through a quilt either horizontally or vertically, changing in hue or value from one side to the other. These gradients can also be mirrored, moving vertically or horizontally from a chosen spot on the quilt.These are often the easiest gradients to create, and they are big impact designs.

From left to right: monochromatic horizontal linear gradient, monochromatic vertical linear gradient, monochromatic mirrored linear gradient.

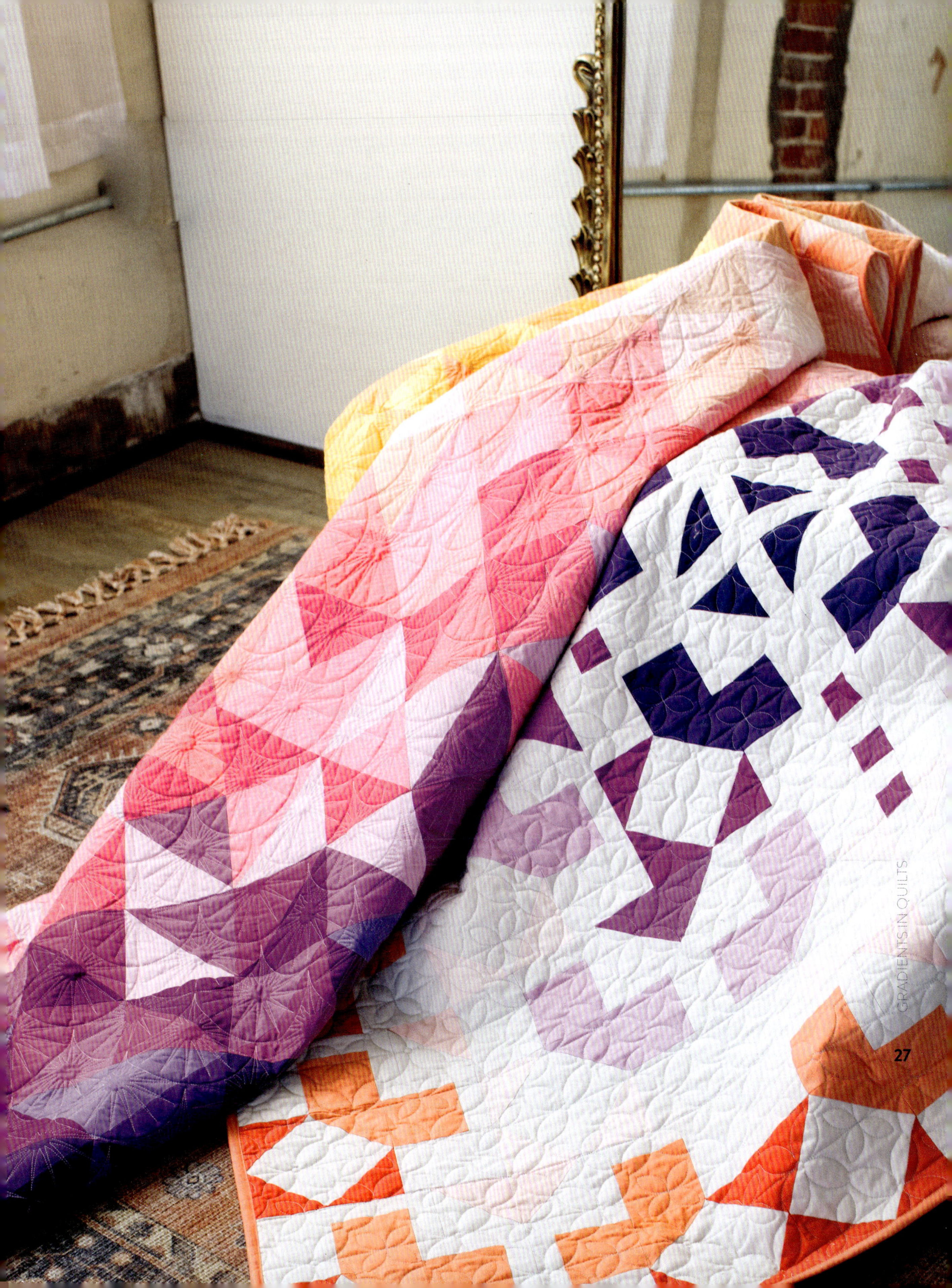

DIAGONAL GRADIENT

Diagonal gradients move through a quilt from corner to corner. They can be mirrored as well, though I personally think they have the biggest impact when they aren't.

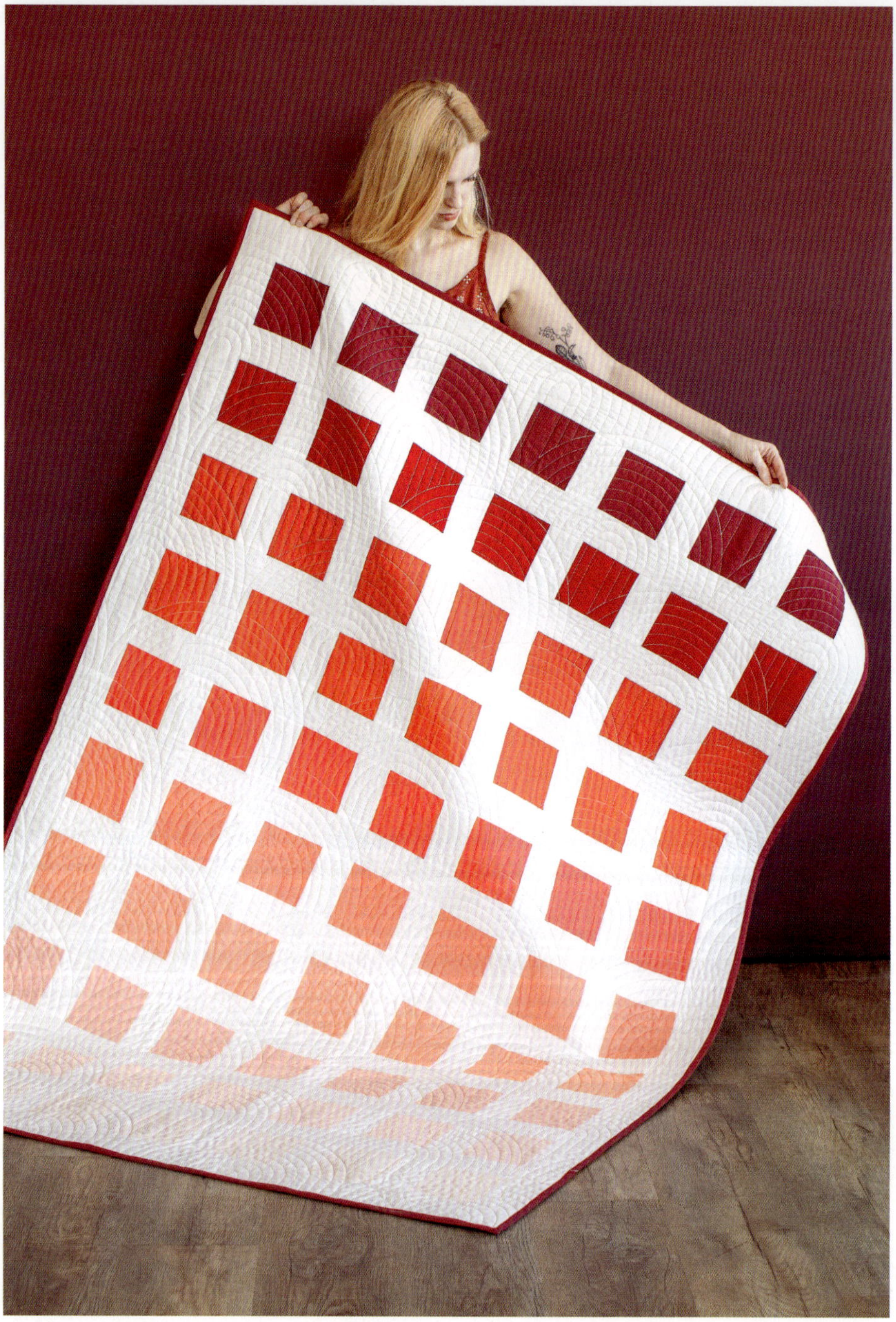

From top to bottom: monochromatic diagonal gradient, complementary diagonal gradient, analogous diagonal gradient, monochromatic mirrored diagonal gradient.

It's easy to spot that *Gradient Grid* (page 40) has a vertical linear gradient, but it actually has a diagonal gradient too! Ombré quilts can often have multiple gradient types hidden within the same design, which makes them even more interesting.

RADIAL GRADIENTS

Radial gradients can create an illusion of depth and movement. The hue or value change moves from the perimeter of the quilt into the center. I find that patterns using this type of gradient look quite different depending on the direction of change and palette.

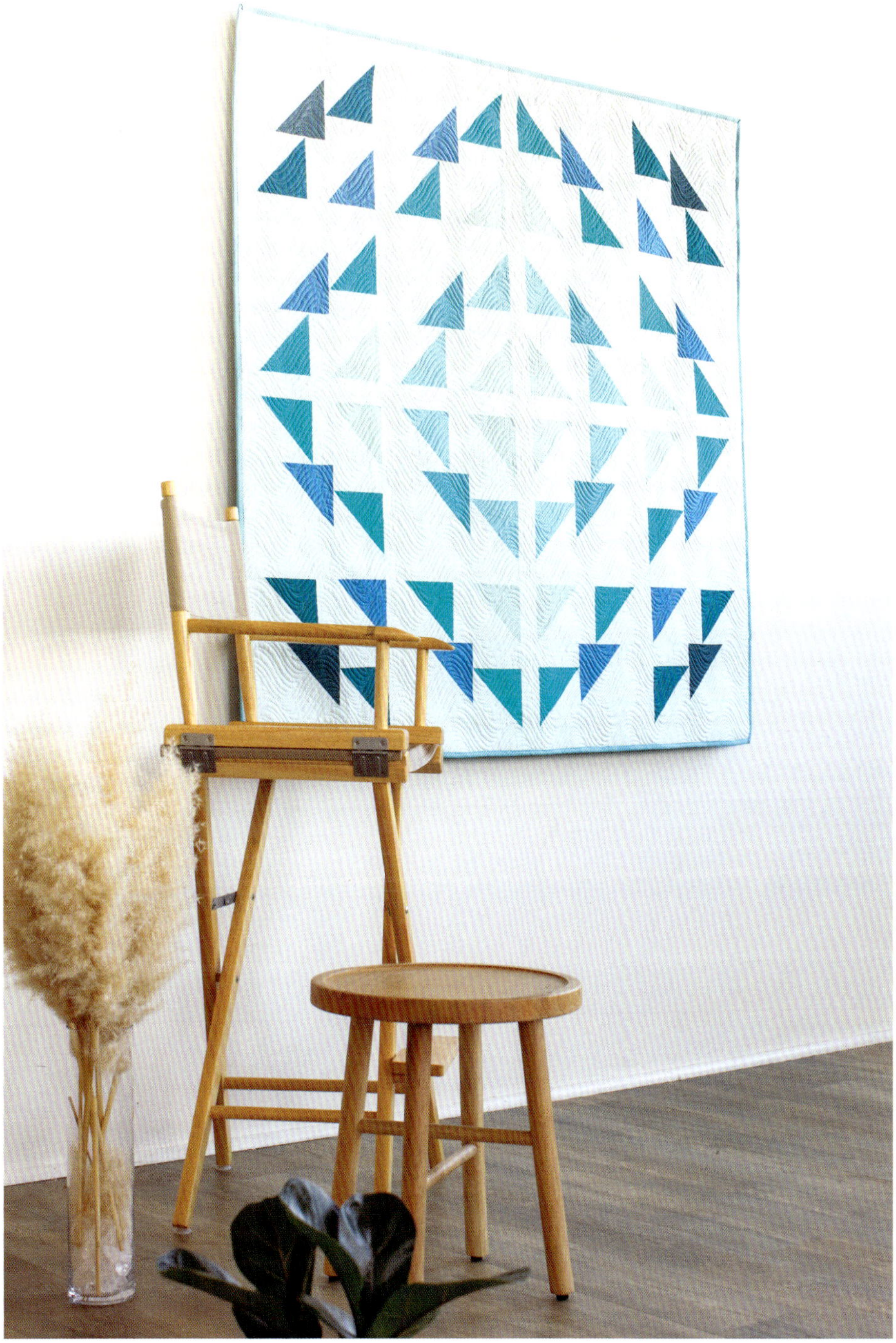

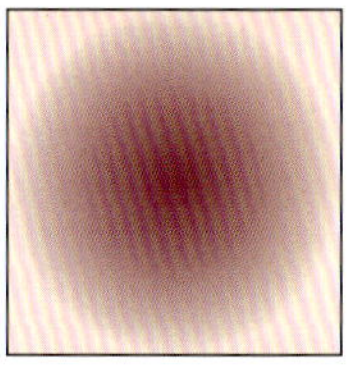

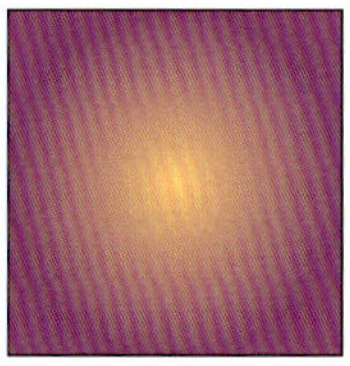

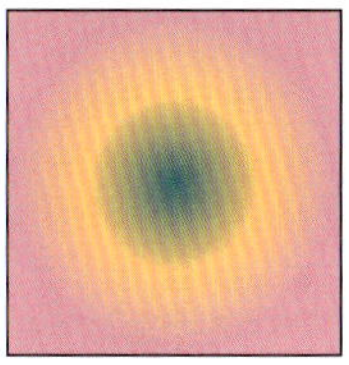

From top to bottom: monochromatic radial gradient moving from dark to light, monochromatic radial gradient moving from light to dark, complementary radial gradient, triadic radial gradient.

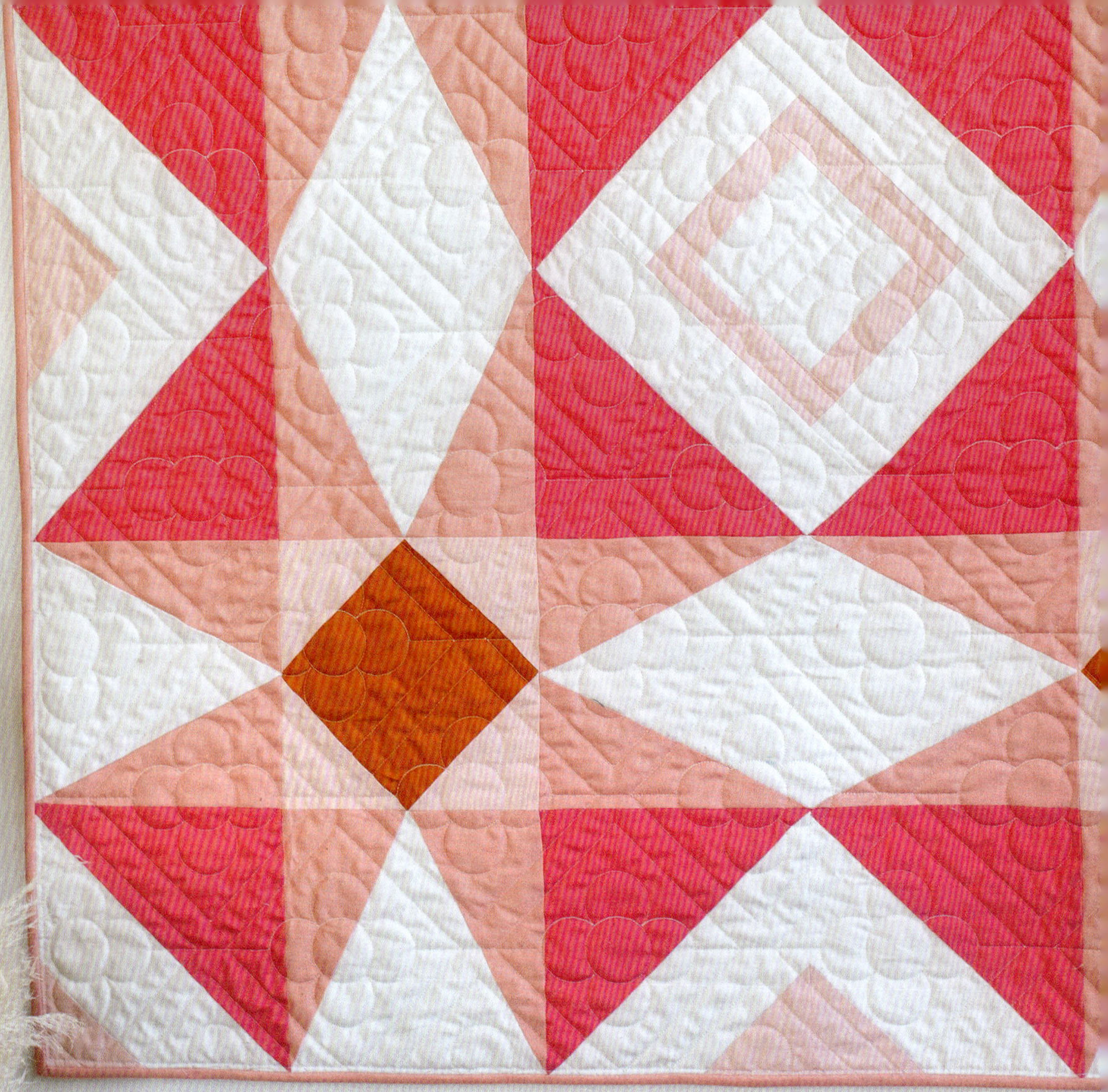

BLOCK GRADIENTS

Block gradients are a bit different from the other layouts that we've discussed so far. While the other gradients are seen on a macro scale, with the gradient flowing throughout the full quilt, in this case, the gradients are isolated to each individual block. This can result in a more subtle, but equally beautiful, gradient quilt. To get the full gradient effect with this more subtle design layout, I suggest using a monochromatic gradient. The below example is from *Primula* (page 92).

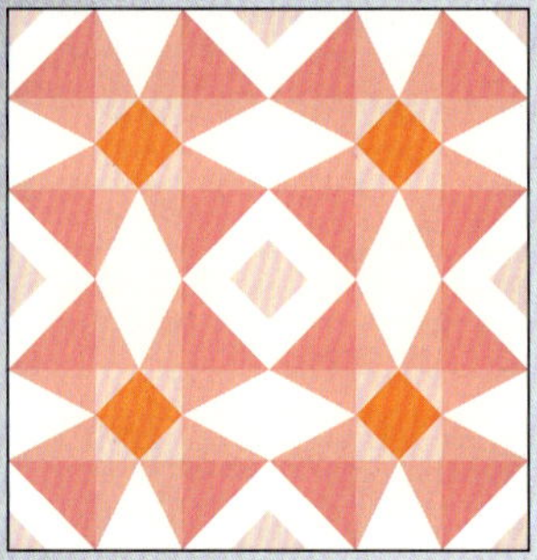

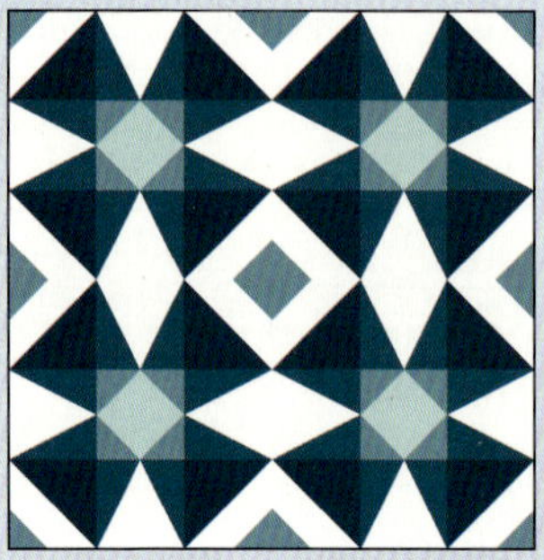

Left: analogous block gradient
Right: monochromatic block gradient

Selecting Fabrics

A true gradient is a continuous blending of one hue or value to another. Because you must pick a limited palette of individual colors for a quilt, the challenge is in replicating this effect with your color choices. To create a color palette that will give the ombré feel you're looking for, pay close attention to both hue and value. Refer to Color Theory (page 20) for a refresher on color relationships and these terms.

First, determine how many fabrics you'll need. This book has patterns that range from using only three fabrics to using up to 22 fabrics! Once you know how many fabrics you'll be working with, you'll be able to make the important decisions around how to build your palette.

BUILDING A GRADIENT AROUND VALUE

Focusing on value with a monochromatic color scheme will create a gorgeous ombré quilt. This is one of the easiest ways to build a palette, as you only have so many fabric options to choose from within one hue! Once you've picked the desired hue, take a look at a few different fabric lines to see which might have the most options for the chosen hue.

Next, you need to decide how large the jumps in value should be between each fabric, and what other variations you'll accept in your palette. Again, this depends on the number of fabrics needed for your project. For instance, you may decide to make a green ombré quilt. A fabric line may have greens ranging from dark hunter green to bright chartreuse to muted sage. Though these are all greens, they vary in hue, saturation, and value.

In general, especially if you're using a small number of fabrics, you want to select a range of greens that have similar hues and saturations, meaning they primarily differ in value. This will create a smooth, flowing ombré palette instead of one that feels jarring or that jumps too far around the color wheel.

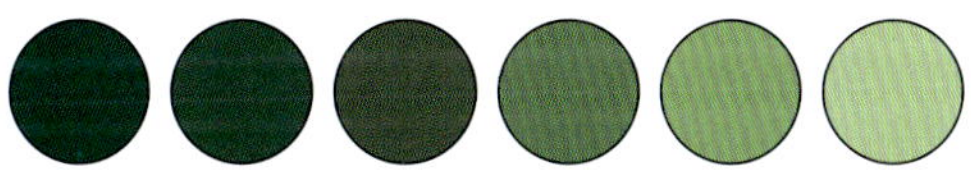

This green ombré palette is pleasing to the eye. The hues and saturations vary a bit, but they are close enough that they feel cohesive, making the main focus on the differing values.

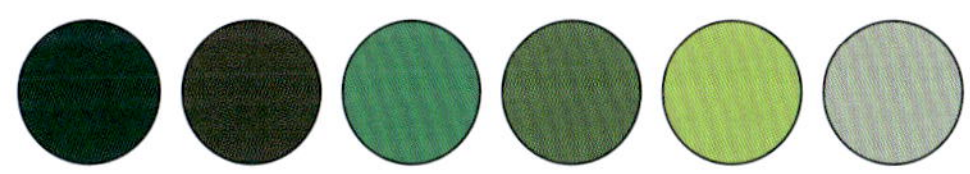

This green ombré palette is incongruous and does not blend well together. The saturation level varies across the colors, and the hues are wide–ranging. So, while this palette is monochromatic and the range does differ in value, it does not emphasize a value gradient.

BUILDING A GRADIENT AROUND HUE

When you want to create a gradient quilt that flows from one color to another, you'll need to pull out some color mixing skills and a color wheel! Quilts that blend from one color to another require a careful consideration of hue to ensure the transition is as seamless as possible.

For instance, in a complementary palette, you want to transition between two hues that are far from one another on the color wheel. So, to create a gentle blend, include all the secondary and tertiary colors between those two hues. There are no rules about what colors you may want to pair together for a gradient quilt like this, but analogous, complementary, and even triadic color pairs/trios are all a great starting point in color selection.

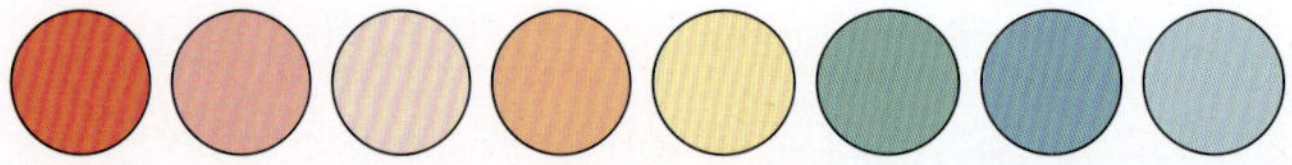

In this example, I started with a tertiary palette (muted primary colors), adding more hues for a smooth gradient. Tertiary schemes often have a rainbow effect. This palette does not include significant shifts in value.

Sometimes blending from one color to another can be very tricky! Using a light neutral—aka incorporating a value gradient too—can make this a bit easier. Let's take pink and teal (complementary colors). If you fade from a dark to light value in pink, then add a light neutral in the middle, you can naturally move from light to dark value in teal to blend the two differing colors.

Once you've nailed down the hues, it's important to look for fabrics that are similar saturation levels. If you're building a color palette that features bright and bold colors, be consistent with that in each fabric. Likewise, if you're utilizing a more muted color scheme, ensure that you don't have oversaturated fabrics mixed in unless you're intentionally going for a big pop of color. Like I mentioned, a value gradient pairs beautifully with a hue gradient, but saturation should be homogenous within a palette.

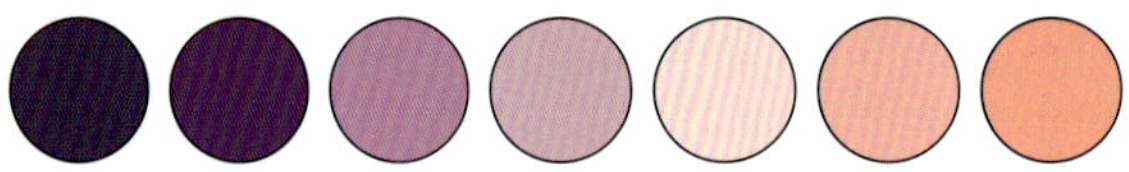

This palette could be considered both complementary or analogous, as it blends neighboring hues, but starts with two complementary colors. It also uses a value gradient, with darker values on both extremes and lighter values in the middle. The saturation of each color is consistent. Note that the fourth and fifth colors are a purple that lean a bit pink and a pink that leans a bit blue to create a natural shift from purple to coral.

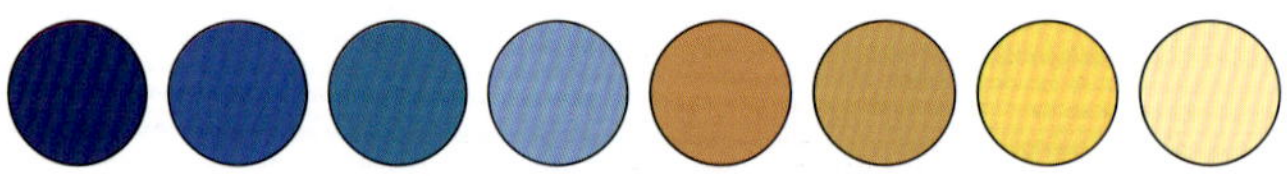

This palette attempts to create a complementary gradient, but it falls a bit short. There is no blending between the two colors. Within each hue family, there is inconsistency in hue, value, and saturation. To improve this palette, there should be a transition point between the fourth color (light blue) and the fifth color (mustard yellow) and more consistency between the hues.

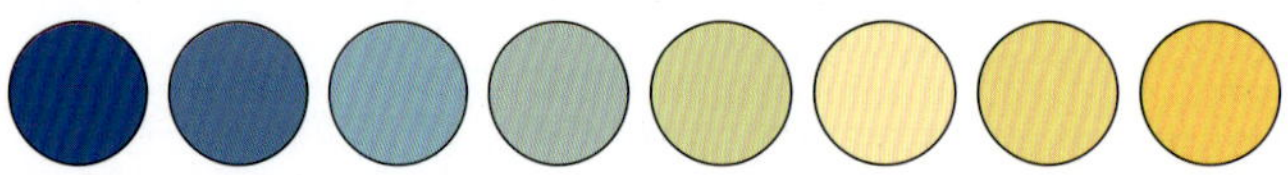

This palette successfully creates the blue—yellow complementary gradient attempted in the previous example. The inclusion of an aqua blue and a green—leaning yellow provides a transition point, and the hues step more consistently from blue to yellow.

USING PRINTS VS. SOLIDS

It is easiest to create ombré and gradient color palettes using solid fabrics, but that doesn't mean it can't be done with prints. While following the same guidelines explored in this chapter, also consider the following:

- Choose prints that feature mostly one hue. While a print that has one primary hue and a couple of supporting colors may work well, a print that has several different main/featured colors will be difficult to tie into an ombré or gradient palette.
- Pay close attention to the value of the dominant color in the print. This is sometimes the background color, but not always! It can be a bit trickier to determine the value of a print than a solid fabric, but it's still very important in ensuring your palette turns out correctly. Converting a photo of your fabric pull to black and white can help determine the value variation in the fabrics.
- Prints are a great time to utilize light neutrals when transitioning from one color to another, as they add a bit of interest in a neutral area without being too distracting with too many colors.

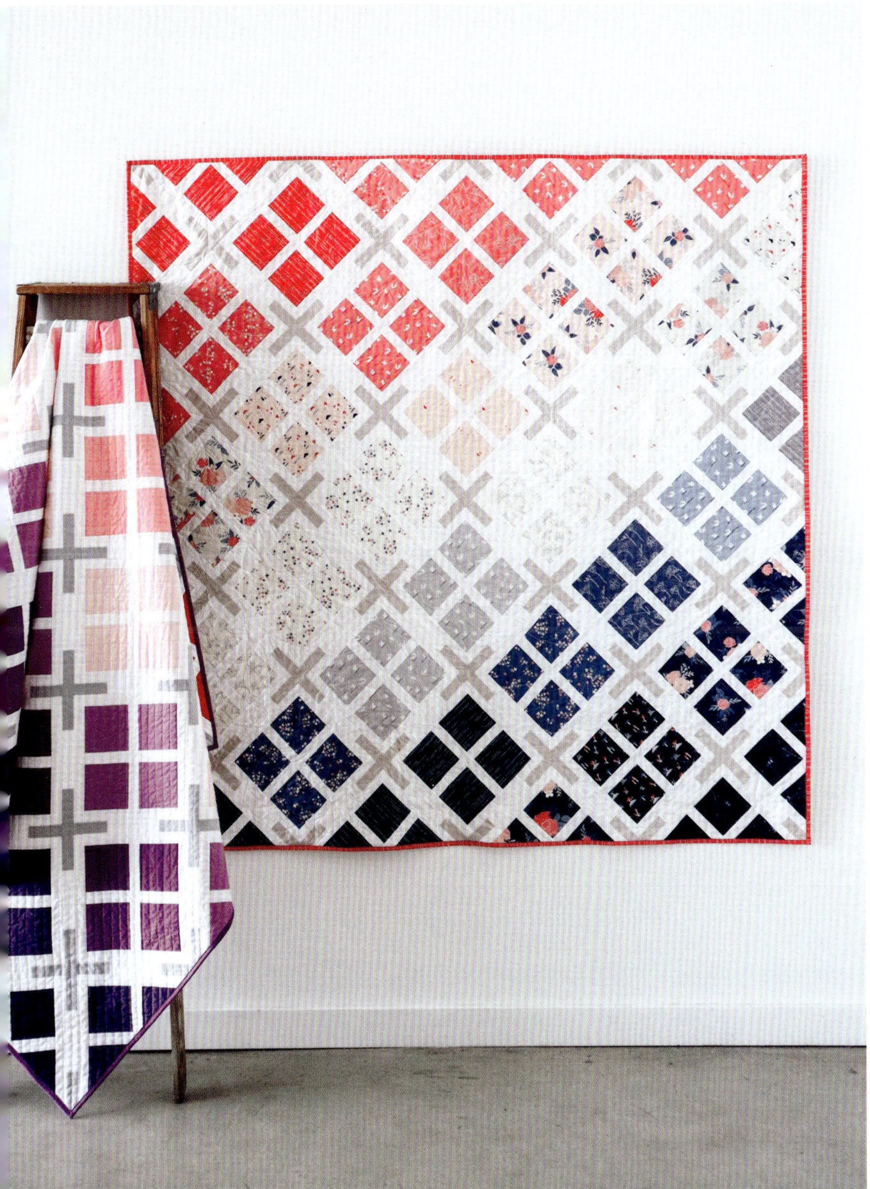

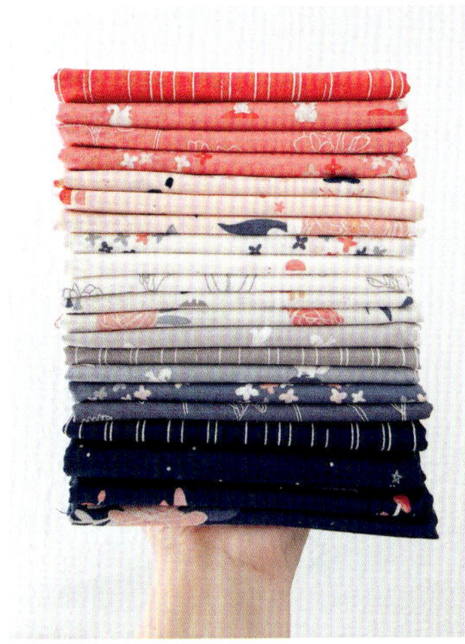

Photos, quilt pattern, and fabric line by Fran Gulick of Cotton and Joy

Adapting Quilt Patterns for Gradient Palettes

While this book contains many projects specifically designed as ombré quilts, you may be wondering how you can adapt patterns you already have or want to make to take advantage of your new gradient knowledge. This can be easy or tricky depending on the pattern! Keep in mind:

- Fat—quarter friendly patterns tend to work well for gradients depending on how the designer uses them. Are they used in a row—based design, where each row features a different fat quarter? This would lend itself well to an ombré quilt. Are they mixed together in the blocks throughout the pattern, and could this be used to create an ombré effect? This takes some careful consideration of how the pattern is constructed.

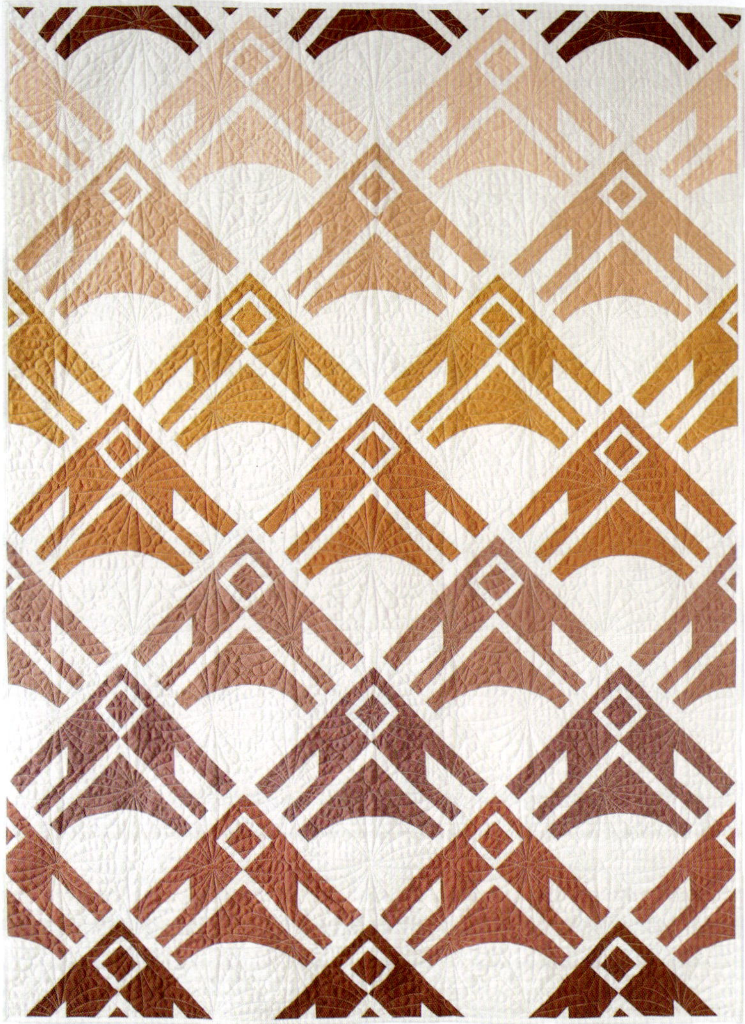

Patterns that utilize row—based color blocking are some of the easiest for making an ombré quilt. Persephone pattern by Alderwood Studio.

- Patterns that use a limited color palette of three or four colors can usually be easily adapted to create a quilt with an ombré effect, even if it's a bit more subtle. Stick to monochromatic color schemes in these instances for maximum impact.

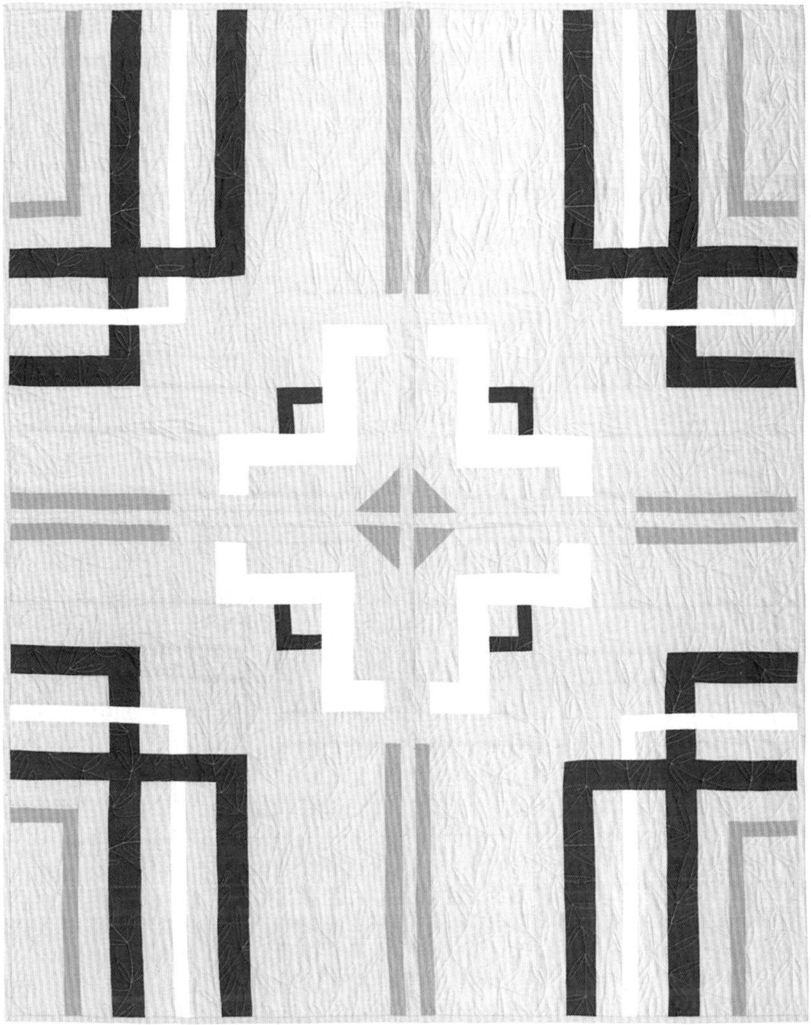

A limited color palette can easily be made ombré with the right fabric choices. Boxwood pattern by Alderwood Studio.

- Look critically at the design of the pattern you want to adapt and how color is used. If the designer uses a variety of colors across a few elements, could you instead homogenize the design, using the same color across multiple elements, before blending into the next gradient shade? If the designer instead used only a few colors, could you expand the number of fabrics used to create an ombré effect?

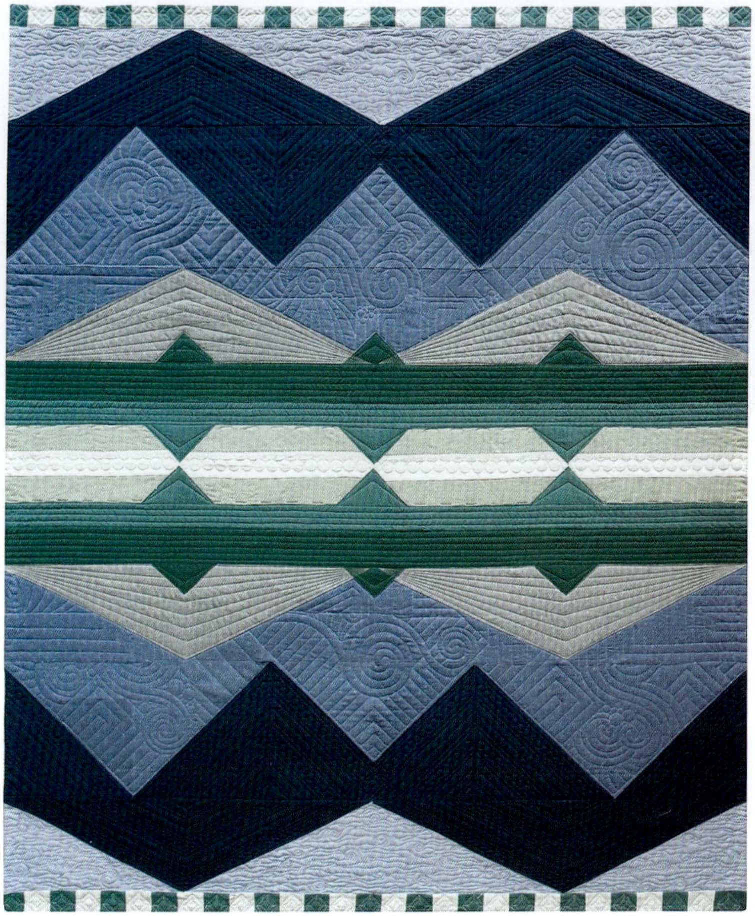

Patterns that follow a linear layout are easy to adapt for gradients. Cascadia pattern by Alderwood Studio.

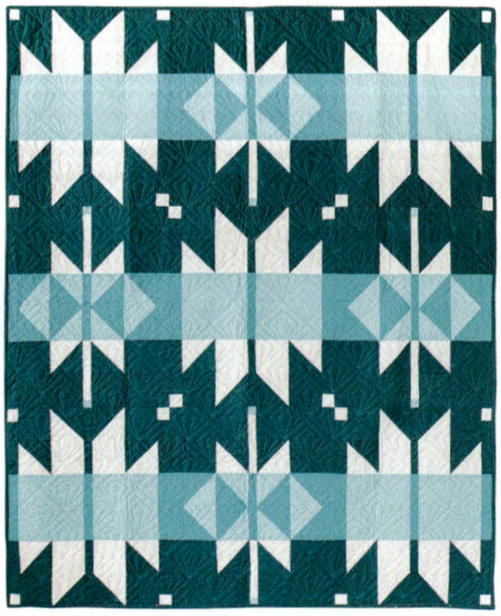

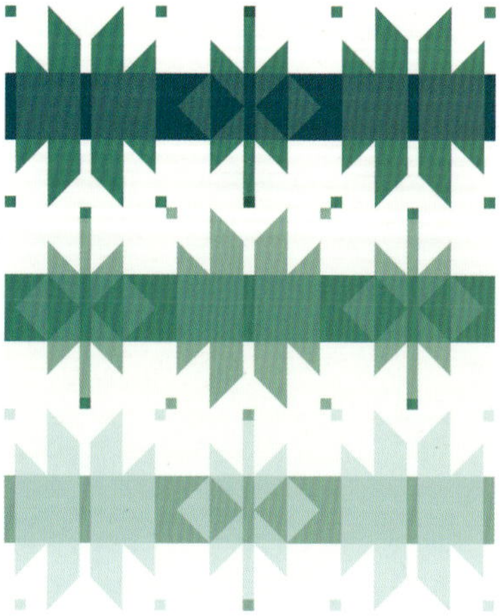

This pattern lends itself well to ombré as written (left), but by adding additional colors it can give a more striking gradient impact (right). Courgette pattern by Alderwood Studio and Great Heron Thread Co.

Color Palette Inspiration

Once you've mastered the basics of selecting fabrics for gradients, you can start to get a bit more creative with mixing hue and value shifts. These color palettes show both straightforward and more complex gradients:

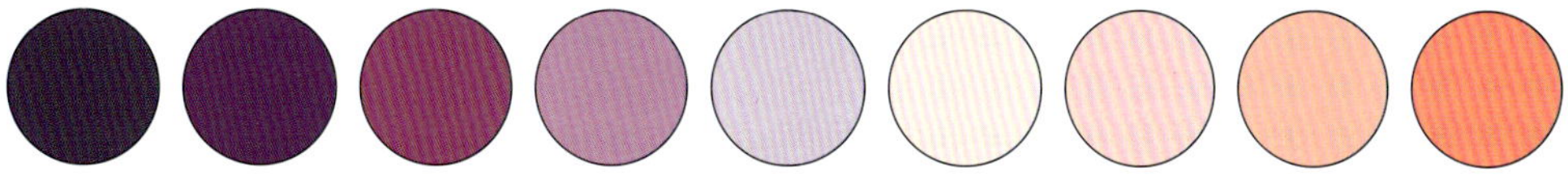

This complementary palette shifts in hue from violet to peach, but has a mirrored value gradient, with lighter values in the middle.

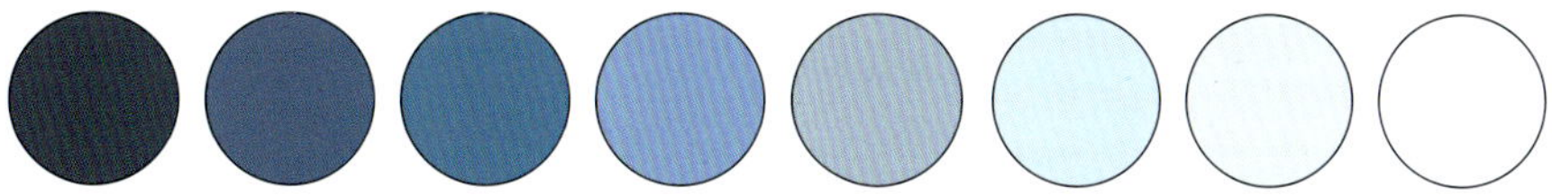

This monochromatic blue palette keeps it simple by shifting only in value from dark to light.

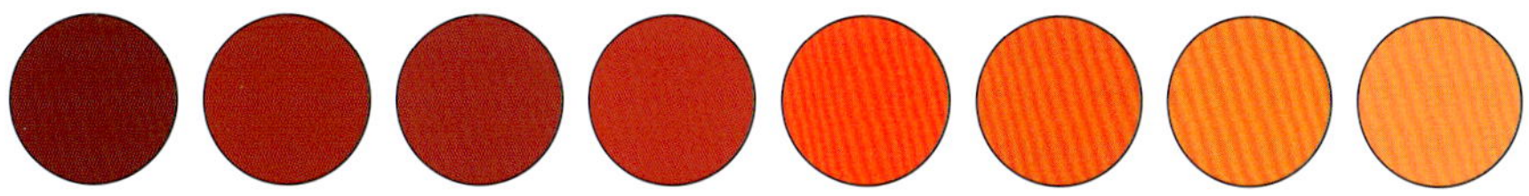

This analogous palette shifts in hue from red to orange.

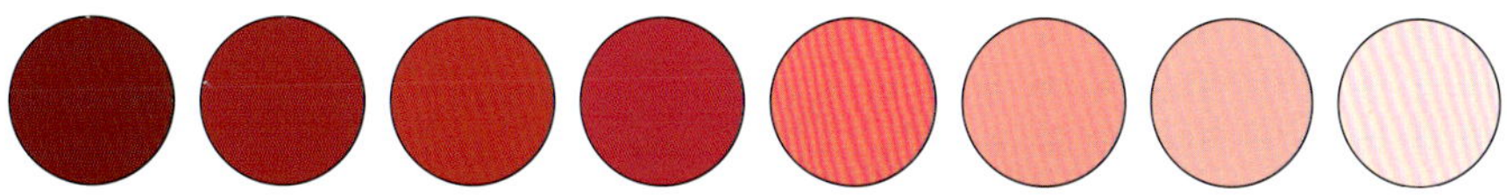

This monochromatic red palette shifts in value to pink.

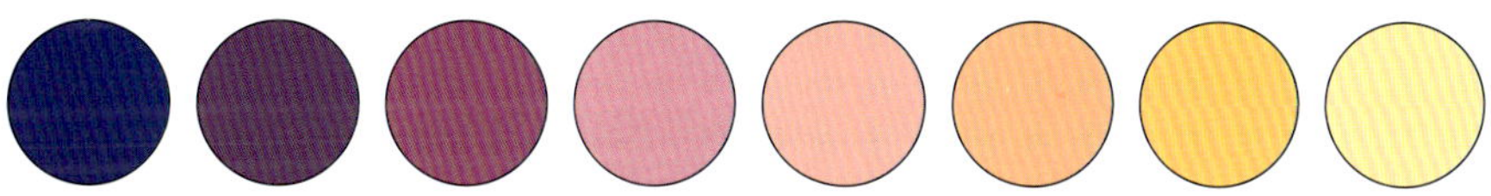

This complementary color palette moves from blue to yellow using fairly saturated colors.

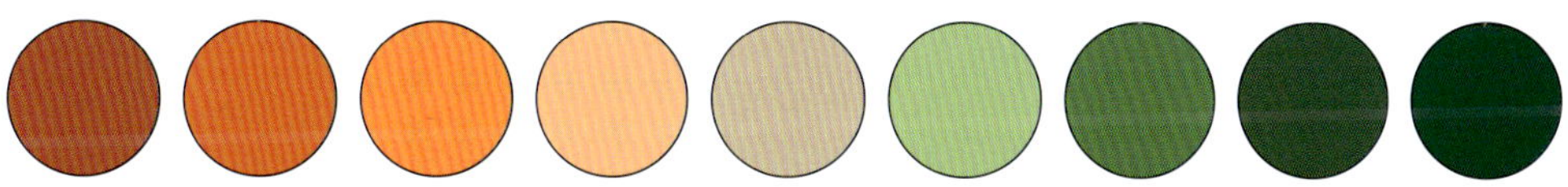

This complementary color palette uses similar—value colors and a muted neutral to blend cohesively.

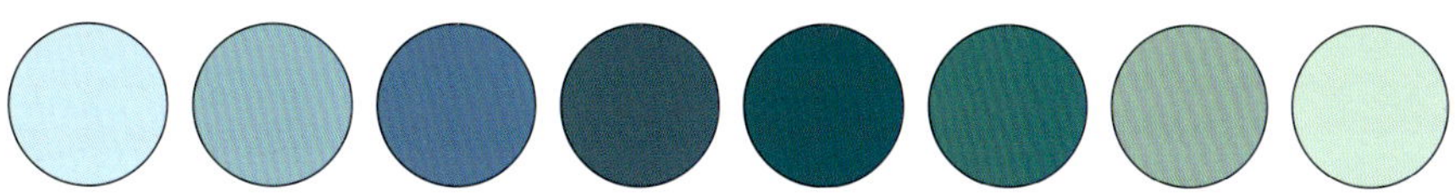

This analogous palette shifts in hue from blue to green, and has a mirrored value gradient, with darker values in the middle.

QUILT PROJECTS

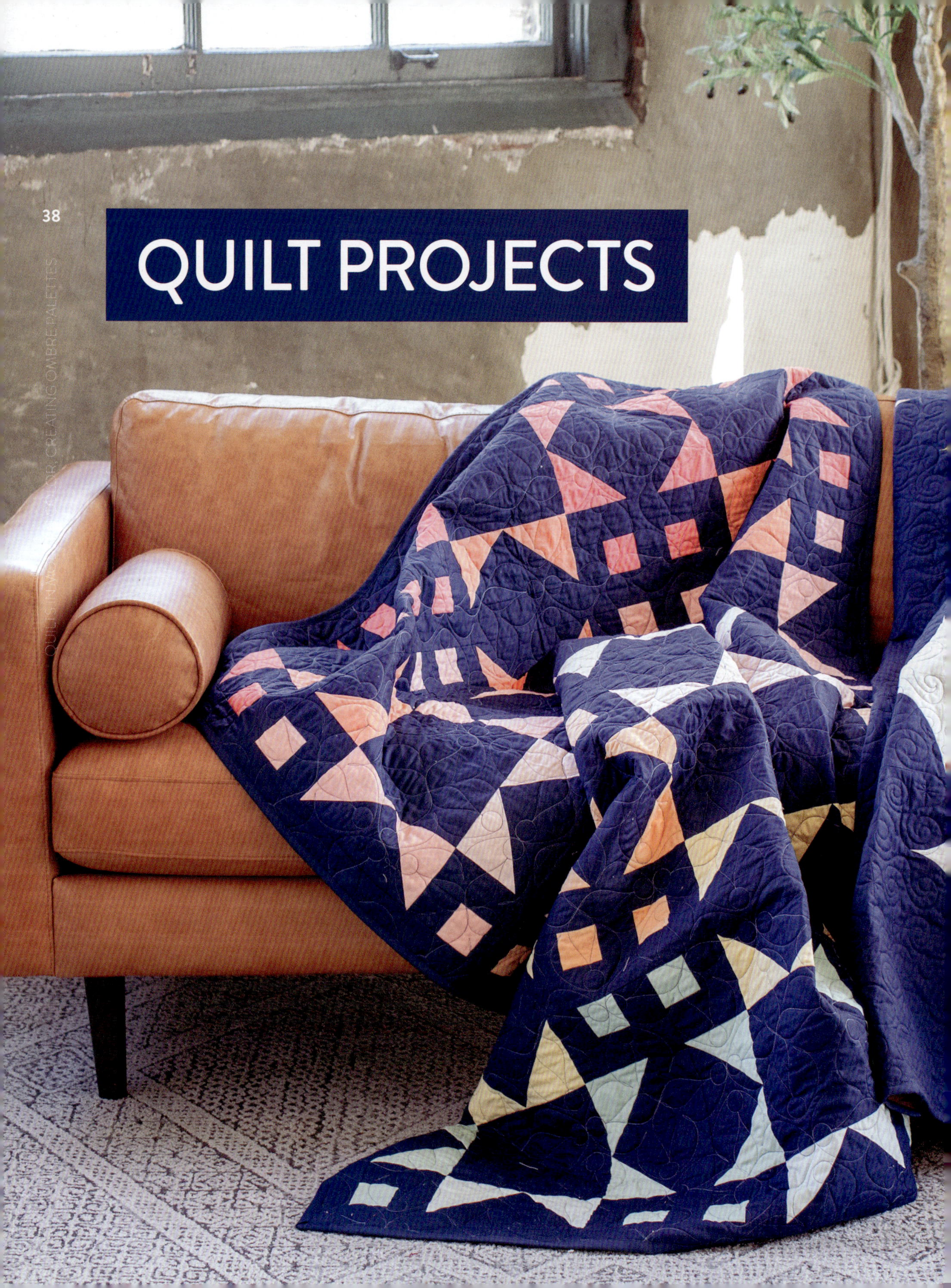

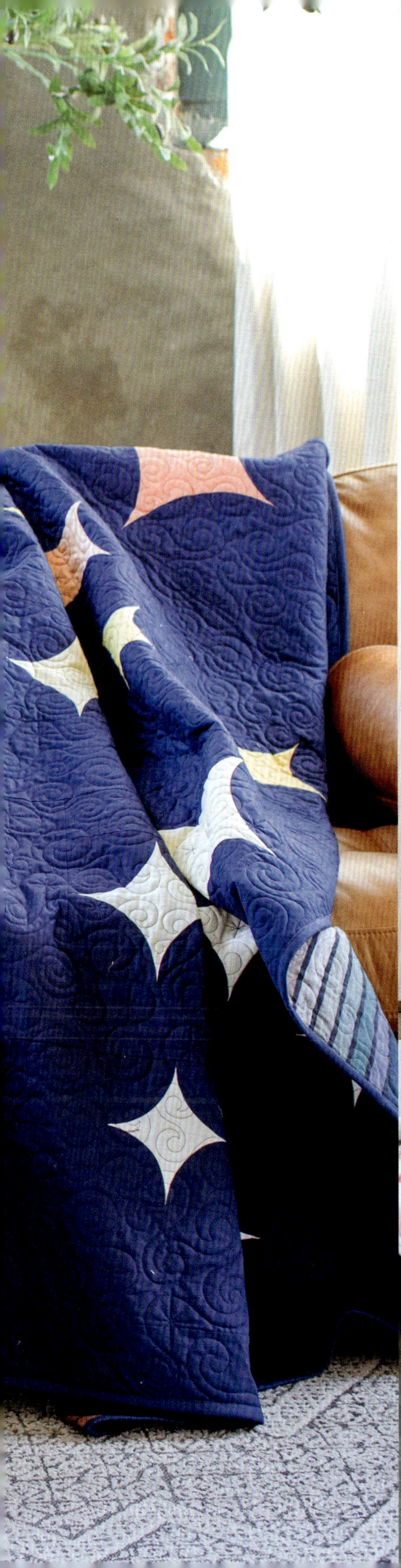
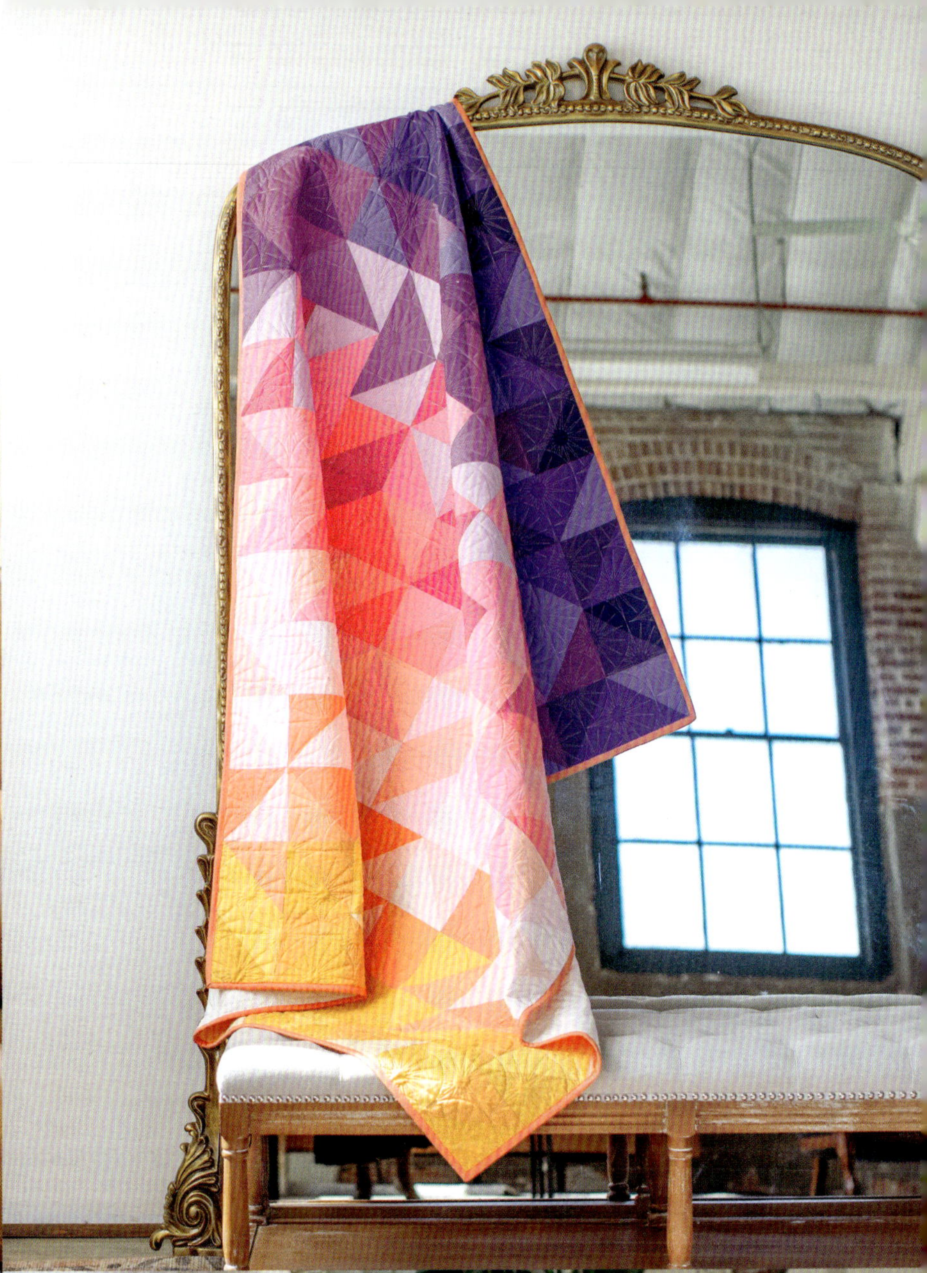
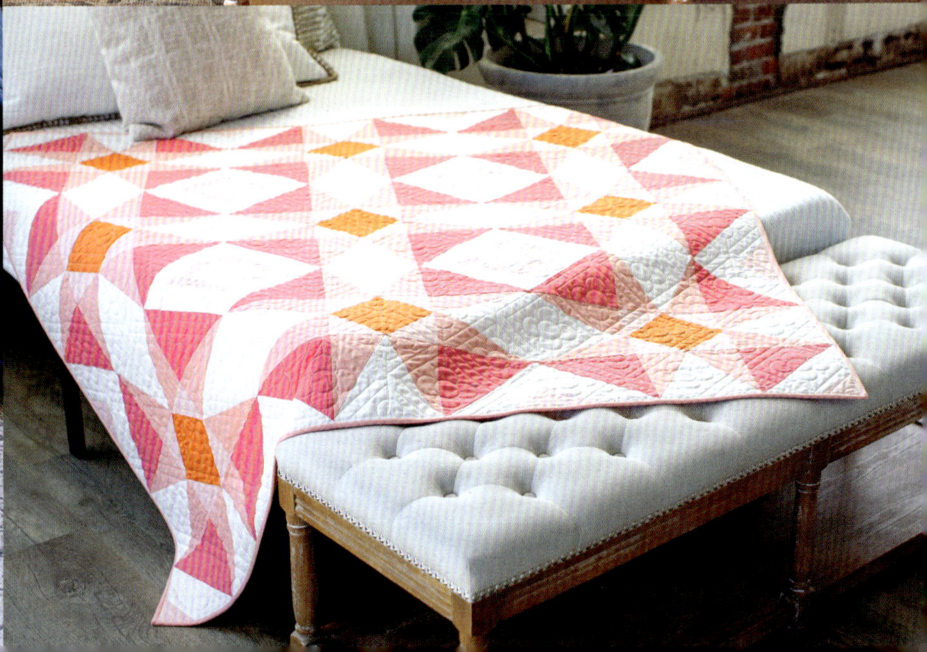

Gradient Grid Quilt

BABY SIZE 37″ × 44″ * THROW SIZE 60″ × 74″

Gradient Grid is a beginner friendly gradient project. It has a modern, minimalist vibe and is a quick sew, making it a great last minute gift! This pattern is a great place to get started with ombré and gradient sewing. Its simple design allows for several different layouts, including vertical, diagonal, and radial gradients. It tends to be most striking with a value—based monochromatic palette, but it would also be lovely with a complementary palette.

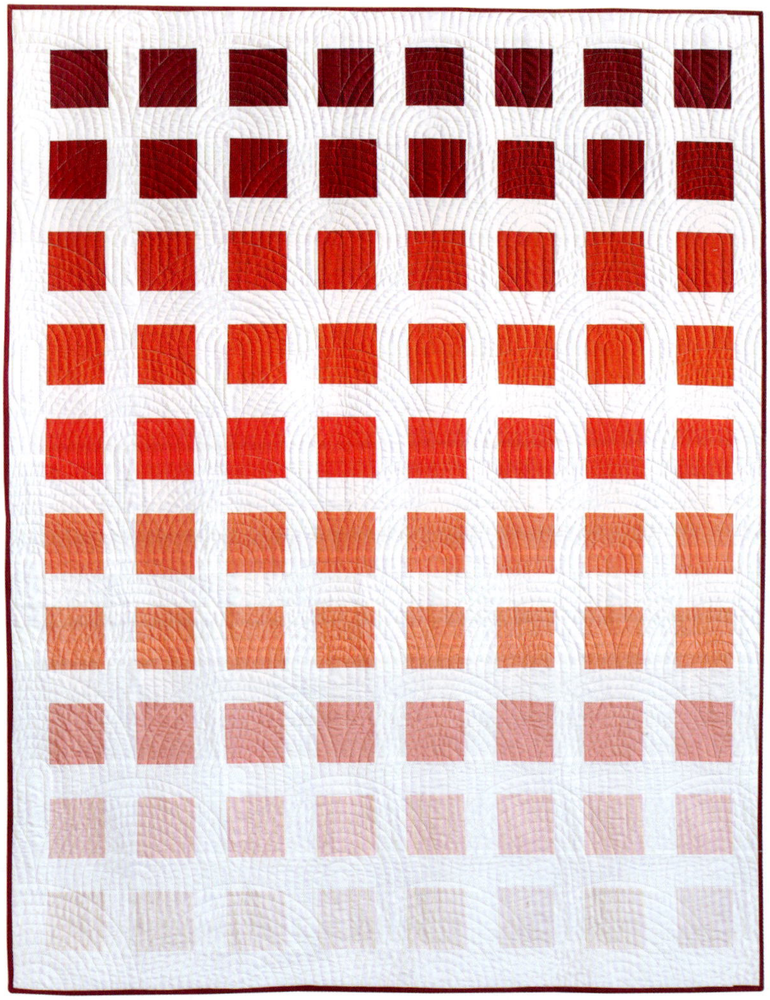

I've included two sizes. The baby quilt has four fewer rows and three fewer columns. So, make sure you consider the size of your palette (aka the number of fabrics you can use) before finalizing your fabric pull. For more on choosing a gradient palette, see Gradients in Quilts (page 26).

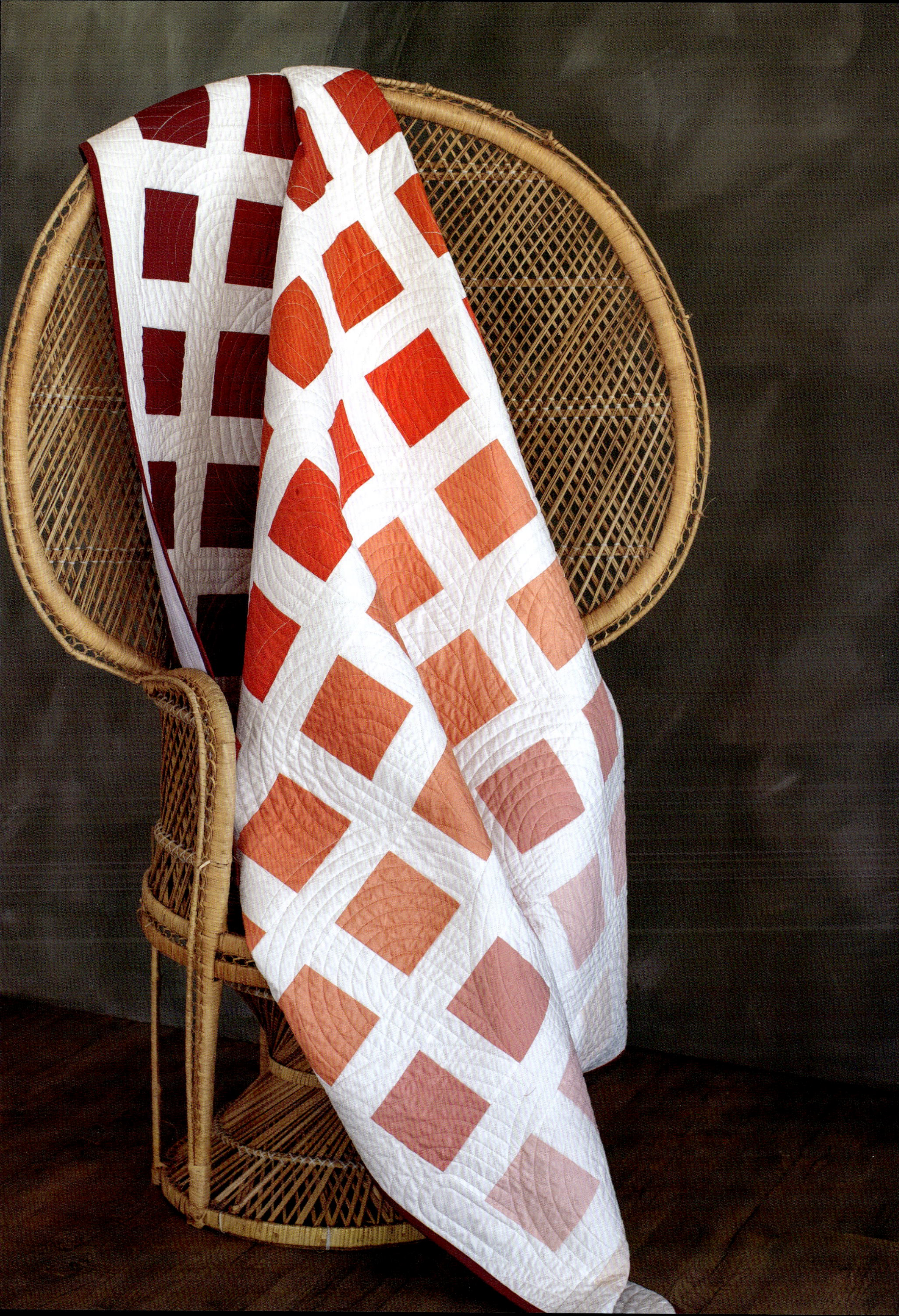

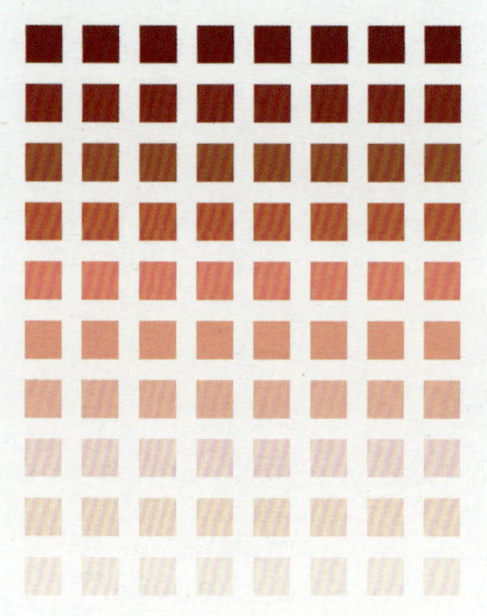

Vertical gradient

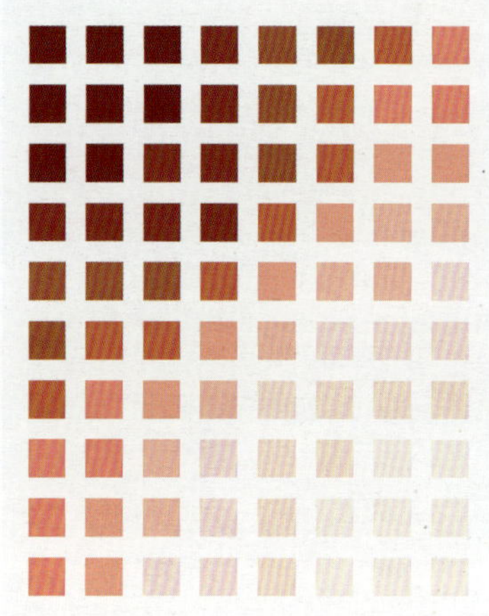

Diagonal gradient

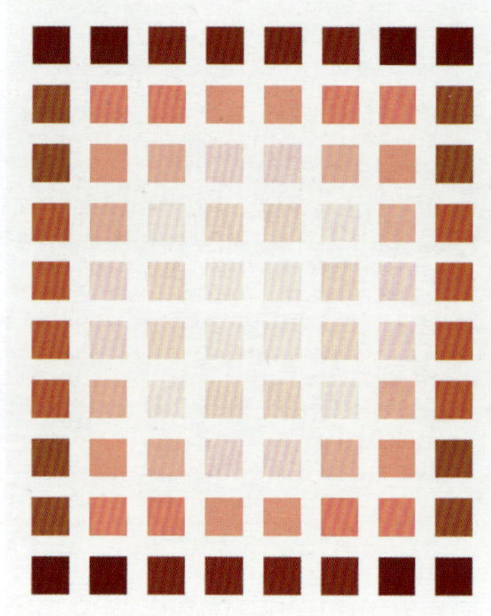

Radial gradient

Fabric Requirements

Fabric *Riley Blake Confetti Cotton Solids*		**Baby (37″ × 44″)**	**Throw (60″ × 74″)**
	Fabric A • *Wine*	¼ yard	¼ yard
	Fabric B • *Dahlia Red*	¼ yard	¼ yard
	Fabric C • *Burnt Orange*	¼ yard	¼ yard
	Fabric D • *Autumn*	¼ yard	¼ yard
	Fabric E • *Lipstick*	¼ yard	¼ yard
	Fabric F • *Salmon*	¼ yard	¼ yard
	Fabric G • *Apricot Blush*	-	¼ yard
	Fabric H • *Grapefruit*	-	¼ yard
	Fabric I • *Peaches and Cream*	-	¼ yard
	Fabric J • *Shell*	-	¼ yard
	Fabric K • *Off White*	1⅜ yard	2¾ yard

Cutting Instructions

Fabric	Baby	Throw
A-F (baby) A-J (throw)	*Cut 1 — 5″ × WOF strip; subcut into* 1 — 5″ × 5″ square (**A2—F2**) 1 — 5″ × 37″ strip (**A1—F1**)	*Cut 1 — 5″ × WOF strip; subcut into* 1 — 5″ × 5″ squares (**A2—J2**) 1 — 5″ × 37″ strips (**A1—J1**)
K	*Cut 10 — 3″ × WOF strips; subcut into* 5 — 3″ × 37″ strips (**K1**) 5 — 3″ × 33″ strips (**K2**) *Cut 4 — 2¾″ × WOF strips; subcut into* 2 — 2¾″ × 40″ strips (**K3**) 2 — 2¾″ × 37½″ strips (**K4**)	*Cut 21 — 3″ × WOF strips, sewn together and subcut into* 10 — 3″ × 37″ strips (**K1**) 9 — 3″ × 54″ strips (**K2**) *Cut 7 — 3¾″ × WOF strips, and sew them together; subcut into* 2 — 3¾″ × 68″ strips (**K3**) 2 — 3¾″ × 60½″ strips (**K4**)

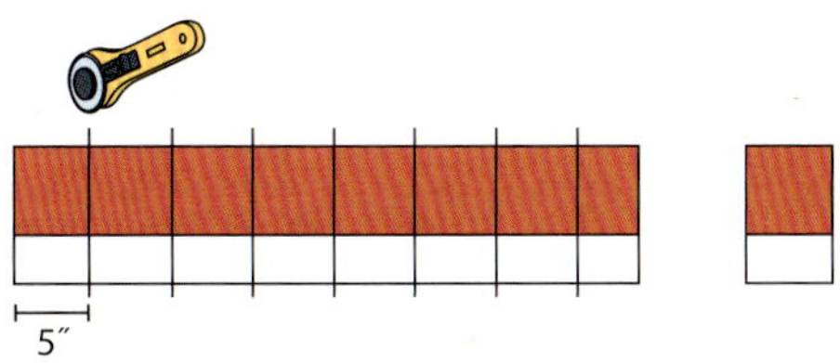

Strip Unit Assembly

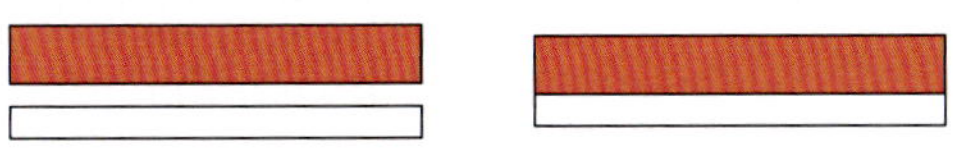

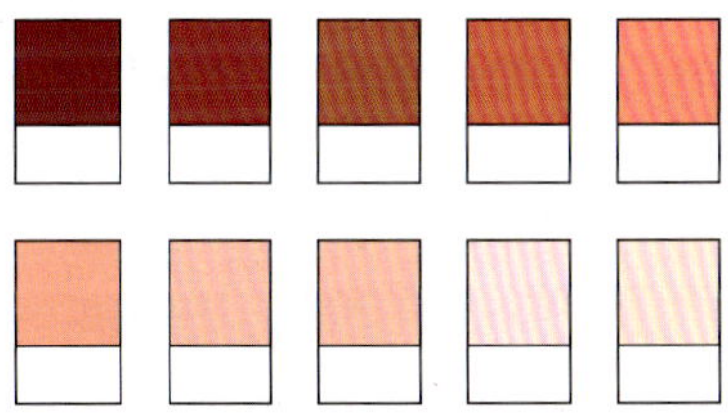

The baby size will have four of each of the first six units shown here. The throw size will have seven of each unit shown.

1. Sew the A1–F1 (baby) or A1–J1 (throw) strips each to a K1 strip. Press each unit toward the darker fabric.

2. Subcut each unit from Step 1 into 4 (baby) or 7 (throw) 5″ × 7½″ Strip Units. Call them Strip Unit A–Strip Unit F (baby) or Strip Unit A–Strip Unit J (throw).

Quilt Assembly

Each row of this quilt is made up of 4 (baby) or 7 (throw) Strip Units and one A2–F2 square (baby) or A2–J2 square (throw). There are many different ways to lay out these units to achieve different gradient effects. The instructions will proceed assuming you are creating the same quilt as shown in the sample, but you can arrange the Strip Units however you like in the next steps to create your desired effect. The diagrams in the following steps will show the assembly of the throw size quilt; the baby size will be the same with fewer units.

1. Rotate and arrange the Strip Units. Arrange 7 Strip Units (throw) or 4 Strip Units (baby) into each row. Sew the Strip Units together, using the same fabric for each row. Then sew a matching A2–F2 square (baby) or A2–J2 square (throw) to one end of each row. There should be 6 (baby) or 10 (throw) rows. The rows measure 5″ × 33″ (baby) or 5″ × 54″ (throw). Trim if needed.

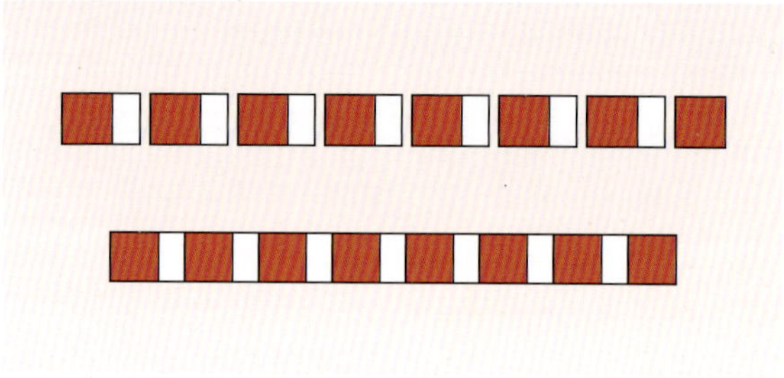

2. Arrange a K2 strip between each row from Step 1. Sew together all of the rows. Press the seams open or toward the darker fabric. The quilt top should now measure 33″ × 40″ (baby) or 54″ × 68″ (throw).

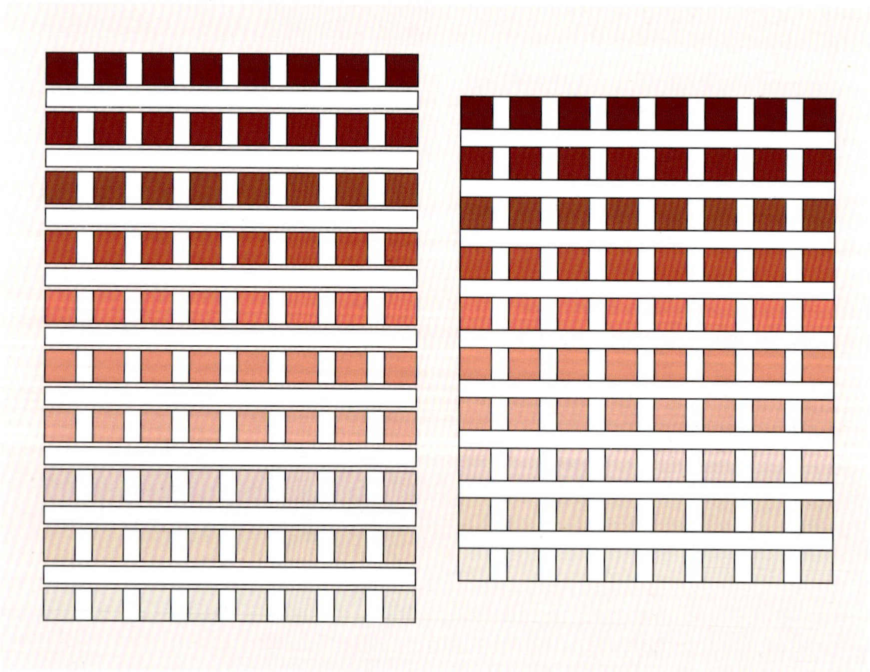

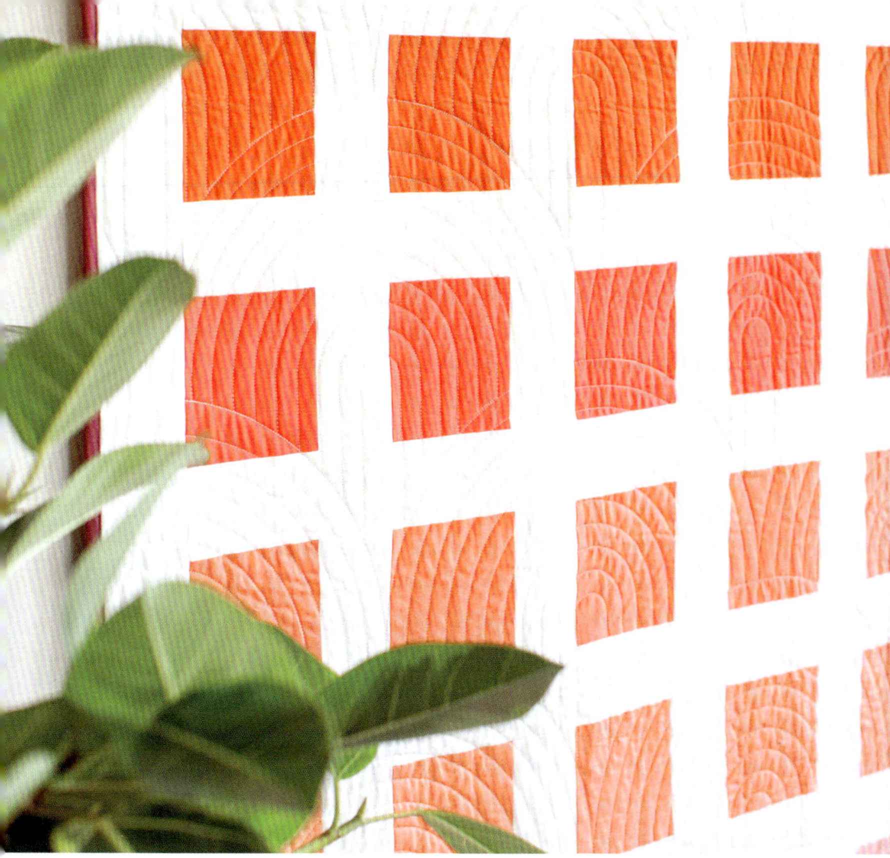

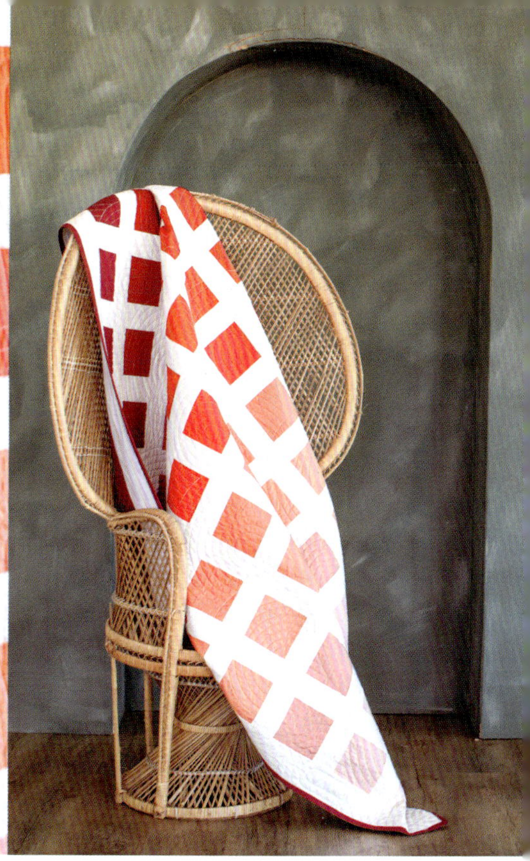

Sample quilt longarm quilted by Jenn B Quilts.

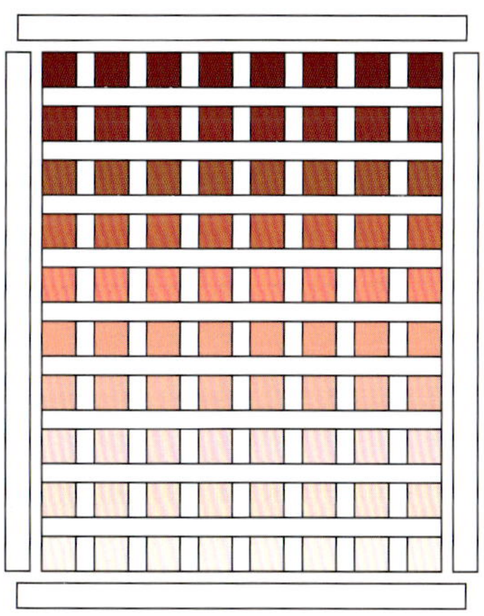

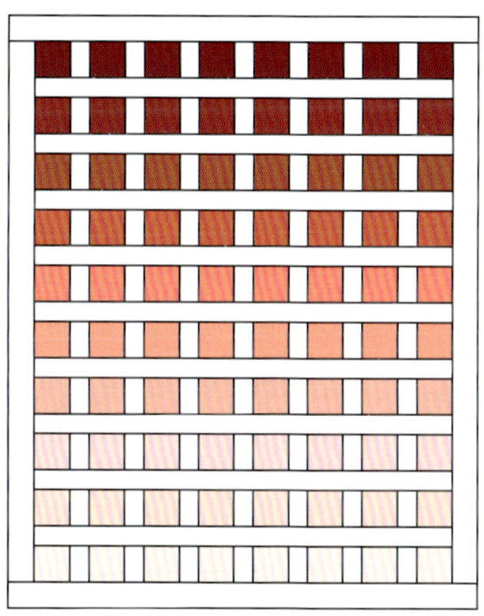

Final throw version

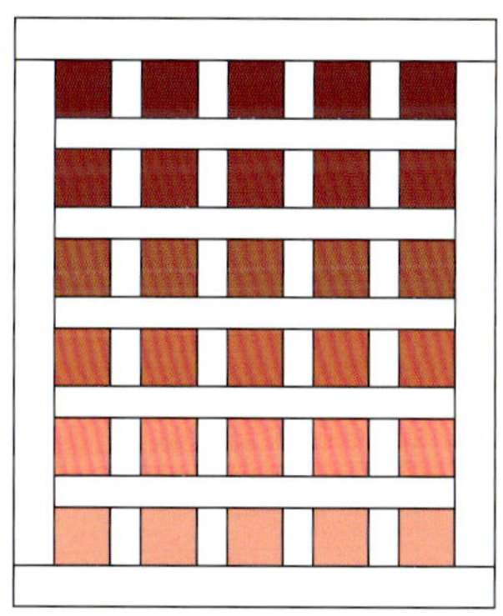

Final baby version

3. Sew a K3 strip to each of the 2 long sides of the quilt top. Press the seams toward the quilt interior. Sew a K4 strip to the top and bottom of the quilt, again pressing toward the quilt interior.

Ombré Stars Quilt

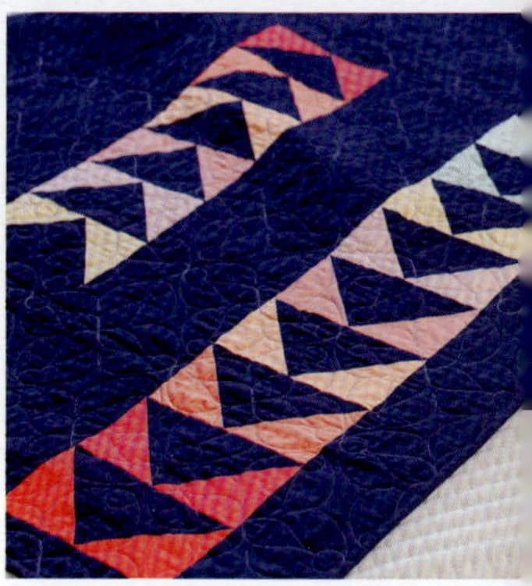

BABY SIZE 42″ × 42″ • THROW SIZE 56″ × 74″

There's nothing more classic than a Sawtooth Star, and sometimes it's fun to go back to basics… with a twist. This pattern does just that, mixing negative space with a linear ombré pattern to create a fresh take on this traditional block. Utilizing Flying Geese and simple strip piecing, this pattern is a great option for a confident beginner!

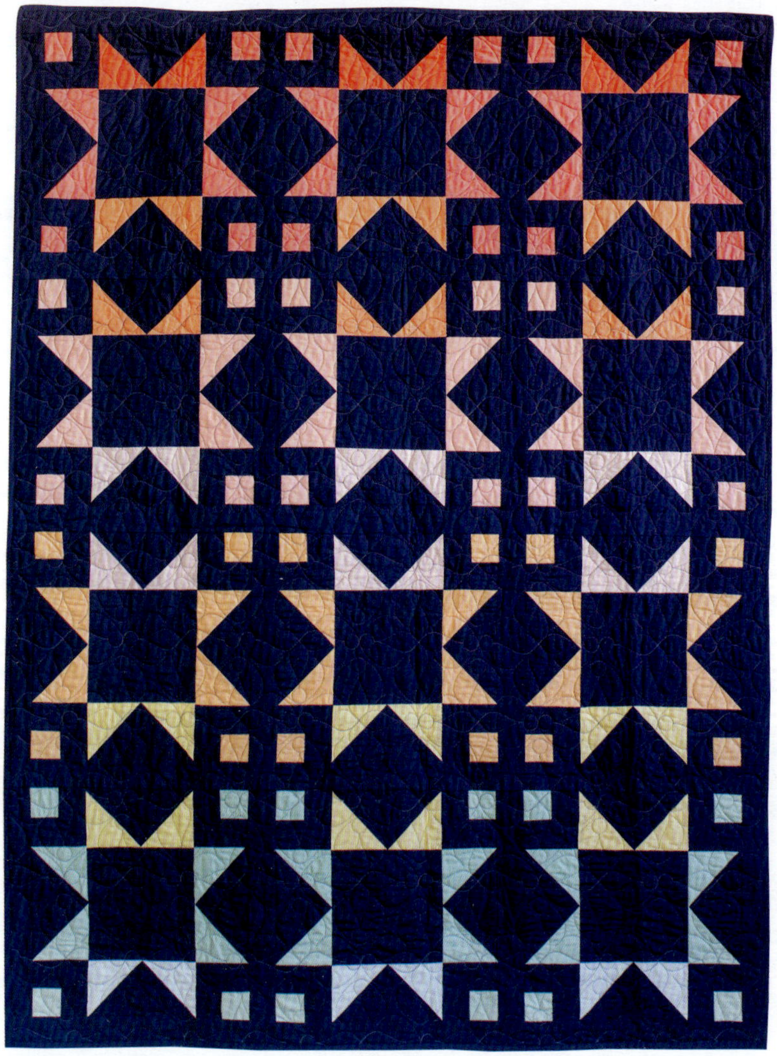

I've included two sizes. The baby quilt has one fewer row. So, make sure you consider the size of your palette (aka the number of fabrics you can use) before finalizing your fabric pull. For more on choosing a gradient palette, see Gradients in Quilts (page 26).

This pattern will show the construction of the throw version, which has 4 different blocks. The baby version construction is the same, but with only three blocks instead. When constructing this pattern, you will have one to two extra flying geese of each color. I suggest sewing these together and adding them to your backing (shown above) to create an extra fun quilt with ombré on both sides!

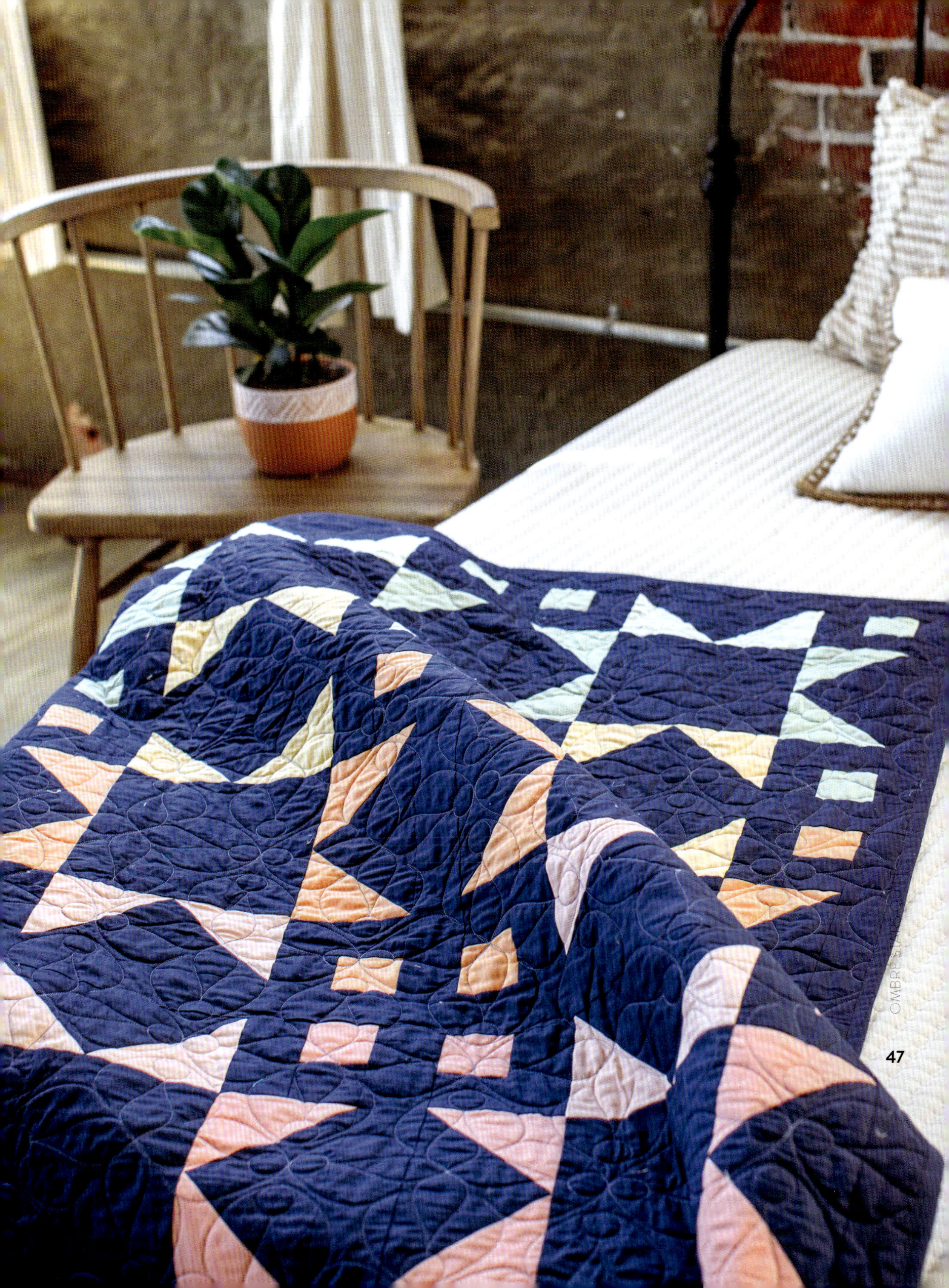

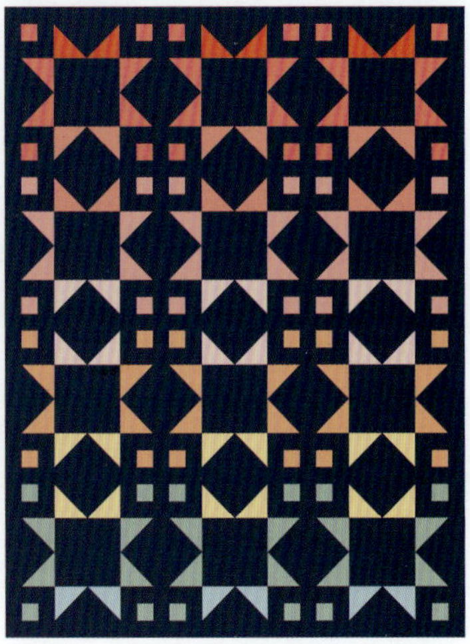

Linear gradient

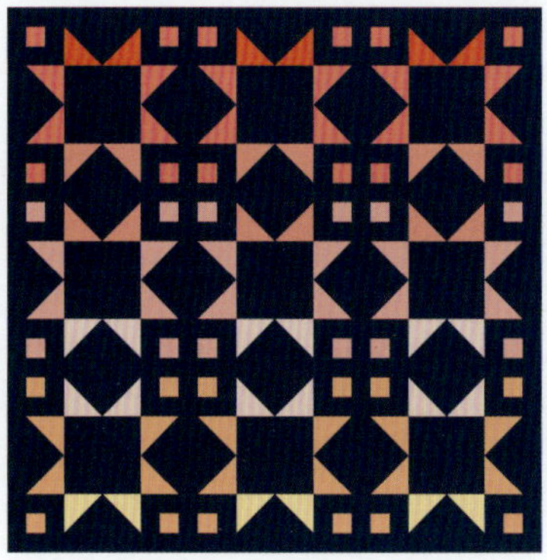

Baby size linear gradient

Fabric Requirements

Fabric *Riley Blake Confetti Cotton Solids*	**Baby (42″ × 42″)**	**Throw (56″ × 74″)**
Fabric A • *Rouge*	⅛ yard or 1 FE	¼ yard or 1 FE
Fabric B • *Lipstick*	¼ yard or 1 FQ	¼ yard or 1 FQ
Fabric C • *Salmon*	¼ yard or 1 FQ	¼ yard or 1 FQ
Fabric D • *Grapefruit*	¼ yard or 1 FQ	¼ yard or 1 FQ
Fabric E • *Peaches and Cream*	¼ yard or 1 FQ	¼ yard or 1 FQ
Fabric F • *Marmalade*	¼ yard or 1 FQ	¼ yard or 1 FQ
Fabric G • *Sunshine*	⅛ yard or 1 FE	¼ yard or 1 FQ
Fabric H • *Sage*	-	¼ yard or 1 FQ
Fabric I • *Misty*	-	¼ yard or 1 FE
Fabric J • *Riley Navy*	2¼ yards	3⅝ yard

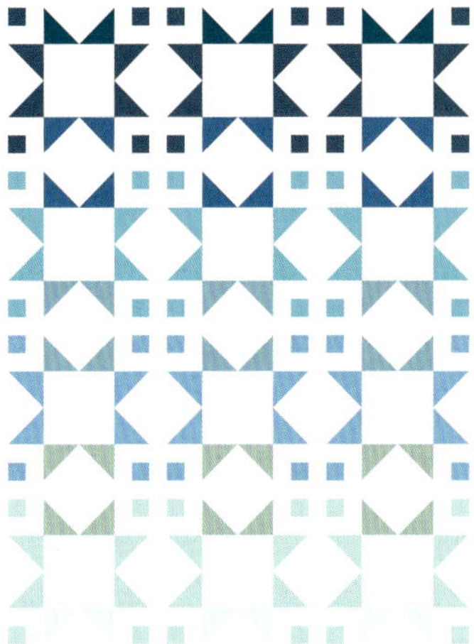

Linear gradient

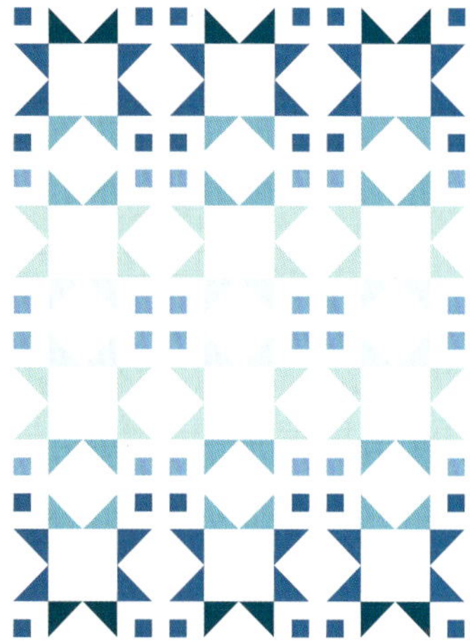

Mirrored linear gradient: By replacing fabrics F – I with duplicates of fabrics A – D, you create a reflected gradient.

Cutting Instructions

Fabric	Baby	Throw
A (baby) **A, I (throw)**	*Cut 1 – 4″ × WOF strip; subcut into* 4 – 4″ × 4″ squares (**A1**)	*Cut 1 – 5″ × WOF strip; subcut into* 4 – 5″ × 5″ squares (**A1, I1**)
B, D, F (baby) **B, D, F, H (throw)**	*Cut 1 – 4″ × WOF strip; subcut into* 8 – 4″ × 4″ squares (**B1, D1, F1**) *Cut 1 – 2″ × WOF strip; subcut into* 2 – 2″ × 14″ rectangles (**B2, D2, F2**)	*Cut 1 – 5″ × WOF strip; subcut into* 8 – 5″ × 5″ squares (**B1, D1, F1, H1**) *Cut 1 – 2½″ × WOF strip; subcut into* 2 – 2½″ × 16″ rectangles (**B2, D2, F2, H2**)
C, E (both sizes)	*Cut 1 – 4″ × WOF strip; subcut into* 8 – 4″ × 4″ squares (**C1, E1**)	*Cut 1 – 5″ × WOF strip; subcut into* 8 – 5″ × 5″ squares (**C1, E1**)
G (both sizes)	*Cut 1 – 4″ × WOF strip; subcut into* 4 – 4″ × 4″ squares (**G1**)	*Cut 1 – 5″ × WOF strip; subcut into* 8 – 5″ × 5″ squares (**G1**)
J (both sizes)	*Cut 3 – 7½″ × WOF strips; subcut into* 12 – 7½″ × 7½″ squares (**J1**) 6 – 2″ × 12½″ rectangles (**J5**)** *Cut 2 – 6½″ × WOF strips; subcut into* 12 – 6½″ × 6½″ squares (**J4**) *Cut 4 – 2″ × WOF strips; subcut into* 48 – 2″ × 3½″ rectangles (**J3**) *Cut 12 – 2″ × WOF strips; subcut into* 10 – 2″ × 12½″ rectangles (**J5**)** 6 – 2″ × 14 rectangles (**J2**) 5 – 2″ × 42½″ strips (**J6**)*	*Cut 3 – 9¼″ × WOF strips; subcut into* 12 – 9¼″ × 9¼″ squares (**J1**) *Cut 9 – 2½″ × WOF strips; subcut into* 8 – 2½″ × 16″ rectangles (**J2**) 48 – 2½″ × 4½″ rectangles (**J3**) *Cut 3 – 8½″ × WOF strips; subcut into* 12 – 8½″ × 8½″ squares (**J4**) *Cut 8 – 2½″ × WOF strips; subcut into* 16 – 2½″ × 16½″ rectangles (**J5**) *Cut 7 – 2½″ × WOF strips, and sew them together; subcut into* 5 – 2½″ × 56½″ strips (**J6**)

**Note that these WOF strips assume that you can get 42½″ usable inches out of a WOF. If you cannot, utilize some of the remnants created in this cutting section to piece the J6 strips.*

***You will cut 16 total J5 pieces*

Flying Geese Assembly

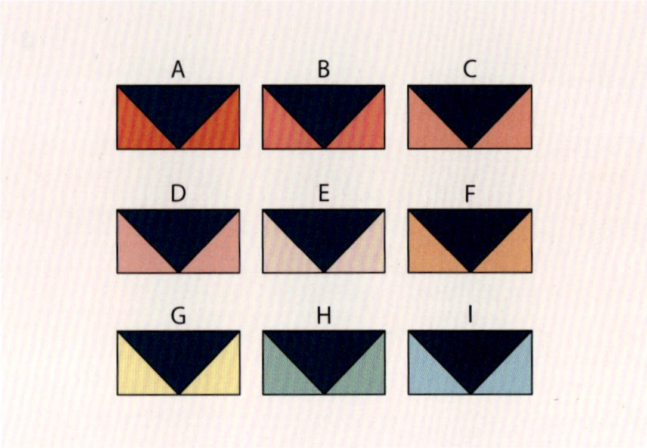

1. Match 4 of each A1–G1 (baby) or A1–I1 (throw) squares with one J1 square, then follow the instructions in Flying Geese: Four-at-a-Time (page 18) to make the number of units listed in Table 1. Trim the Flying Geese to 3½″ × 6½″ (baby size) or 4½″ × 8½″ (throw size).

Table 1

Flying Geese Unit	Baby	Throw
A	4	4
B	8	8
C	8	8
D	8	8
E	8	8
F	8	8
G	4	8
H	-	8
I	-	4

Block Assembly

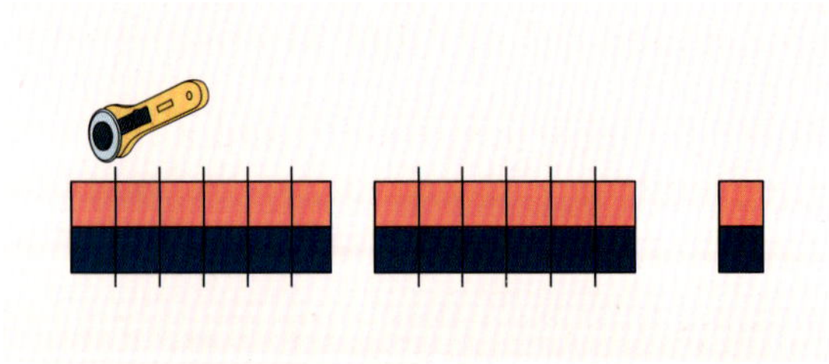

1. Sew each B2, D2, F2, and H2 (H2: throw only) piece to a J2 piece. Press toward the darker fabric. Subcut each strip pair into 6 rectangles 2″ × 3½″ (baby) or 2½″ × 4½″ (throw). There will be 12 units total of each color.

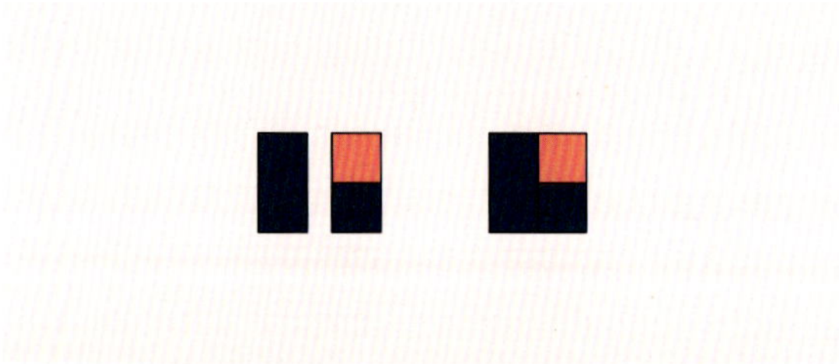

2. Sew a J3 rectangle to the left side of each unit from Step 1. If needed, trim to 3½″ × 3½″ (baby) or 4½″ × 4½″ (throw). There will be 12 total units of each color.

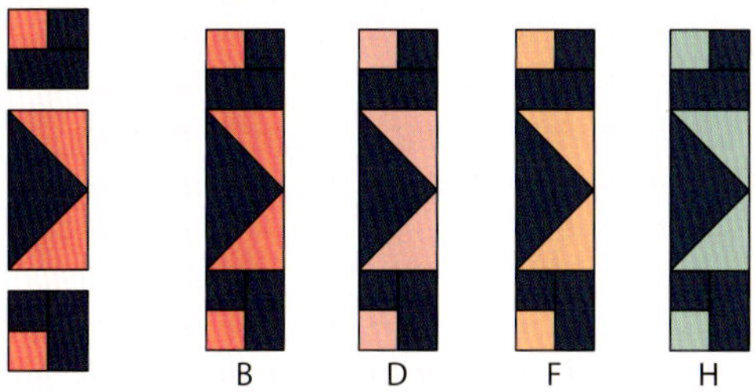

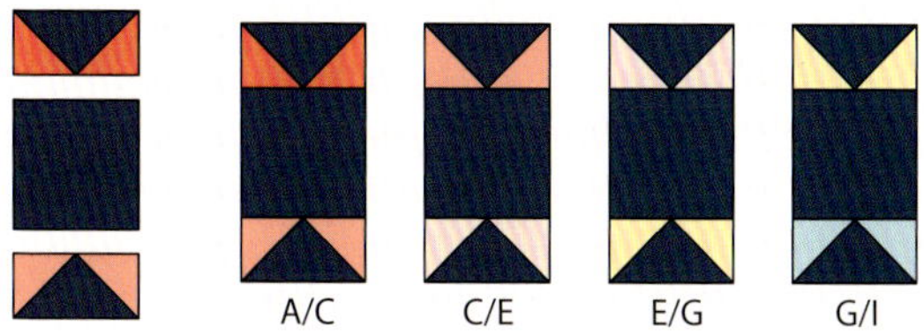

3. Sew a unit from Step 2 to the top and bottom of a matching color flying geese unit, as shown. If needed, trim to 3½″ × 12½″ (baby) or 4½″ × 16½″ (throw). These (6 per color) are called B, D, F, and H Side Units (H: throw only).

4. Pair together sets of flying geese in the following colors: A/C, C/E, E/G, and G/I (G/I: throw only). Sew these pairs on opposite sides of a J4 square. If needed, trim to 6½″ × 12½″ (baby) or 8½″ × 16½″ (throw). These (3 per color) are called A/C, C/E, E/G, and G/I Center Units (G/I: throw only).

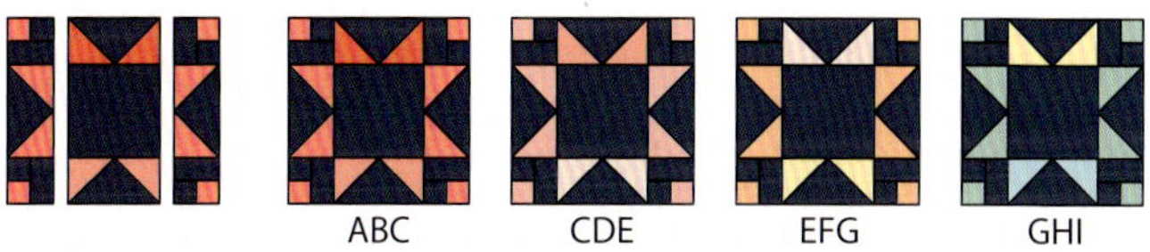

Star Block label diagram

5. Sew the Side Units to the Center Units, using the combinations shown in Table 2. Make 3 of each combination. If needed, trim to 12½″ × 12½″ (baby) or 16½″ × 16½″ (throw). Refer to the Star Block label diagram for the name of each unit (based on the colors used).

Table 2

Side Units	Center Units
B	A/C
D	C/E
F	E/G
H	G/I

Quilt Assembly

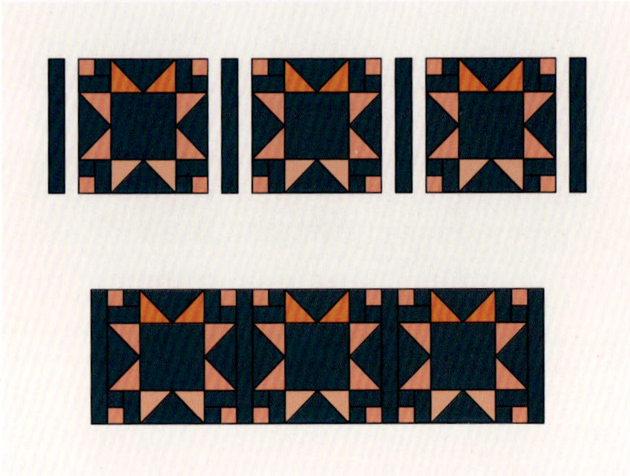

1. Arrange 4 J5 pieces alternating with 3 Star Blocks to create rows as shown. Sew together. Use the same Star Block colorway in each row for a linear gradient. Repeat to create 3 (baby) or 4 (throw) rows, using all the Star Blocks and J5 rectangles. These rows should measure 42½" × 12½" (baby) or 56½" × 16½" (throw). Press the seams away from the Star Blocks.

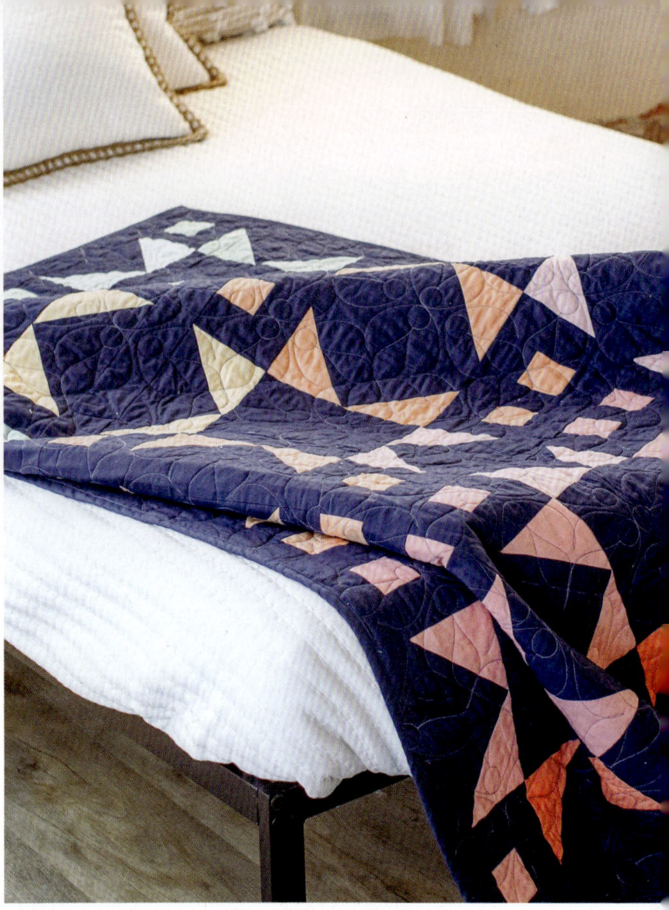

Sample quilt longarm quilted by Jenn B Quilts.

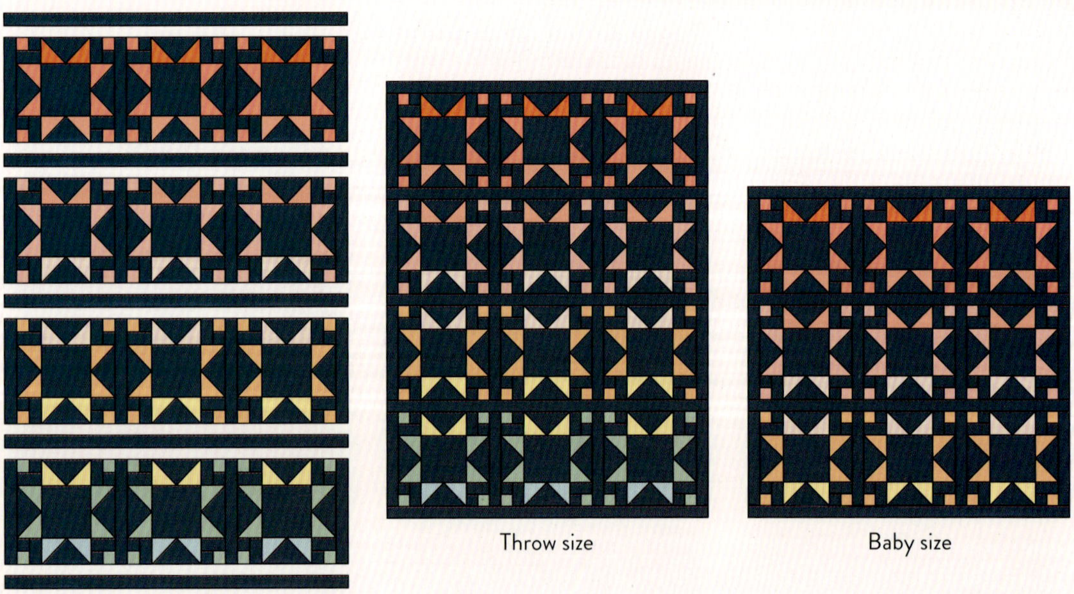

Throw size

Baby size

2. Arrange the J6 strips alternating with the rows created from Step 1. Lay out the rows in alphabetical order from top to bottom, based on the blocks in each row: ABC, CDE, EFG, and GHI (GHI: throw only). Sew together. Press the seams away from the Star Blocks.

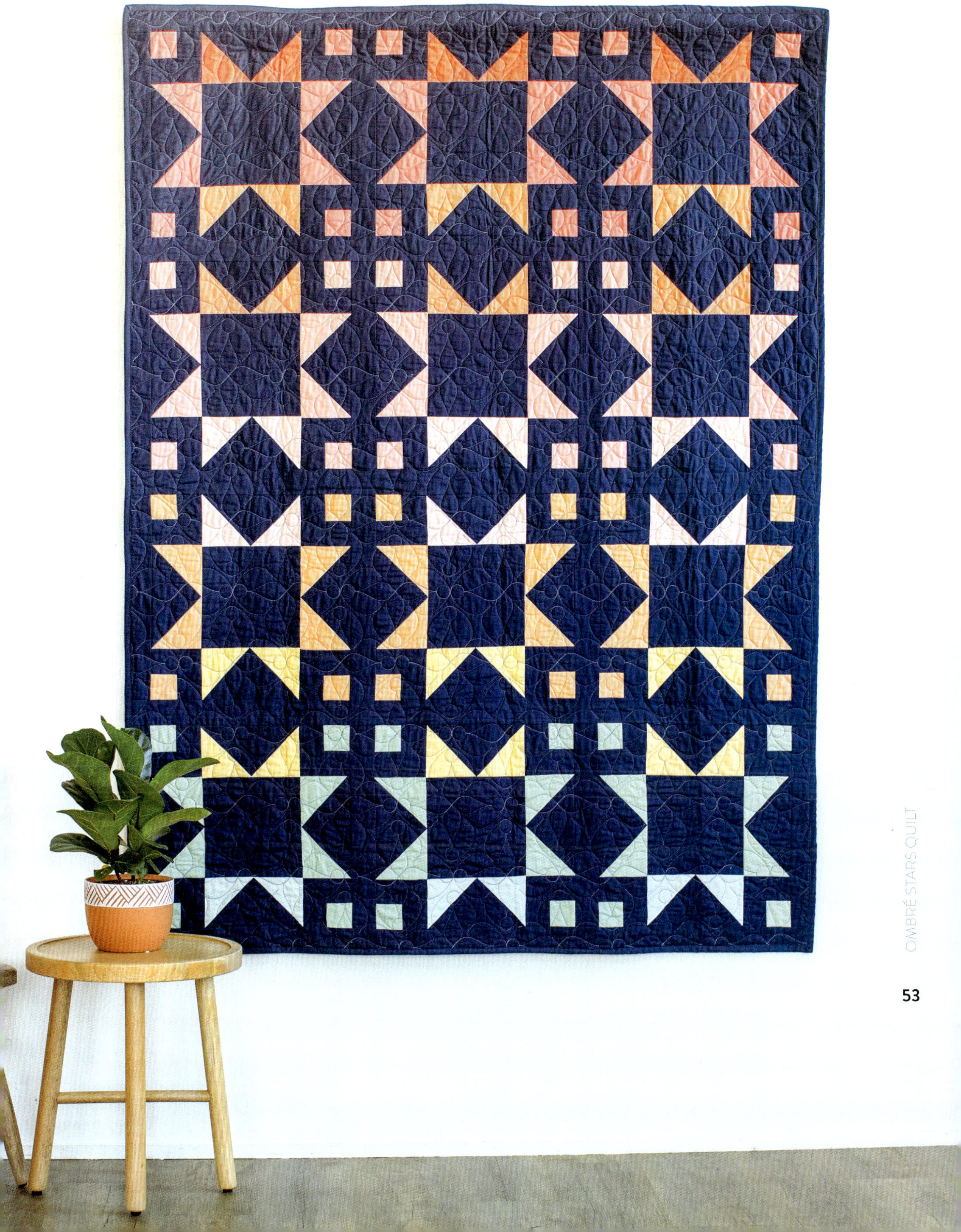

Resonance Quilt

BABY SIZE 36″ × 48″ • THROW SIZE 54″ × 72″

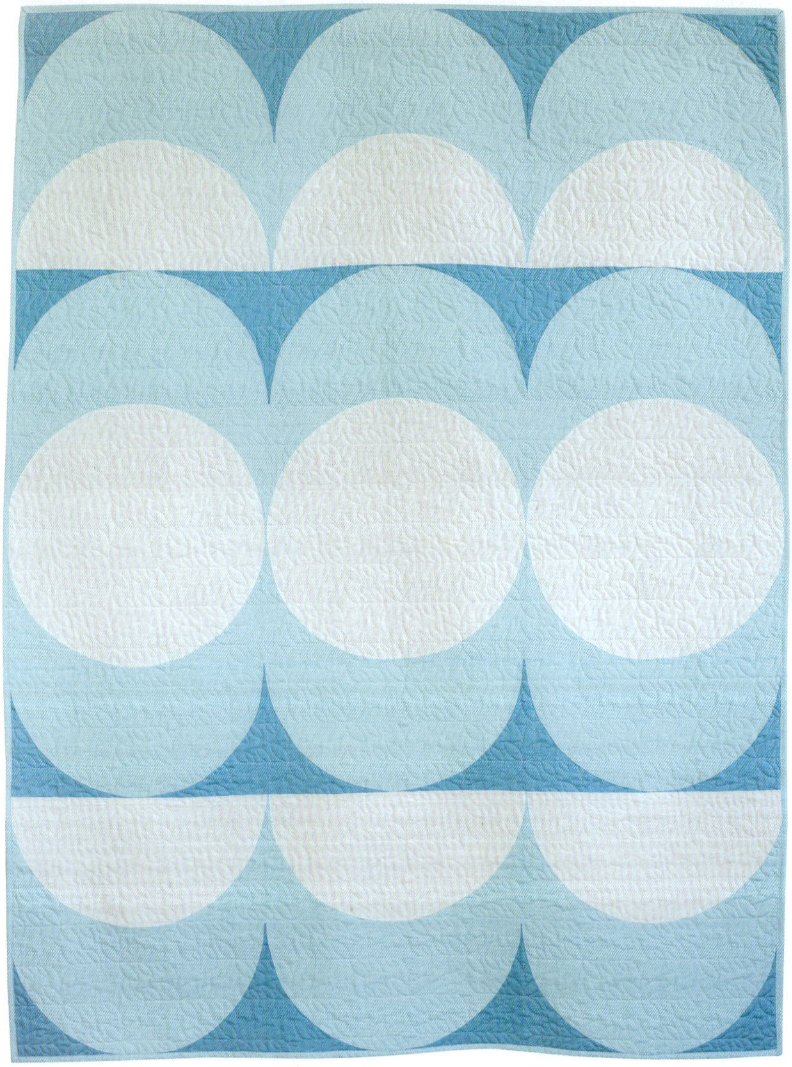

Resonance is an example of using a very small ombré color palette to create a big impact. This quilt only uses three colors, but they are used in a way that evokes a resonating wave or a ripple effect. The large, gentle curves in this pattern make it approachable but interesting, and the reflective gradient grants the big blocks some additional visual interest. This quilt is best made using a monochromatic gradient. Beyond size, there is no difference in the design between the baby and throw options. Prepare Templates 1 and 2 (baby size) or 3 and 4 (throw size) (see Templates, page 126).

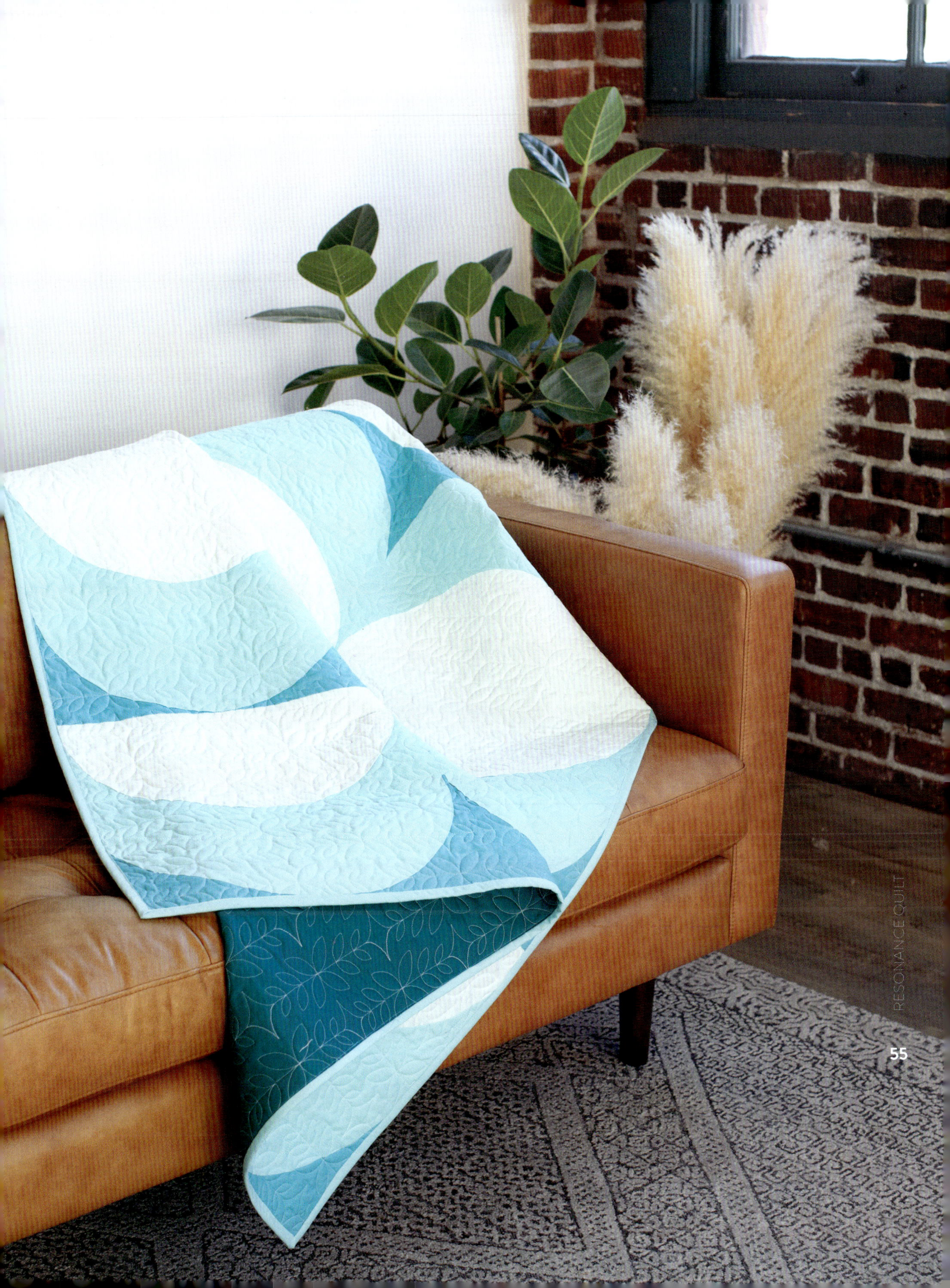

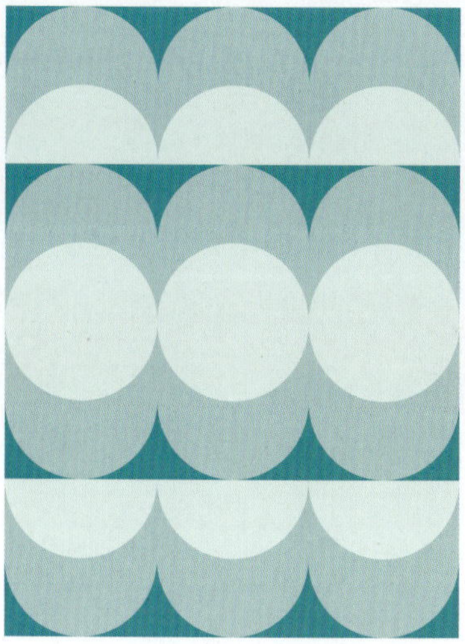

Two mirrored gradients sandwiched together

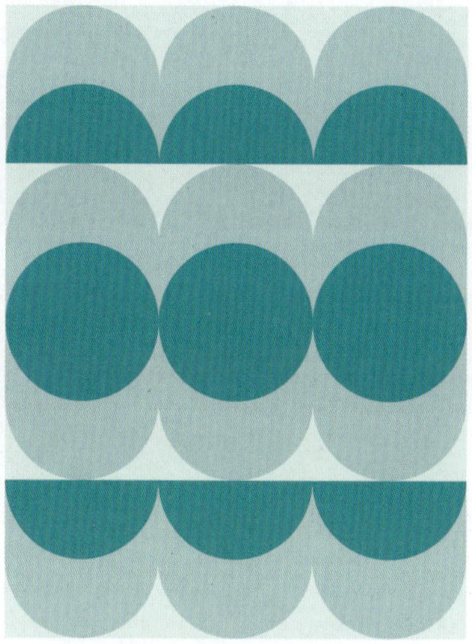

Inverting the color order gives an entirely different feel.

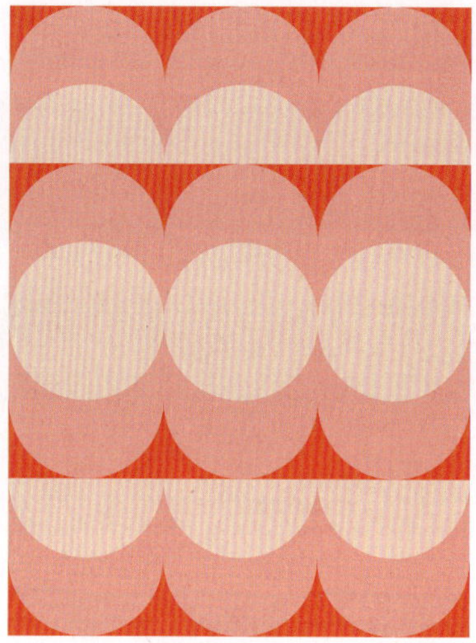

Two mirrored gradients sandwiched together

Fabric Requirements

Fabric *Riley Blake Confetti Cotton Solids*		**Baby (36″ × 48″)**	**Throw (54″ × 72″)**
	Fabric A • *Peacock*	¾ yard	1½ yards
	Fabric B • *Scuba*	1¼ yards	2¼ yards
	Fabric C • *Misty*	⅞ yard	1⅔ yards

Cutting Instructions

Fabric	**Baby**	**Throw**
A	*Cut 3 – 7¼″ × WOF strips; subcut into* Cut 12 – Template 2 (**A1**)*	*Cut 4 – 10½″ × WOF strips; subcut into* Cut 12 – Template 4 (**A1**)*
B	*Cut 3 – 12¾″ × WOF strips; subcut into* Cut 12 – Template 1 (**B1**)** Cut 12 – Template 2 (**B2**)**	*Cut 4 – 18¾″ × WOF strips; subcut into* 12 – Template 3 (**B1**)** 12 – Template 4 (**B2**)**
C	*Cut 2 – 12½″ × WOF strips; subcut into* 12 – Template 1 (**C1**)	*Cut 3 – 18½″ × WOF strips; subcut into* 12 – Template 3 (**C1**)

** Nest templates as shown*

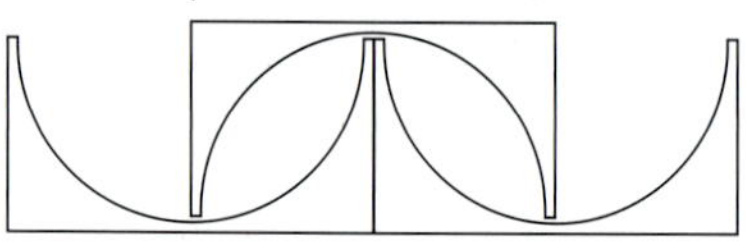

*** Nest templates as shown*

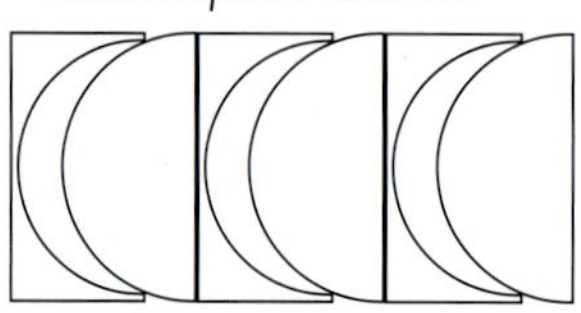

Half Circle Unit Assembly

1. Match each A1 piece with a B1 piece. Match each B2 piece with a C1 piece. Follow the instructions in Sewing Curves (page 15) to create 12 A/B Half Circle Units and 12 B/C Half Circle Units. Trim the Half Circle Units to 6½″ × 12½″ (baby) or 9½″ × 18½″ (throw).

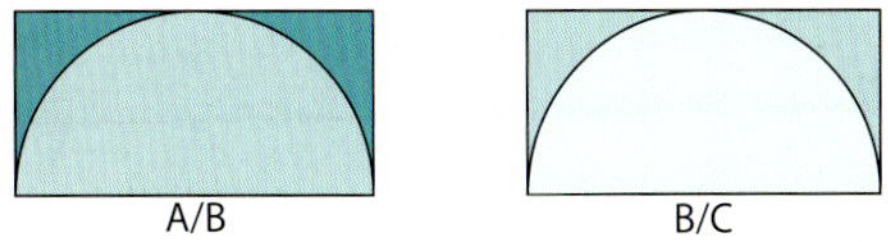

Quilt Assembly

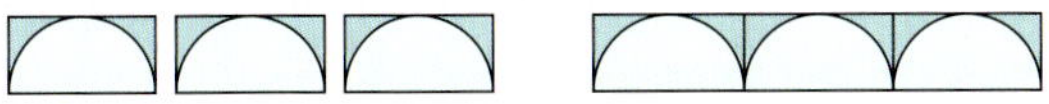

1. Sew together 4 sets of 3 A/B Half Circle Units. Press seams open.

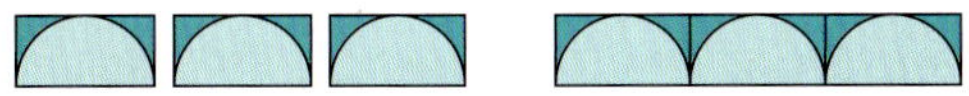

2. Sew together 4 sets of 3 B/C Half Circle Units. Press seams open.

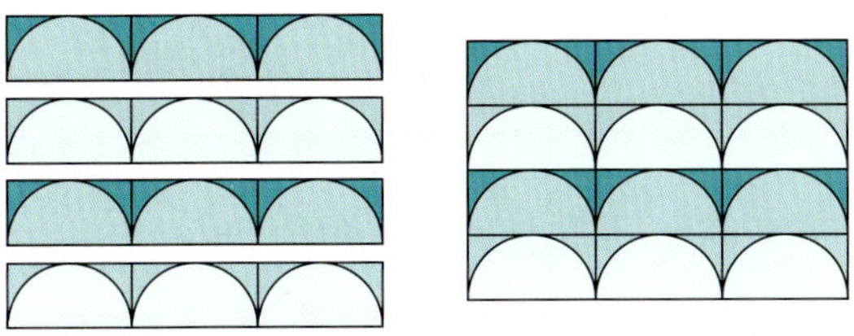

3. Sew together 4 rows from Steps 1 and 2 in an alternating color arrangement as shown. Repeat to make a second unit. Press seams open.

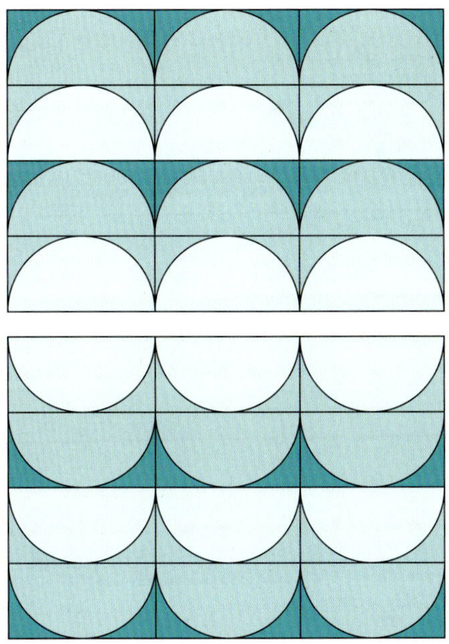

4. Sew the units from Step 3 together as shown, with the designs mirroring one another in the center. Press the seam open.

Sample quilt longarm quilted by Trace Creek Quilting.

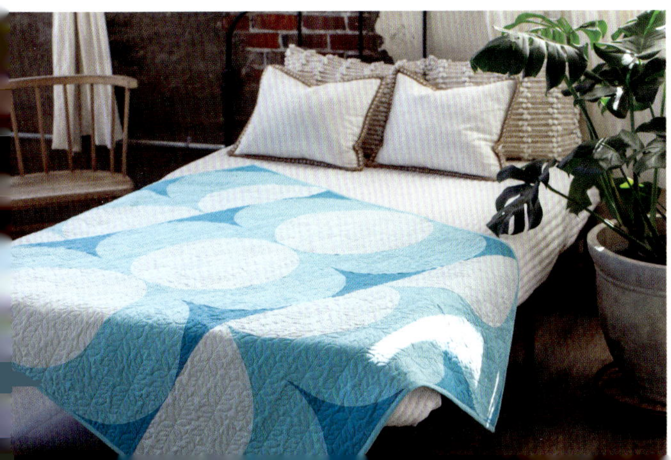

Shimmering Sunset Quilt

BABY SIZE 42″ × 49″ • THROW SIZE 60″ × 70″ • BED SIZE 96″ × 112″

Shimmering Sunset is simply constructed from only HSTs. The real challenge comes in creating a cohesive color palette and layout. This pattern is a great exercise for building a gradient palette that blends multiple colors, and works especially well for a complementary palette. It also gives you a lot of flexibility when it comes to laying out the blocks and rows.

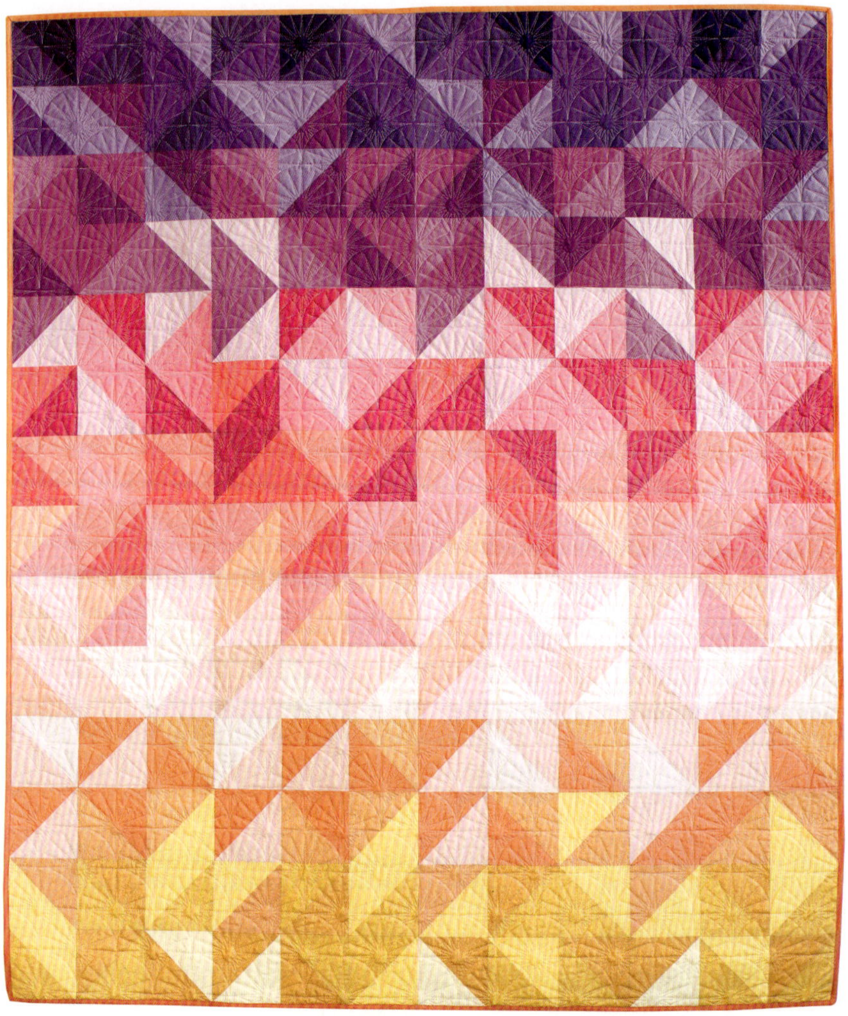

The fabric requirements table lists yardage requirements if you're purchasing new fabric, but this pattern is very scrap friendly; take a look at the cutting instructions to see the sizes of pieces needed, and you might be able to make this one out of your stash or from precuts like 10″ squares! There are two HST methods (see Half-Square Triangles, page 17), which provides more flexibility for fabric usage.

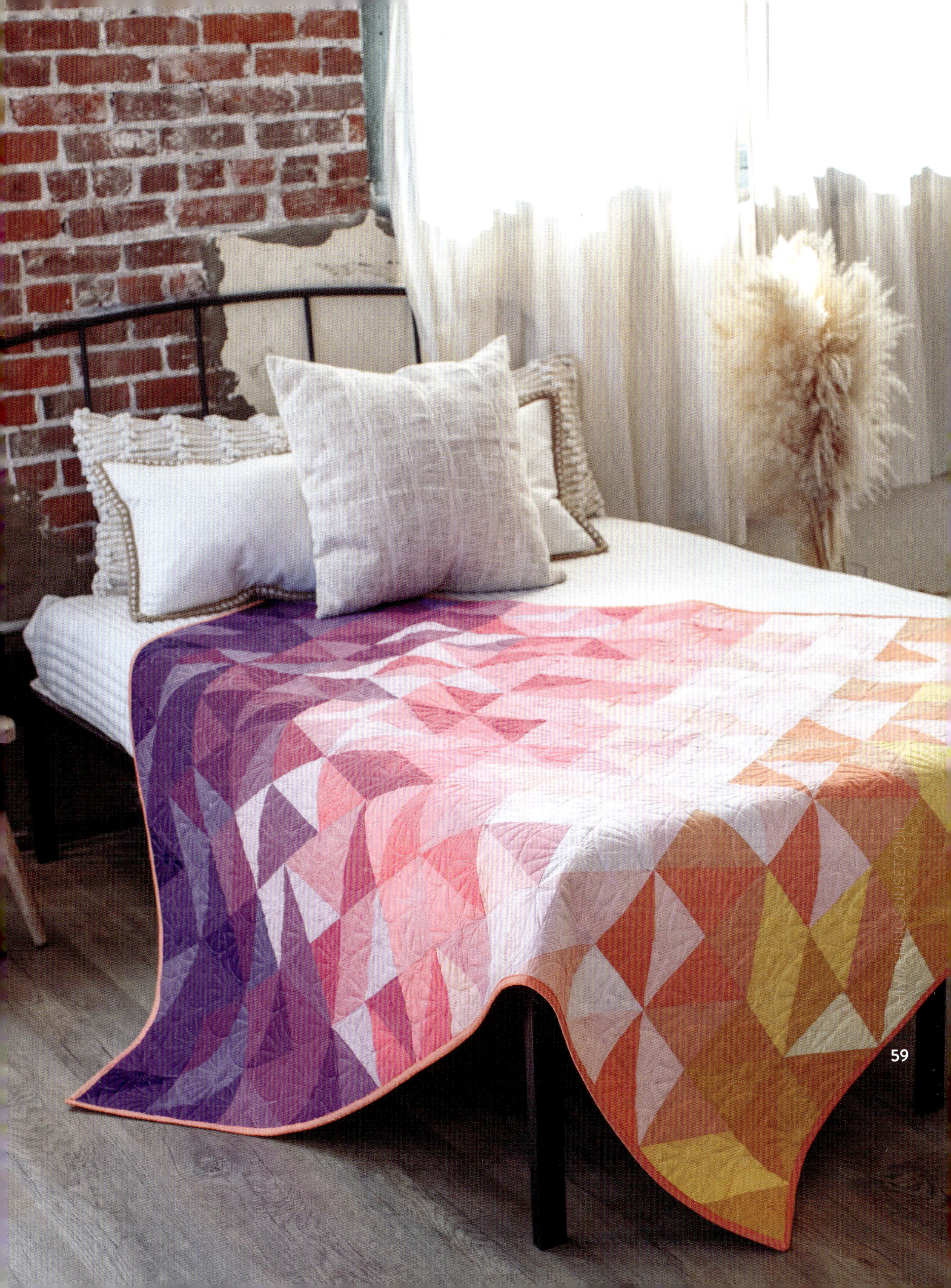

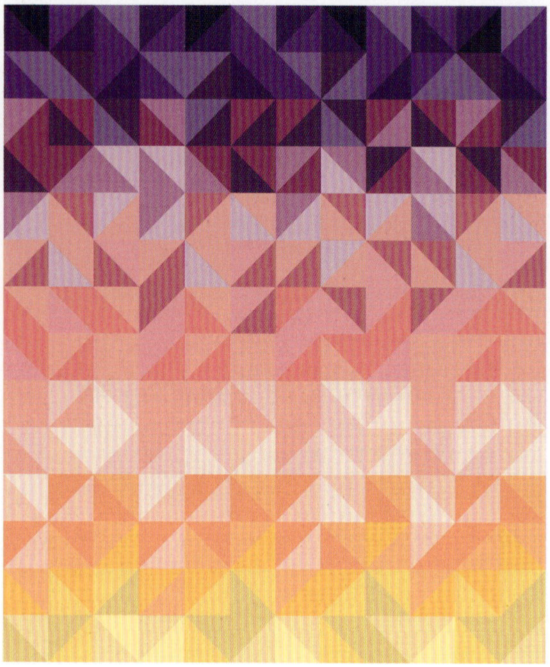

Complementary linear gradient

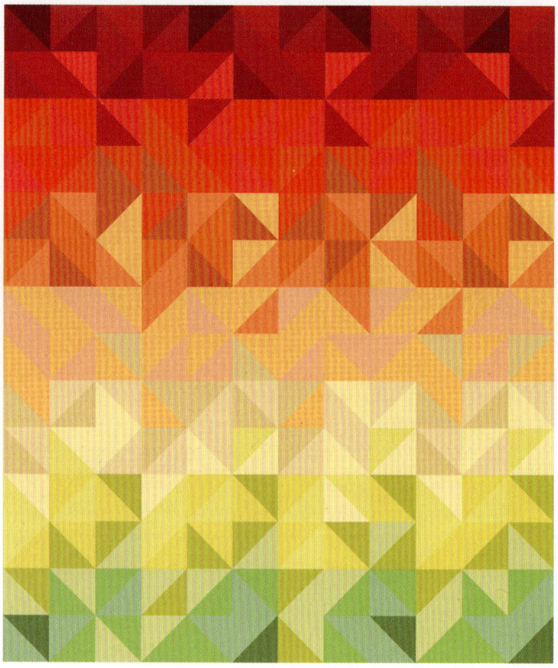

Complementary linear gradient

Fabric Requirements

Fabric *Riley Blake Confetti Cotton Solids*	**Baby (42″ × 49″)**	**Throw (60″ × 70″)**	**Bed (96″ × 112″)**
Fabric A • ***Eggplant***	¼ yard or 1 FE	¼ yard or 1 FE	½ yard or 1 FQ
Fabric B • ***Grape***	¼ yard or 1 FE	¼ yard* or 1 FQ	⅝ yard
Fabric C • ***Iris***	¼ yard or 1 FE	¼ yard* or 1 FQ	¾ yard
Fabric D • ***Amethyst***	¼ yard or 1 FE	¼ yard* or 1 FQ	¾ yard
Fabric E • ***Purple***	¼ yard or 1 FE	¼ yard* or 1 FQ	¾ yard
Fabric F • ***Orchid***	¼ yard or 1 FE	¼ yard* or 1 FQ	¾ yard
Fabric G • ***Violet***	¼ yard or 1 FE	¼ yard* or 1 FQ	¾ yard
Fabric H • ***Princess***	¼ yard or 1 FE	¼ yard* or 1 FQ	¾ yard
Fabric I • ***Peony***	¼ yard or 1 FE	¼ yard* or 1 FQ	¾ yard
Fabric J • ***Hibiscus***	¼ yard or 1 FE	¼ yard* or 1 FQ	¾ yard
Fabric K • ***Rose***	¼ yard or 1 FE	¼ yard* or 1 FQ	¾ yard
Fabric L • ***Sugar Pink***	¼ yard or 1 FE	¼ yard* or 1 FQ	¾ yard

Fabric *Riley Blake Confetti Cotton Solids*	Baby (42″ × 49″)	Throw (60″ × 70″)	Bed (96″ × 112″)
Fabric M • *Riley Coral*	¼ yard or 1 FE	¼ yard* or 1 FQ	¾ yard
Fabric N • *Grapefruit*	¼ yard or 1 FE	¼ yard* or 1 FQ	¾ yard
Fabric O • *Frosting*	¼ yard or 1 FE	¼ yard* or 1 FQ	¾ yard
Fabric P • *Ballerina*	¼ yard or 1 FE	¼ yard* or 1 FQ	¾ yard
Fabric Q • *Peaches N Cream*	¼ yard or 1 FE	¼ yard* or 1 FQ	¾ yard
Fabric R • *Apricot Blush*	¼ yard or 1 FE	¼ yard* or 1 FQ	¾ yard
Fabric S • *Marmalade*	¼ yard or 1 FE	¼ yard* or 1 FQ	¾ yard
Fabric T • *Daisy*	¼ yard or 1 FE	¼ yard* or 1 FQ	¾ yard
Fabric U • *Riley Yellow*	¼ yard or 1 FE	¼ yard* or 1 FQ	¾ yard
Fabric V • *Honey*	¼ yard or 1 FE	¼ yard* or 1 FQ	⅝ yard
Fabric W • *Beehive*	¼ yard or 1 FE	¼ yard or 1 FE	½ yard or 1 FQ

** If you're using the two-at-a-time method, ⅜ yard or 1 FQ is required.*

Cutting Instructions

The cutting instructions are divided based on the HST assembly method. Choose whichever method you prefer, and cut accordingly.

Fabric	Baby	Throw	Bed
A, W	*For the four-at-a-time* 1 – 6½″ square **OR** *For the two-at-a-time* 2 – 4½″ squares	*For the four-at-a-time* 1 – 8½″ square **OR** *For the two-at-a-time* 2 – 6″ squares	*For the four-at-a-time* 1 – 13″ square **OR** *For the two-at-a-time* 2 – 9″ squares
C – U	*For the four-at-a-time* 4 – 6½″ squares **OR** *For the two-at-a-time* 8 – 4½″ squares	*For the four-at-a-time* 4 – 8½″ squares **OR** *For the two-at-a-time* 8 – 6″ squares	*For the four-at-a-time* 4 – 13″ squares **OR** *For the two-at-a-time* 8 – 9″ squares
B, V	*For the four-at-a-time* 3 – 6½″ squares **OR** *For the two-at-a-time* 6 – 4½″ squares	*For the four-at-a-time* 3 – 8½″ squares **OR** *For the two-at-a-time* 6 – 6″ squares	*For the four-at-a-time* 3 – 13″ squares **OR** *For the two-at-a-time* 6 – 9″ squares

Half-Square Triangle Unit Assembly

Following the instructions in Half-Square Triangles (page 17), create the HST Units shown in Table 1 using the method of your choice. Trim each HST to 4″ × 4″ (baby), 5½″ × 5½″ (throw), or 8½″ × 8½″ (bed).

Table 1

HST Name	Fabric 1	Fabric 2	Number of units
HST 1	A	B	4
HST 2	B	C	8
HST 3	C	D	8
HST 4	D	E	8
HST 5	E	F	8
HST 6	F	G	8
HST 7	G	H	8
HST 8	H	I	8
HST 9	I	J	8
HST 10	J	K	8
HST 11	K	L	8
HST 12	L	M	8
HST 13	M	N	8
HST 14	N	O	8
HST 15	O	P	8
HST 16	P	Q	8
HST 17	Q	R	8
HST 18	R	S	8
HST 19	S	T	8
HST 20	T	U	8
HST 21	U	V	8
HST 22	V	W	4

Quilt Assembly

For each row of this quilt, you will use 4 sets of 3 different HSTs. To achieve the look of the pattern sample, randomize the order and orientation of these HSTs while laying out the rows. While you can follow the rows shown in this pattern exactly, experimenting with your own orders and orientations for each row will create a unique quilt!

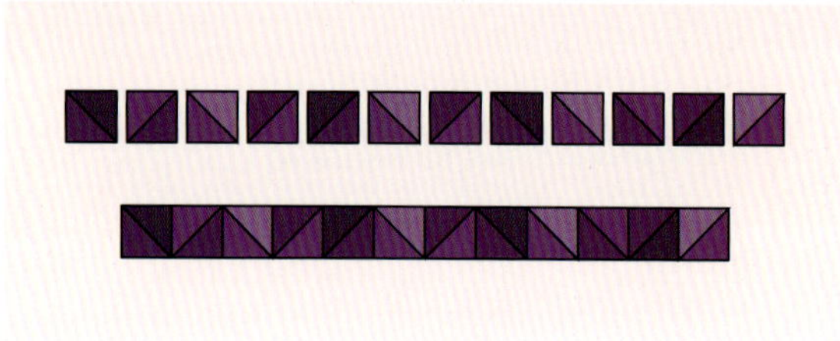

1. Sew together 4 of HST 1, 4 of HST 2, and 4 of HST 3 in a random order and orientation, as shown. Press all seams to the right.

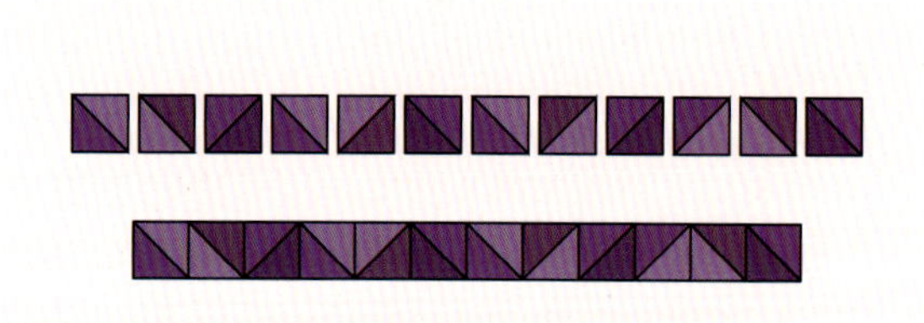

2. Sew together the remaining 4 of HST 2, remaining 4 of HST 3, and 4 of HST 4 in a random order and orientation as shown. Press all seams to the left.

3. Repeat Steps 1–2 to sew together each row. Use Table 2 to determine which HSTs to use for each row. Continue to alternate seam pressing direction so that the seams will nest: For odd numbered rows, press seams to the right; for even numbered rows, press seams to the left.

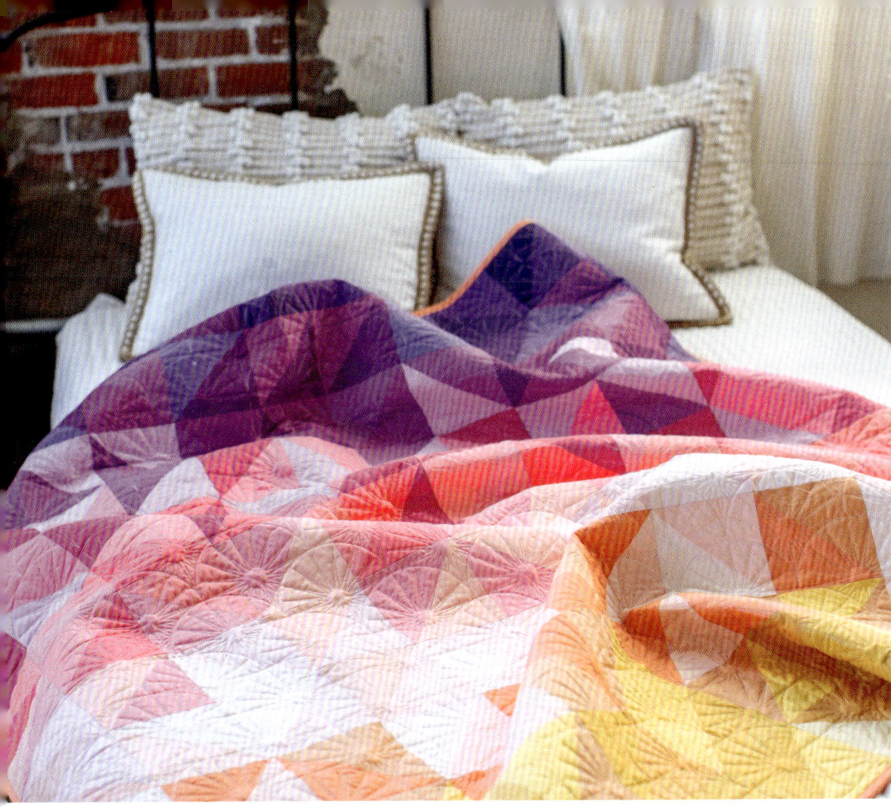

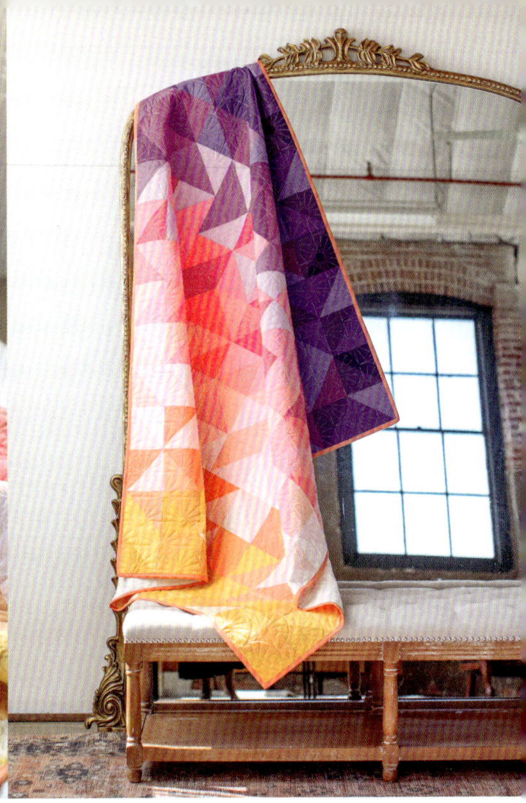

Sample quilt pieced by Katie Dean, longarm quilted by Trace Creek Quilting.

Table 2

Row Number	HSTs Used
1	1, 2, 3
2	2, 3, 4
3	4, 5, 6
4	5, 6, 7
5	7, 8, 9
6	8, 9, 10
7	10, 11, 12
8	11, 12, 13
9	13, 14, 15
10	14, 15, 16
11	16, 17, 18
12	17, 18, 19
13	19, 20, 21
14	20, 21, 22

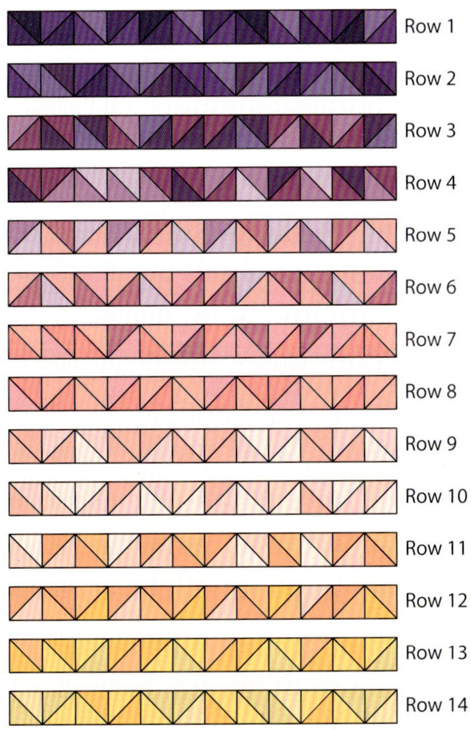

4. Sew together the rows in order. Press all seams open.

Crossroads Quilt

BABY SIZE 40″ × 48″ • THROW SIZE 60″ × 72″ • BED SIZE 90″ × 108″

This quilt is a quick finish with a big impact. This pattern lends itself well to almost any type of gradient and color palette, so it's a great design to experiment with.

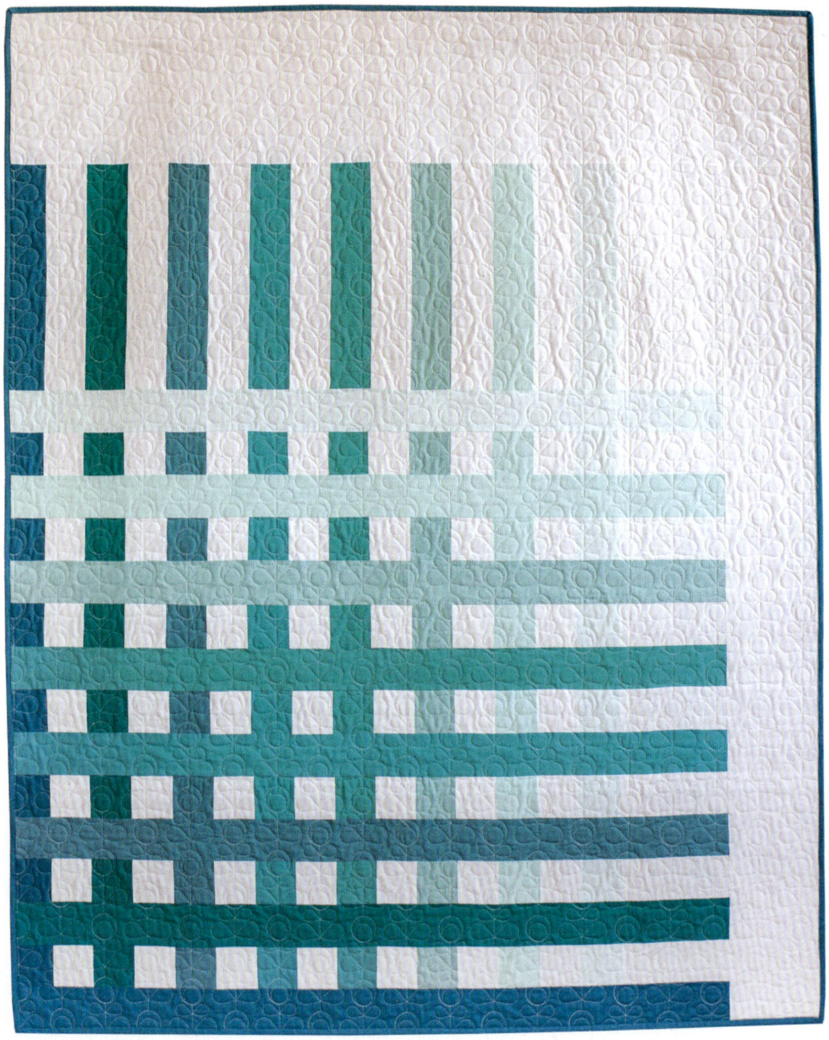

Because there is strip piecing in this quilt, make sure to use a consistent *scant* ¼″ seam allowance (see Seam Allowances, page 12). If your seam allowances end up a bit too large and your blocks end up on the smaller side, this pattern is very forgiving; just trim strips J3 and J4 as needed to fit the size of the unit in Assembly Step 2 (page 68).

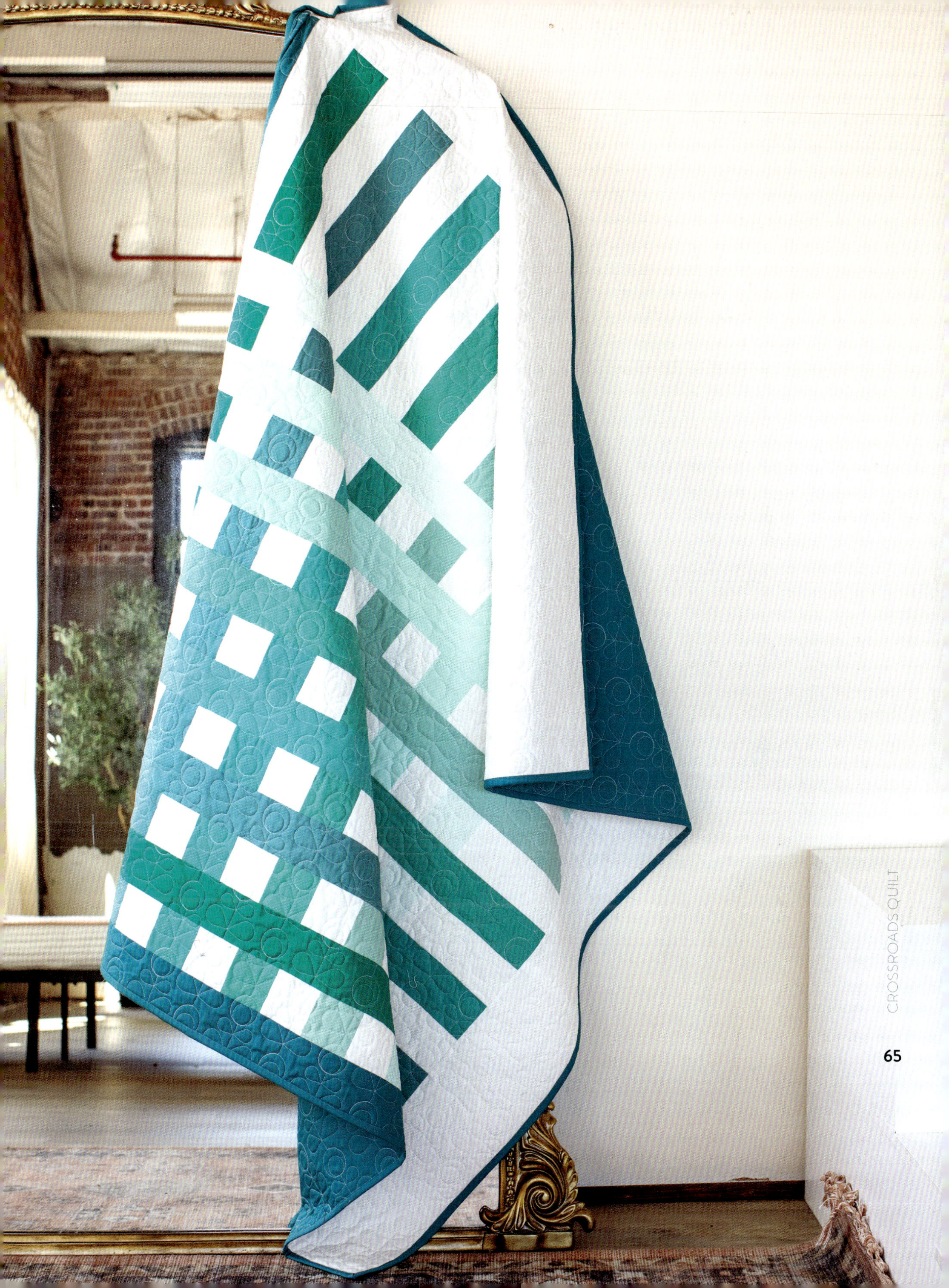

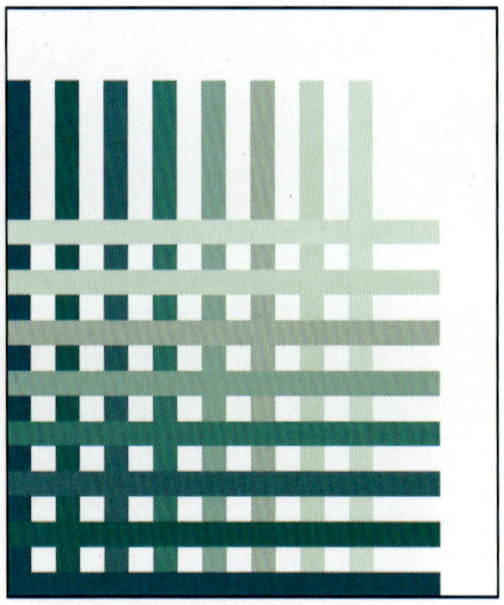

Monochromatic linear gradient, both horizontal and vertical

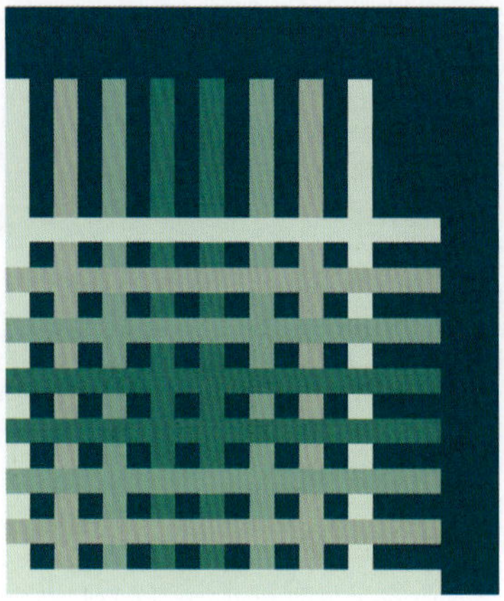

Mirrored linear gradient, both horizontal and vertical

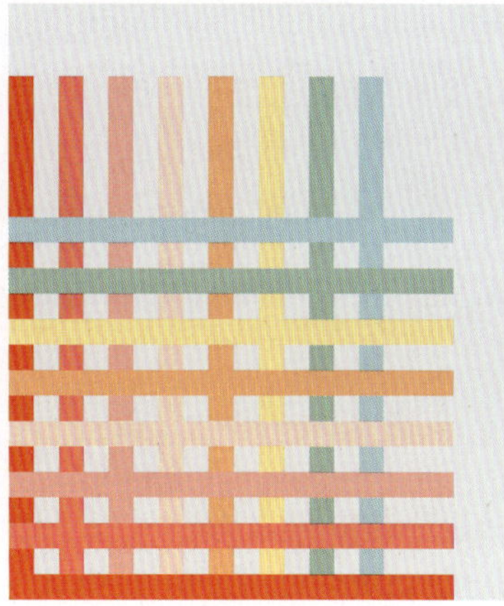

Triadic linear gradient

Fabric Requirements

Fabric *Riley Blake Confetti Cotton Solids*	**Baby (40″ × 48″)**	**Throw (60″ × 72″)**	**Bed (90″ × 108″)**
Fabric A • *Oceanside*	¼ yard	⅓ yard	¾ yard
Fabric B • *Poseidon*	¼ yard	⅓ yard	¾ yard
Fabric C • *Riley Teal*	¼ yard	⅓ yard	¾ yard
Fabric D • *Vivid*	¼ yard	⅓ yard	¾ yard
Fabric E • *Rain Forest*	¼ yard	⅓ yard	¾ yard
Fabric F • *Seafoam*	¼ yard	⅓ yard	¾ yard
Fabric G • *Hint of Mint*	¼ yard	⅓ yard	¾ yard
Fabric H • *Misty*	¼ yard	⅓ yard	¾ yard
Fabric J • *Off White*	1¼ yards	2 yards	5 yards

Cutting Instructions

Fabric	Baby Size	Throw Size	Bed Size
Fabrics A–H	*Cut 2 – 2½" × WOF strips* (A1–H1)	*Cut 3 – 3½" × WOF strips* (A1–H1)	*Cut 4 – 4½" × WOF strips* (A1–H1)
J	*Cut 7 – 2½" × WOF strips* (**J1**) *Cut 2 – 5½" × WOF strips* (**J2**) *Cut 1 – 7½" × WOF strip* (**J4**)	*Cut 7 – 3½" × WOF strips* (**J1**) *Cut 1 – 8½" × WOF strip* (**J2**) *Cut 2 – 11½" × WOF strips, and sew them together; subcut into* 1 – 11½" × 60½" strip (**J4**) *Cut 1 – 7½" × WOF strip.* Trim remnant from J4 to 7½" wide. Join the strip and remnant together and trim to 1 – 7½" × 61½" strip (**J3**)	*Cut 14 – 5" × WOF strips* (**J1**) *Cut 3 – 17" × WOF strips, and sew them together; subcut into* 1 – 17" × 90½" strips (**J4**) *Cut 2 – 13" × WOF strips, and sew together; subcut into* 1 – 13" × 61½" strip (**J2**) *Cut 2 – 10½" × WOF strips.* Trim remnant from J4 to 10½" wide. Join the strips and remnant together and trim to 1 – 10½" × 92" strip (**J3**)

Strip Unit Assembly

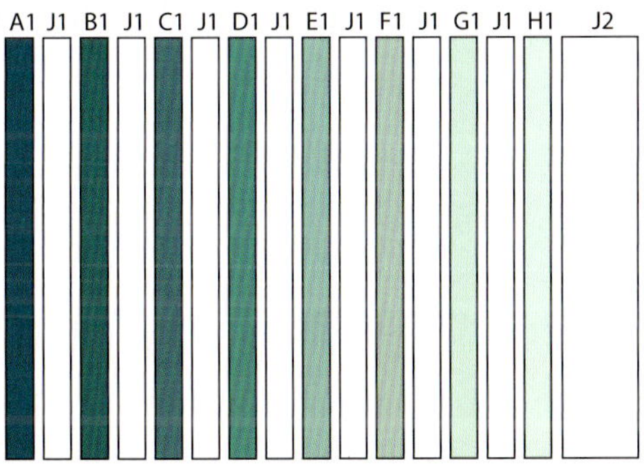

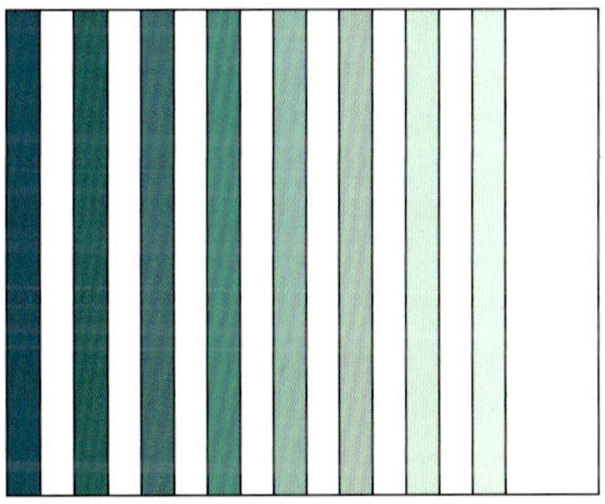

1. Arrange strips A1, B1, C1, D1, E1, F1, G1, and H1 with a J1 strip in between each as shown, ending with a J2 strip. Sew all the strips together. Repeat to make a second unit for bed size only. There will be 1 (baby) or 2 (throw, bed) remaining A1 – H1 strips. Trim the bottom of the unit(s) to remove any uneven edges.

tip *To prevent the fabric from warping as you strip piece, press the strips toward the darker fabric only after all the strips have been sewn together. Be sure to pin the strips together securely as well.*

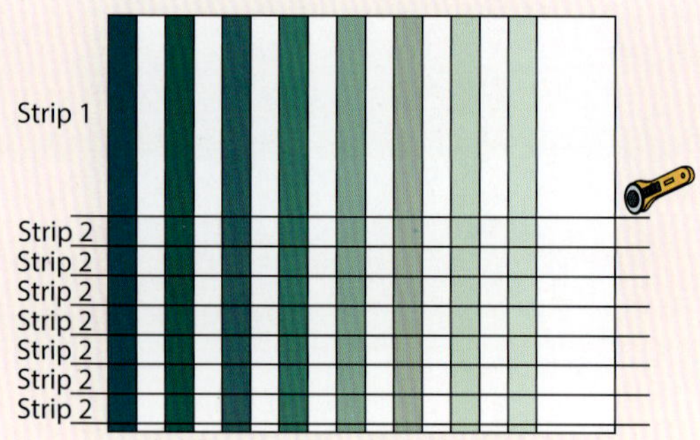

Strip 1 Unit Size

Baby Size	Throw Size	Bed Size
11½" × 35½"	16½" × 53½"	24½" × 80½"

Strip 2 Unit Size

Baby Size	Throw Size	Bed Size
2½" × 35½"	3½" × 53½"	5" × 80½"

2. Cut the unit horizontally into 1 — Strip 1 Unit and 7 — Strip 2 Units using the dimensions in the above tables.

3. For the throw and bed sizes only, pair the remaining matching A1 — H1 strips and sew together (i.e, sew both A1 strips together, both B1 strips together, and so on). Trim each strip to 3½" × 53½" (throw) or 4½" × 80½" (bed). These double—wide strips will still be referred to as A1—H1.

QUILT ASSEMBLY

1. Using lots of pins, sew together the strips shown in Diagram 1 along the long sides, paying close attention to the strip order.

2. Press all the seams towards the solid colored strips. If needed, trim to 35½" × 41½" (baby), 53½" × 61½" (throw), or 80½" × 92" (bed).

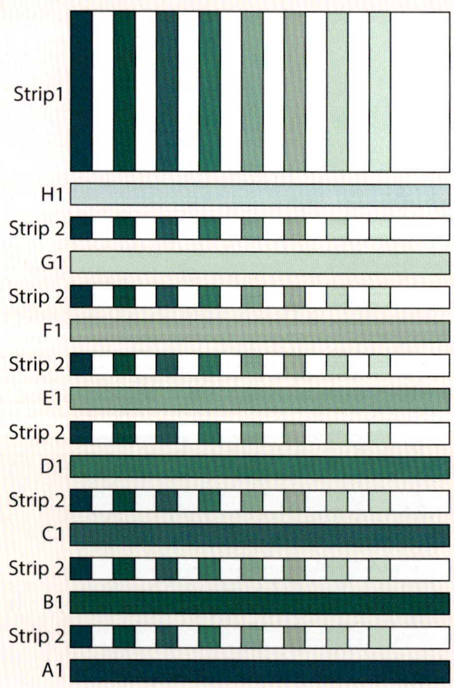

Diagram 1

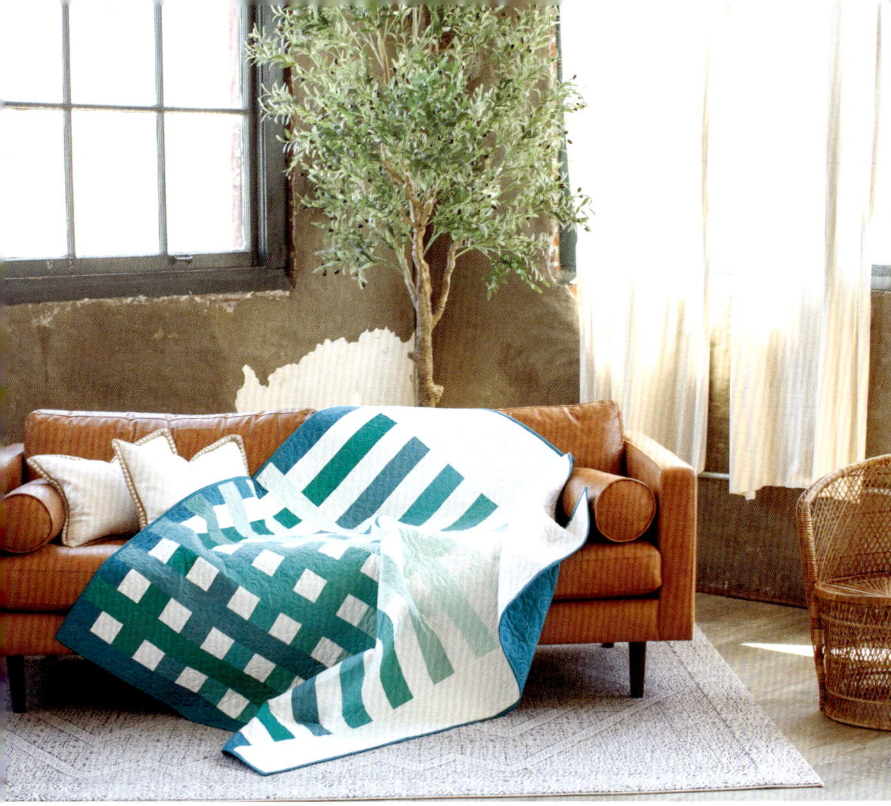

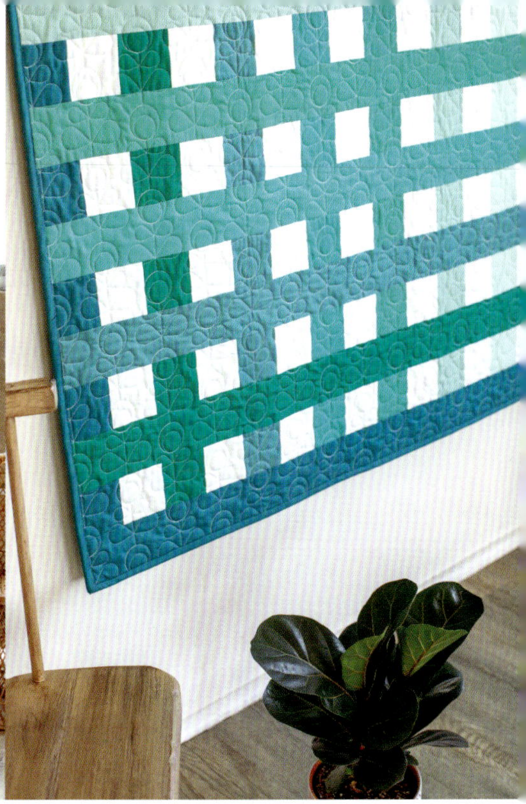

Sample quilt pieced by Christina West, longarm quilted by Trace Creek Quilting.

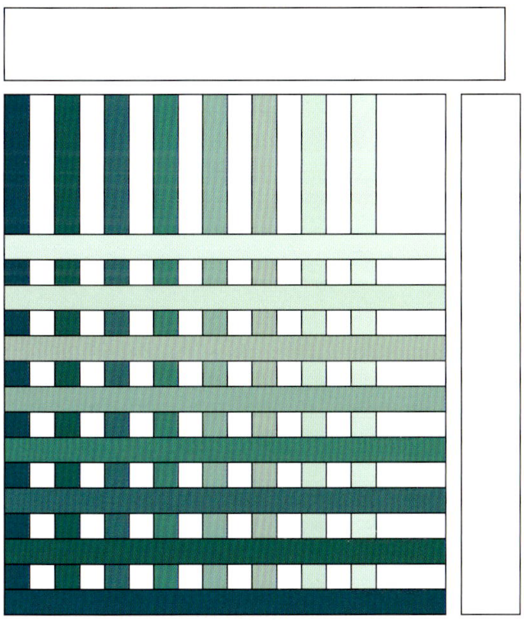

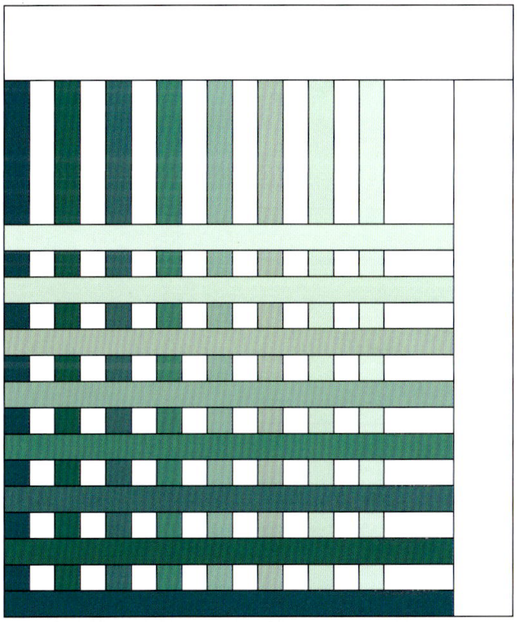

3. Sew a J2 (baby) or J3 (throw, bed) strip to the right edge of the quilt. Press the seam away from the J2/J3 piece. Sew a J4 strip to the top of the quilt. Press the seam away from the J4 piece.

Kinetic Quilt

BABY SIZE 45″ × 45″ • THROW SIZE 58″ × 58″

Many ombré quilt designs evoke a feeling of *flow*, with smooth transitions from one color to the next. *Kinetic* contrasts this feeling with sharp shapes and edges, staggering the gradient effect to achieve more visual movement and interest. Use a monochromatic or analogous color palette to keep the design from looking too busy.

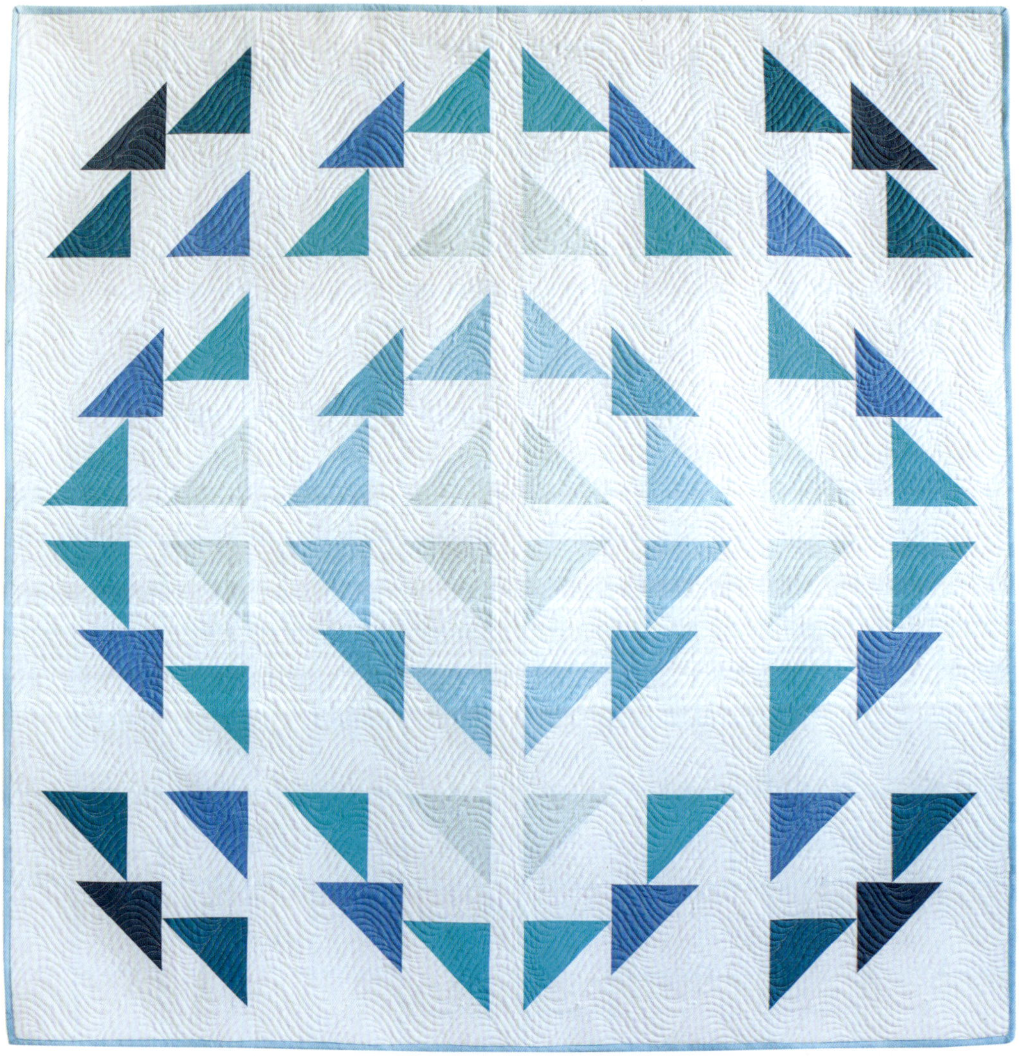

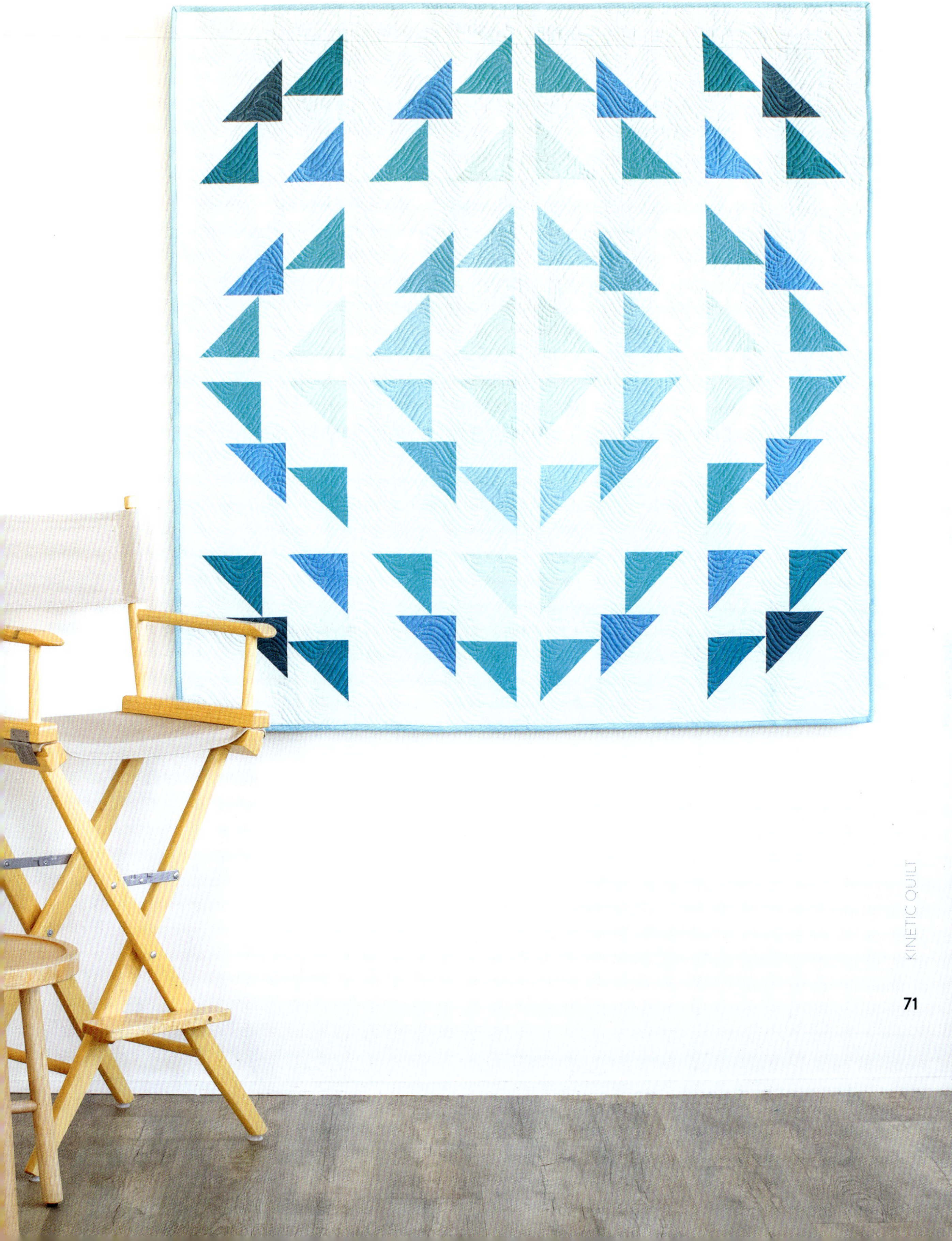

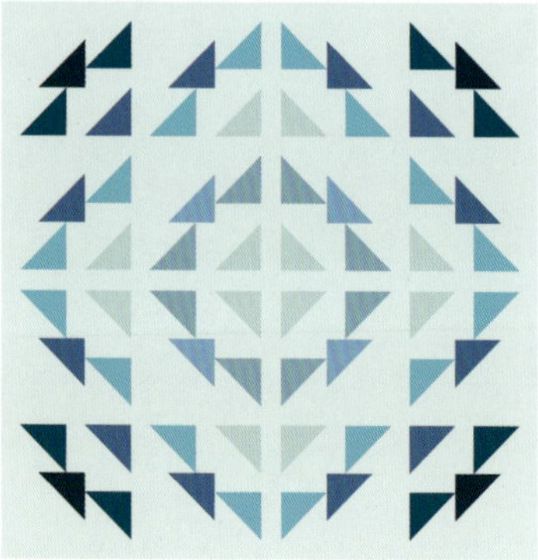
Monochromatic radial gradient

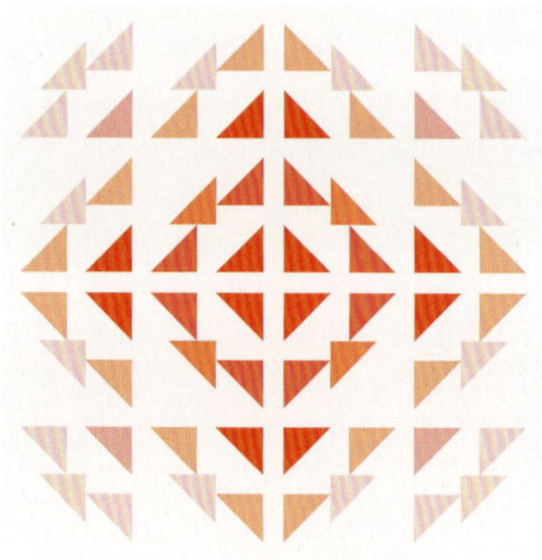
Analogous radial gradient

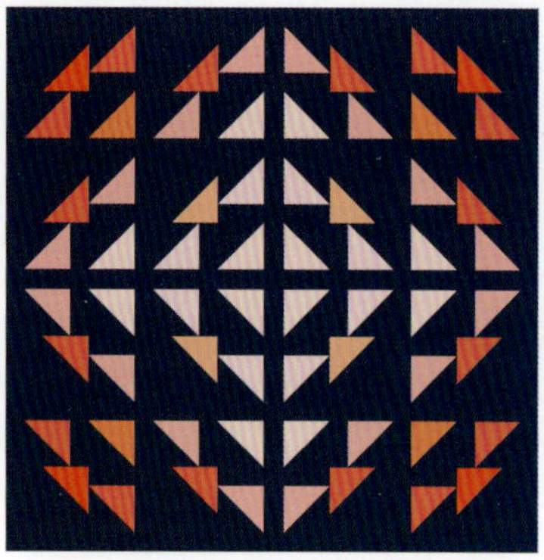
Analogous radial gradient with a complementary background.

Fabric Requirements

Fabric *Riley Blake Confetti Cotton Solids*		Baby (45″ × 45″)	Throw (58″ × 58″)
	Fabric A • *Cape Verde*	¼ yard or 1 FE	¼ yard or 1 FE
	Fabric B • *Oceanside*	¼ yard or 1 FE	¼ yard or 1 FQ
	Fabric C • *Deep Water*	¼ yard or 1 FQ	¼ yard or 1 FQ
	Fabric D • *Peacock*	¼ yard or 1 FQ	¼ yard or 1 FQ
	Fabric E • *Riley Aqua*	¼ yard or 1 FQ	¼ yard or 1 FQ
	Fabric F • *Bear Lake*	¼ yard or 1 FE	¼ yard or 1 FE
	Fabric G • *Songbird*	¼ yard or 1 FE	¼ yard or 1 FQ
	Fabric H • *Bleached Denim*	2 yards	2¾ yards

Cutting Instructions

Fabric	Baby	Throw
A	*Cut 1 – 5″ × WOF strip; subcut into* 2 – 5″ × 5″ squares (**A1**)	*Cut 1 – 6″ × WOF strip; subcut into* 2 – 6″ × 6″ squares (**A1**)
B	*Cut 1 – 5″ × WOF strip; subcut into* 4 – 5″ × 5″ squares (**B1**)	*Cut 1 – 6″ × WOF strip; subcut into* 4 – 6″ × 6″ squares (**B1**)
C	*Cut 1 – 5″ × WOF strip; subcut into* 6 – 5″ × 5″ squares (**C1**)	*Cut 1 – 6″ × WOF strip; subcut into* 6 – 6″ × 6″ squares (**C1**)
D	*Cut 1 – 5″ × WOF strip; subcut into* 8 – 5″ × 5″ squares (**D1**)	*Cut 2 – 6″ × WOF strips; subcut into* 8 – 6″ × 6″ squares (**D1**)
E	*Cut 1 – 5″ × WOF strip; subcut into* 6 – 5″ × 5″ squares (**E1**)	*Cut 1 – 6″ × WOF strip; subcut into* 6 – 6″ × 6″ squares (**E1**)
F	*Cut 1 – 5″ × WOF strip; subcut into* 2 – 5″ × 5″squares (**F1**)	*Cut 1 – 6″ × WOF strip; subcut into* 2 – 6″ × 6″ squares (**F1**)
G	*Cut 1 – 5″ × WOF strip; subcut into* 4 – 5″ × 5″ squares (**G1**)	*Cut 1 – 6″ × WOF strip; subcut into* 4 – 6″ × 6″ squares (**G1**)
H	*Cut 4 – 5″ × WOF strip; subcut into* 32 – 5″ × 5″ squares (**H1**) *Cut 4 – 3½″ × WOF strips; subcut into* 16 – 3½″ × 7½″ rectangles (**H3**) *Cut 5 – 4½″ × WOF strips; subcut into* 64 – 2″ × 4½″ rectangles (**H4**) 16 – 4½″ × 3½″ rectangles (**H2**) *Cut 4 – 1½″ × WOF strips; subcut into* 2 – 1½″ × 22½″ strips (**H5**) *Sew 2 remaining strips together; subcut into* 1 – 1½″ × 45½″ strip (**H6**)	*Cut 5 – 6″ × WOF strips; subcut into* 32 – 6″ × 6″ squares (**H1**) *Cut 6 – 5½″ × WOF strips; subcut into* 64 – 2½″ × 5½″ rectangles (**H4**) 16 – 4½″ × 5½″ rectangles (**H2**) *Cut 4 – 4½″ × WOF strips; subcut into* 16 – 4½″ × 9½″ rectangles (**H3**) *Cut 4 – 2½″ × WOF strips; subcut into* 2 – 2½″ × 28½″ strips (**H5**) *Sew 2 remaining strips together; subcut into* 1 – 2½″ × 58½″ strip (**H6**)

Half-Square Triangle Unit Assembly

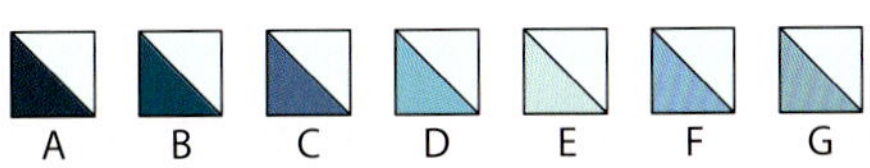

1. Following the instructions in Half-Square Triangles, create the HST Units shown in Table 1 using the Two-at-a-Time method (page 17). Trim each HST to 4½″ × 4½″ (baby) or 5½″ × 5½″' (throw).

Table 1

HST Name	Pieces Used	Number of Units
A HST	A1, H1	4
B HST	B1, H1	8
C HST	C1, H1	12
D HST	D1, H1	16
E HST	E1, H1	12
F HST	F1, H1	4
G HST	G1, H1	8

Block Assembly

Create three variations of the same block with three different color combinations. Each block uses 4 HSTs, but only 3 colorways, meaning 2 of the same HSTs are used in each block. Repeat Steps 1–5 with the colorways listed in Table 2 to make the correct number of Block 1, Block 2, and Block 3 (the 3 block variations). We refer to the three HST colorways used in each block as HST 1, HST 2, and HST 3. HST 2 is the colorway that will be repeated in each block.

Table 2

Block	HST 1	HST 2	HST 3	Number of Blocks
Block 1	B	C	A	4
Block 2	D	E	C	8
Block 3	G	E	F	4

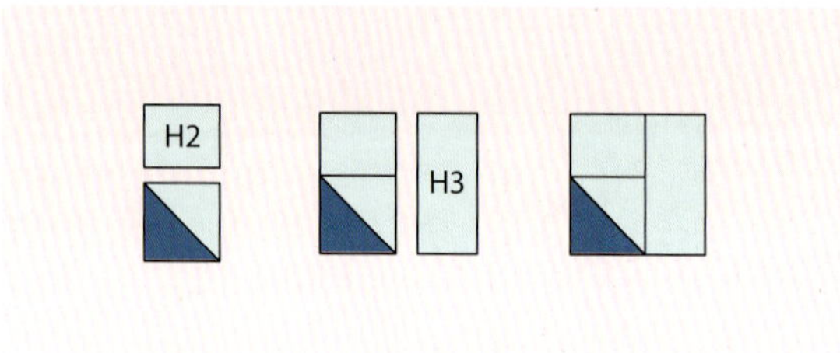

1. Sew an H2 to the top of a HST 3. Then, sew an H3 to the side of the unit.

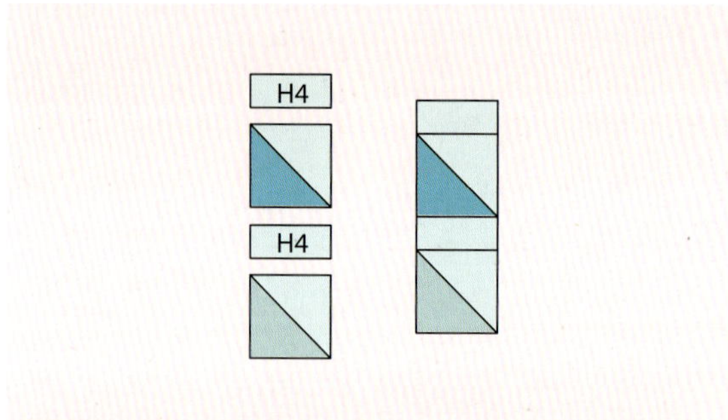

2. Sew together an H4 rectangle, an HST 1, an H4 rectangle, and an HST 2. This unit should measure 4½" × 11½" (baby) or 5½" × 14½" (throw).

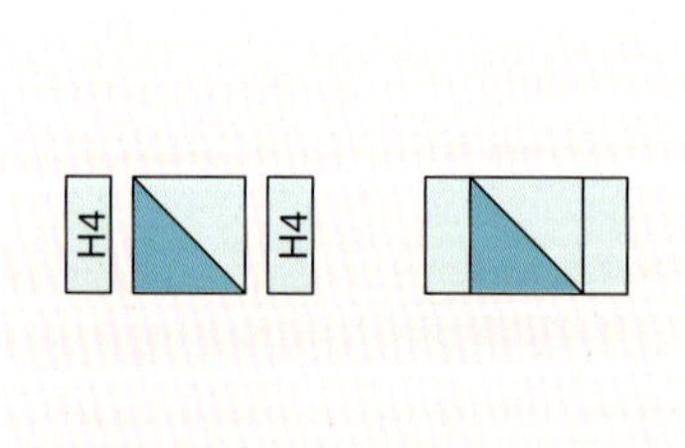

3. Sew an H4 rectangle to each side of a HST 2.

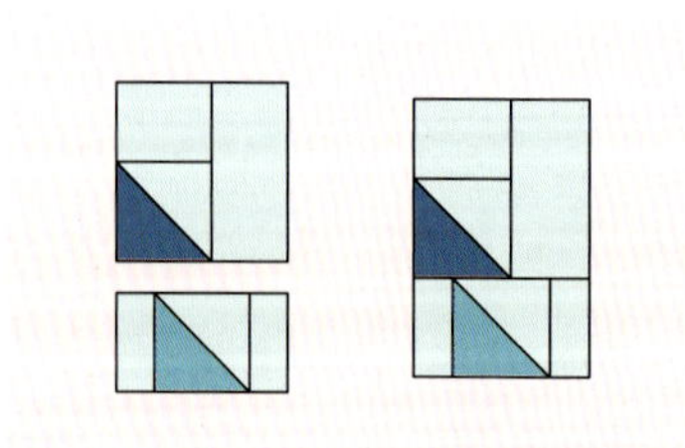

4. Sew together the units created in Steps 2 and 3. This unit should measure 7½" × 11½" (baby) or 9½" × 14½" (throw).

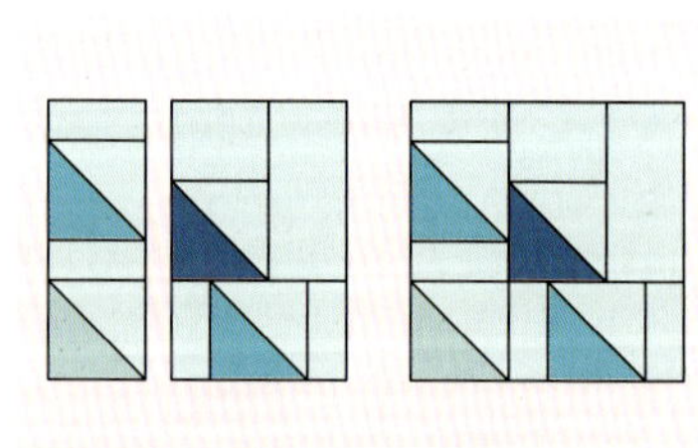

5. Sew together the units created in Steps 1 and 4. This block should now measure 11½" × 11½" (baby) or 14½" × 14½" (throw).

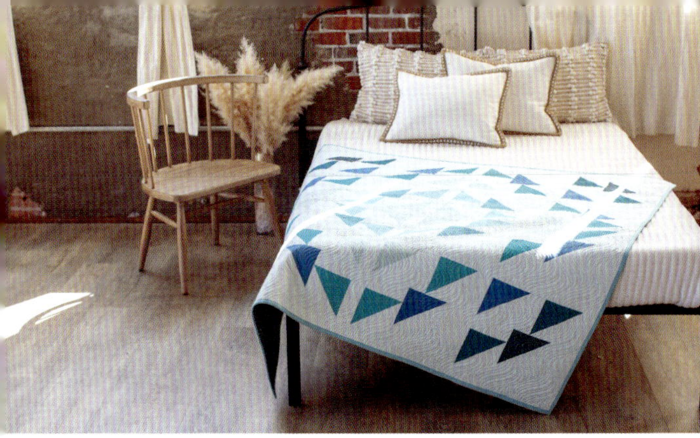

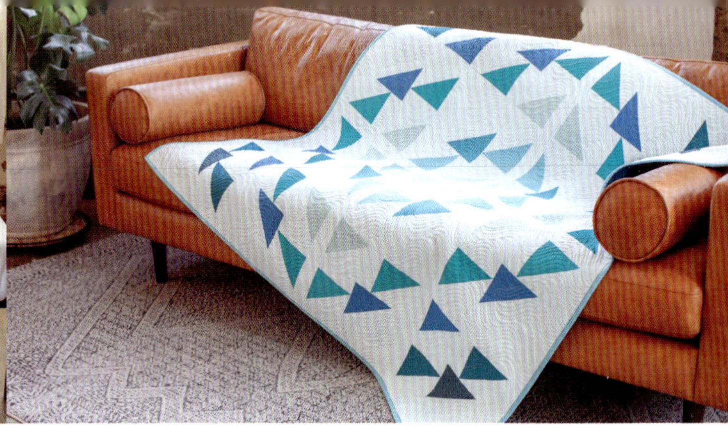

Sample quilt pieced by Katie Dean, longarm quilted by Trace Creek Quilting.

Quilt Assembly

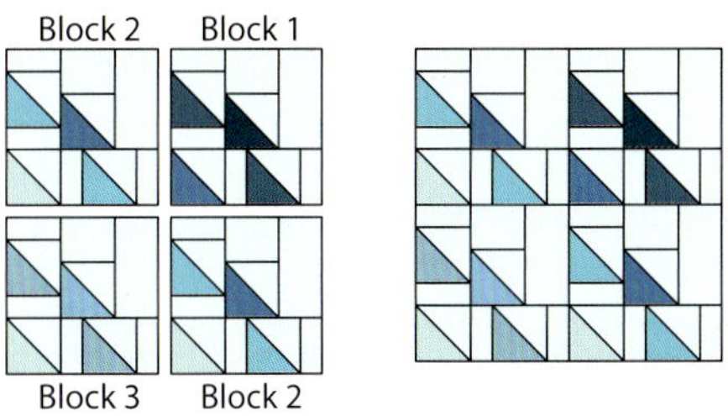

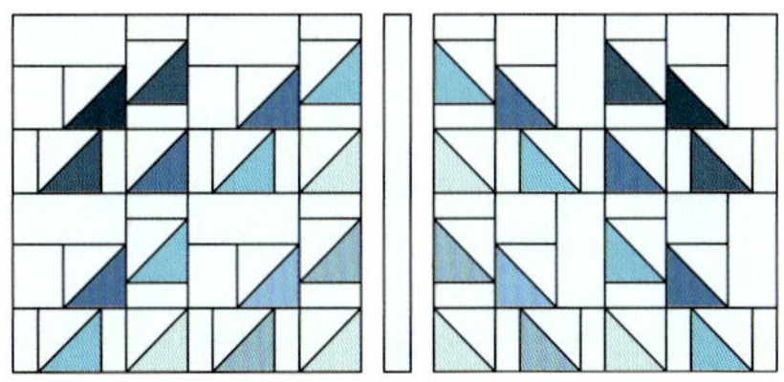

1. Sew each Block 1 to the right side of a Block 2. Press the seam toward Block 1. Then, sew each Block 3 to the right of a Block 2. Press the seam toward Block 2. Then, sew these 2 rows together as shown, nesting the seams. Press open, then repeat these steps to create 4 Quadrants. Each Quadrant will measure 22½″ × 22½″ (baby) or 28½″ × 28½″ (throw).

2. Sew 2 Quadrants together with an H5 piece in between. Press the seams toward the H5 piece. Repeat with the other 2 Quadrants and H5.

3. Sew the 2 rows from Step 2 together with an H6 piece in between. Press the seams toward the H6 piece.

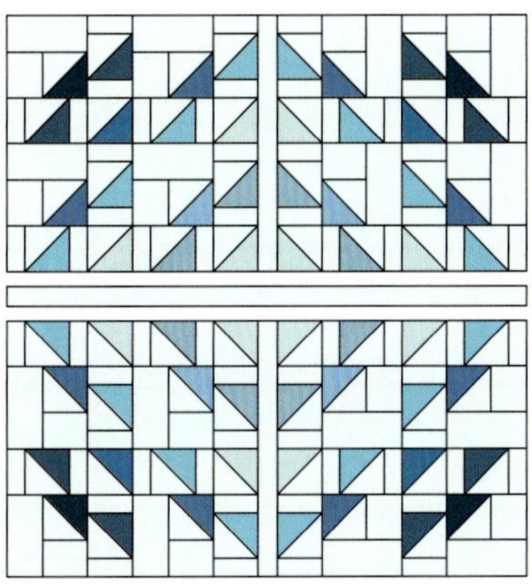

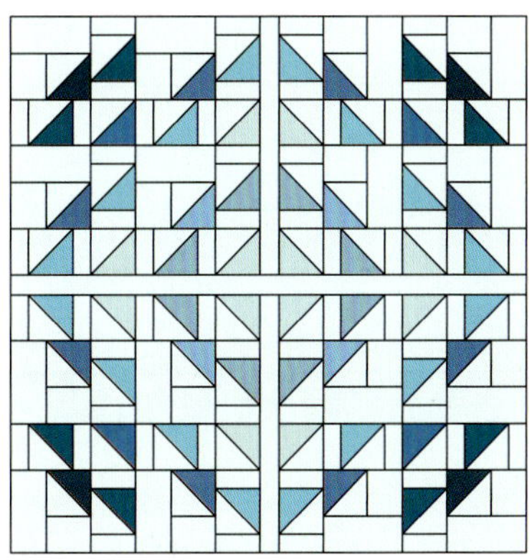

Prisma Quilt

THROW SIZE 61½" × 61½"

In my home, a crystal chandelier hangs in the entryway. When the sun hits the crystal prisms just right, it lights the whole wall up with dancing rainbows. This pattern was inspired by that beautiful afternoon show we get every day.

This pattern is laid out in a radial gradient, and it's a really excellent project to get adventurous with your color palettes. While you can definitely use a palette that transitions evenly through values, using a mirrored gradient effect (going from dark to light and then dark again) can make it more interesting. It's also a good pattern to try throwing in a few *pops* of a contrast hue or value for some fun.

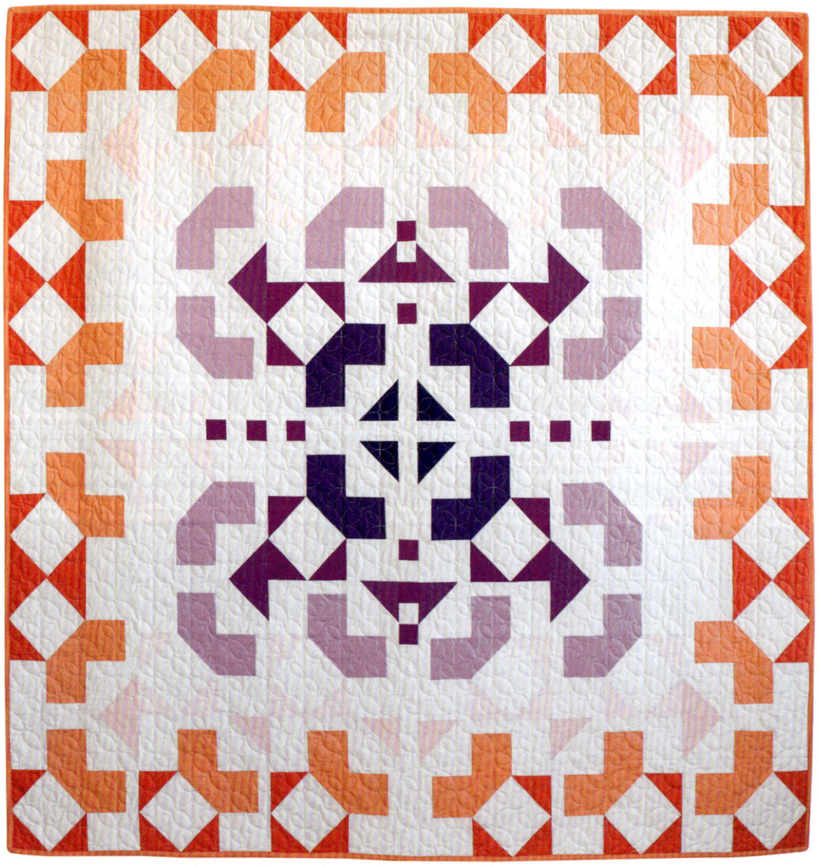

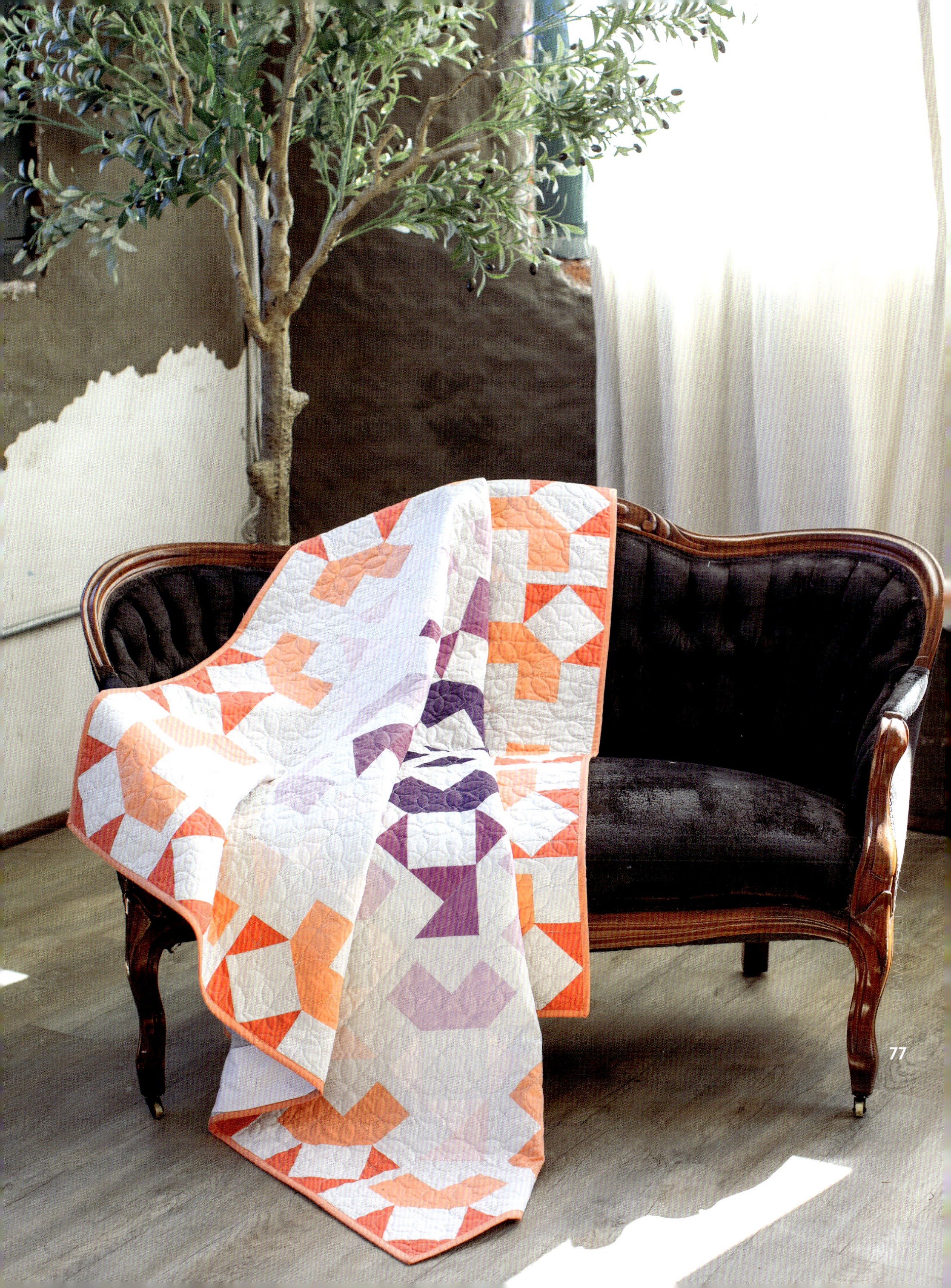

PRISMA QUILT

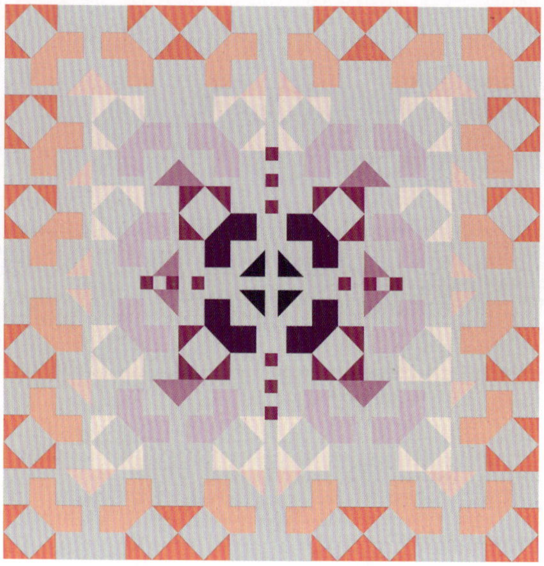

Radial complementary hue gradient, mirrored value gradient

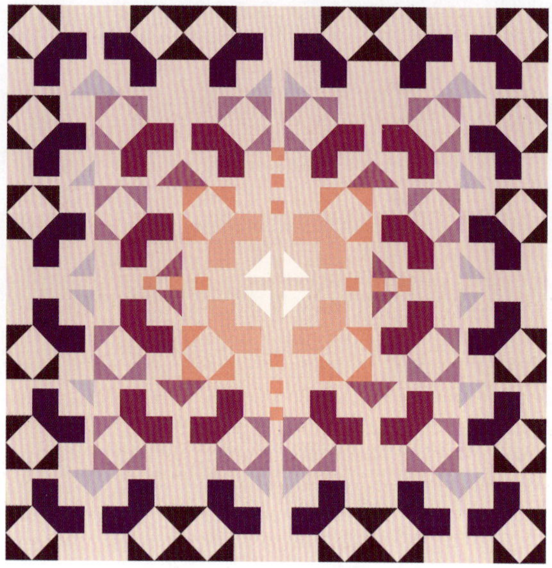

Radial complementary hue gradient with pops of value contrast

Fabric Requirements

Fabric *Riley Blake Confetti Cotton Solids*		**Throw (61½″ × 61½″)**
	Fabric A • *Rouge*	½ yard
	Fabric B • *Apricot Blush*	⅔ yard
	Fabric C • *Peaches N Cream*	¼ yard or 1 FQ
	Fabric D • *Ballerina*	¼ yard or 1 FQ
	Fabric E • *Princess*	⅓ yard
	Fabric F • *Violet*	¼ yard or 1 FQ
	Fabric G • *Orchid*	¼ yard or 1 FQ
	Fabric H • *Grape*	¼ yard or 1 FQ
	Fabric I • *Eggplant*	¼ yard or 1 FE
	Fabric J • *Silver*	2¾ yard

Cutting Instructions

Fabric	Throw
A	*Cut 3 – 4″ × WOF strips; subcut into* 30 – 4″ × 4″ squares (**A1**)
B	*Cut 5 – 4″ × WOF strips; subcut into* 10 – 4″ × 4″ squares (**B1**) 4 – 3½″ × WOF strips (**B2**)
C	*Cut 1 – 4″ × WOF strip; subcut into* 10 – 4″ × 4″ squares (**C1**)
D	*Cut 2 – 4″ × WOF strips; subcut into* 18 – 4″ × 4″ squares (**D1**)
E	*Cut 3 – 3½″ × WOF strips; subcut into* 6 – 4″ × 4″ squares (**E1**) 2– 3½″ × WOF strips (**E2**)
F	*Cut 1 – 4″ × WOF strip; subcut into* 6 – 4″ × 4″ squares (**F1**)
G	*Cut 1 – 4″ × WOF strip; subcut into* 6 – 4″ × 4″ squares (**G1**) *Cut 1 – 2″ × WOF strip; subcut into* 12 – 2″ × 2″ squares (**G2**)
H	*Cut 1 – 4″ × WOF strips; subcut into* 2 – 4″ × 4″ squares (**H1**) 1 – 3½″ × 35″ strip (**H2**)
I	*Cut 1 – 4″ × WOF strip; subcut into* 2 – 4″ × 4 ″ squares (**I1**)
J	*Cut 5 – 4¾″ × WOF strips; subcut into* 36 – 4¾″ × 4¾″ squares (**J2**) *Cut 8 – 4½″ × WOF strips; subcut into* 72 – 4½″ × 3½″ rectangles (**J6**) 36 – 4½″ × 1½″ rectangles (**J4**) *Cut 2 – 4″ × WOF strips; subcut into* 18 – 4″ × 4″ squares (**J1**) *Cut 7 – 1½″ × WOF strips* (**J5**) *Cut 3 – 2″ × WOF strips; subcut into* 5 – 2″ × 16″ rectangles (**J9**) 2 – 2″ × 7½″ rectangles (**J8**) 8 – 2″ × 2″ squares (**J7**) *Cut 3 – 1½″ × WOF strips; subcut into* 36 – 1½″ × 3½″ rectangles (**J3**)

Half-Square Triangle Unit Assembly

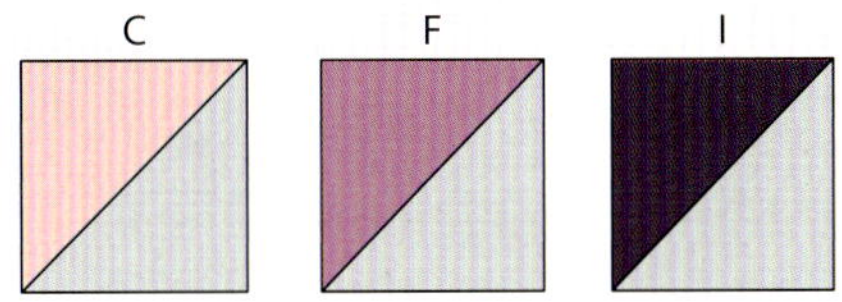

1. Following the instructions in Half-Square Triangle, create the HST Units shown in Table 1 using the Two-at-a-Time method (page 17). Trim each HST to 3½″ × 3½″.

Table 1

HST Name	Pieces Used	Number of HSTs
C HST	C1, J1	20
F HST	F1, J1	12
I HST	I1, J1	4

Square-in-a-Square Unit Assembly

Refer to Table 2 while piecing these units.

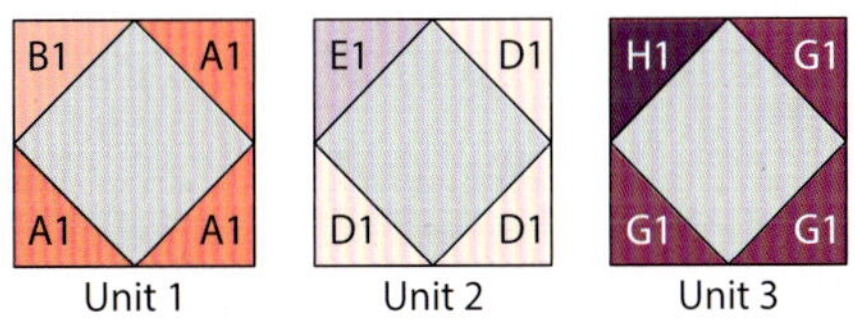

1. Cut each of the required A1, B1, D1, E1, G1, and H1 squares in half diagonally from corner to corner.

Table 2

Unit Name	Pieces Used	Number of Units
Square-in-a-Square Unit 1	30 – A1 10 – B1	20
Square-in-a-Square Unit 2	18 – D1 6 – E1	12
Square-in-a-Square Unit 3	6 – G1 2 – H1	4

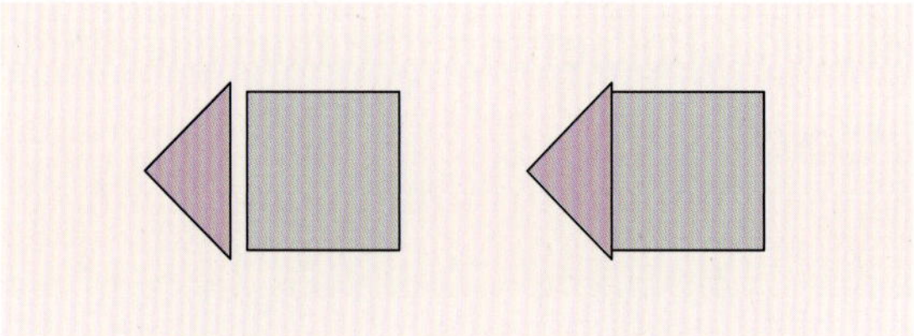

2. Center each cut B1, E1, and H1 triangle on the left side of a J2 square as shown. Sew. Handle these pieces with care, since you will be sewing along a bias edge. Press the seam away from the J2 square.

tip *Fold the triangle and J2 pieces in half, mark the centers, and then match them up to ensure the triangles are properly centered before sewing.*

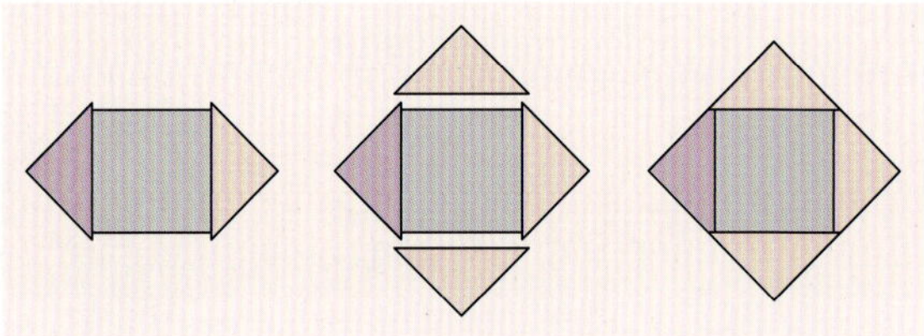

3. Center an A1, D1, or G1 triangle on the right side of each J2 square as shown. Sew. Use Table 2 to determine which fabric to use for each unit. Press the seam away from the J2 square. Repeat this step for the remaining triangles, using the same color in each unit. If needed, trim the final square-in-a-square to 6½″ × 6½″.

Strip Unit Assembly

1. Sew each B2, E2, and H2 strip to a J5 strip. Note that the H2 strip will not be a full WOF; this is ok. Press the seam toward the darker fabric.

2. Subcut each strip from Step 1 into 3½″ pieces to create 40 (B2/J5), 24 (E2/J5), and 8 (H2/J5) 3½″ × 4½″ Strip Units. Moving forward, we will refer to each Strip Unit by its unique color (B, E, and H).

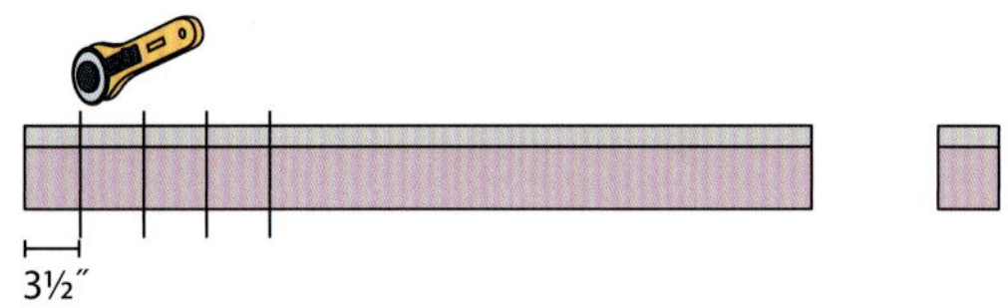

Block Assembly

Create three variations of the same blocks with different color combinations of HST units, strip units, and square units. Repeat Steps 1–5 below to make the correct number of Block 1, Block 2, and Block 3 (the 3 colorways). Table 3 shows which units and pieces are used within each block.

Table 3

Block Name	HST Unit	Strip Unit – 2 each	Square Unit	Number of Blocks
Block 1	C HST	Strip Unit B	Square-in-a-Square Unit 1	20
Block 2	F HST	Strip Unit F	Square-in-a-Square Unit 2	12
Block 3	I HST	Strip Unit H	Square-in-a-Square Unit 3	4

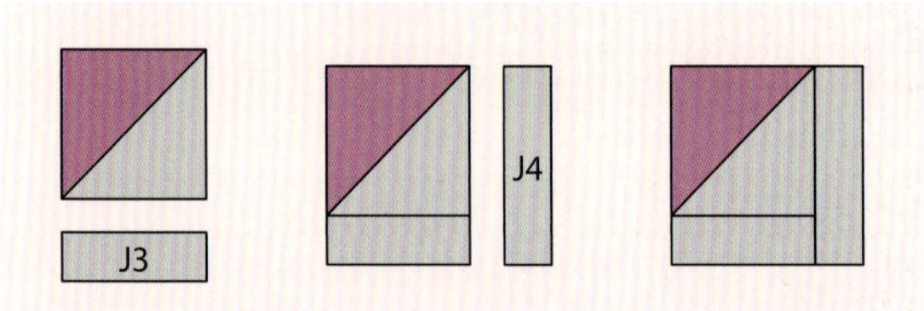

1. Sew a J3 rectangle to the bottom of each C, F, and I HST. Press, then sew a J4 rectangle to the right side of each unit. If needed, trim to 4½″ × 4½″.

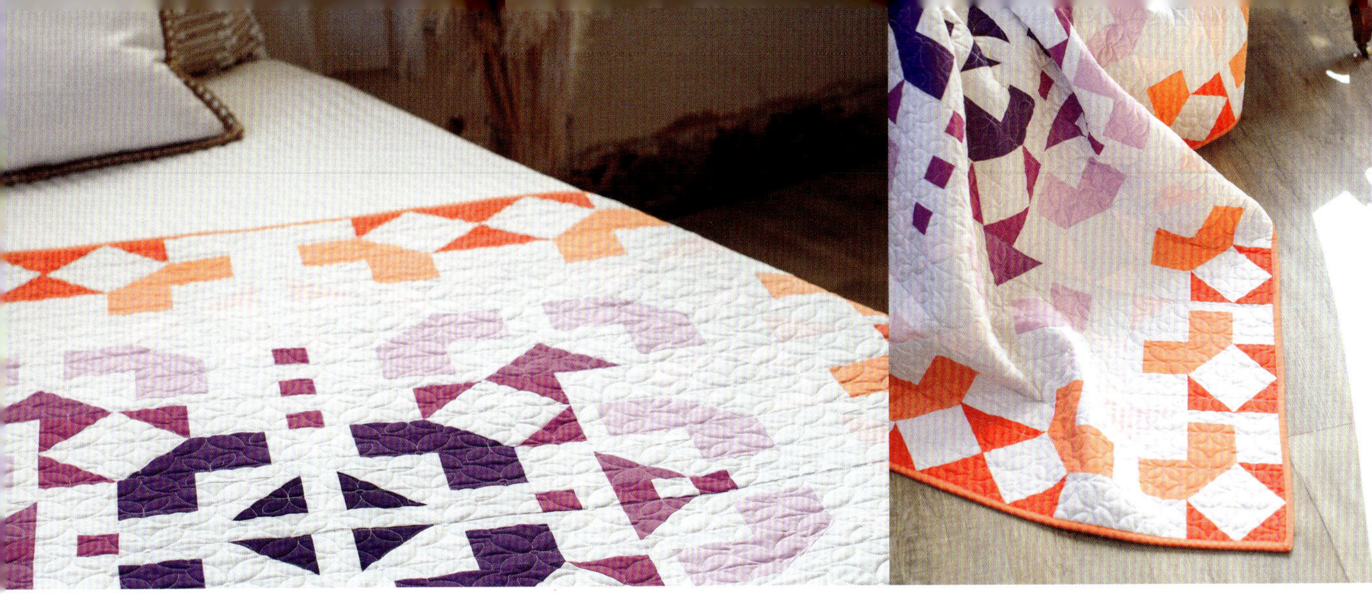

Quilt sample pieced by Katie Dean, longarm quilted by Trace Creek Quilting.

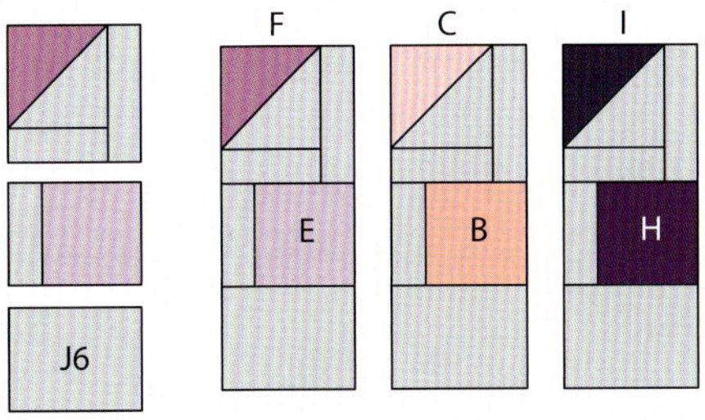

Create 12 of the F HST unit, 20 of the C HST unit, and 4 of the I HST unit.

2. Sew each unit from Step 1 to the corresponding Strip Piece unit and a J6 rectangle in the order shown. You will only use half of the Strip Piece units and J6 rectangles in this step. If needed, trim to 4½" × 10½".

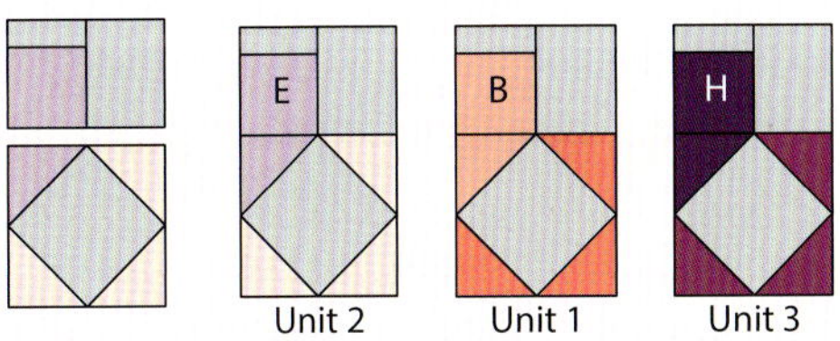

Create 12 of Unit 2, 20 of Unit 1, and 4 of Unit 3.

4. Sew each of the units from Step 3 to each Square-in-a-Square Unit, matching the fabrics of the Strip Unit to the left corner of the Square Unit. If needed, trim to 6½" × 10½".

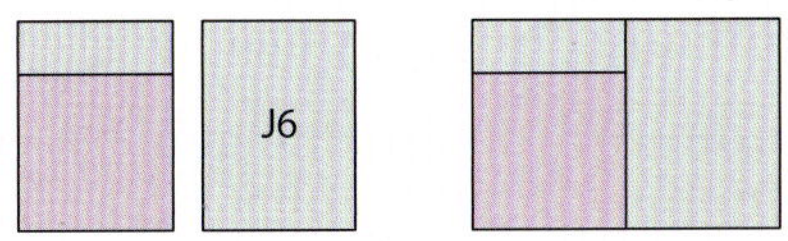

3. Sew the remaining Strip Piece units to the remaining J6 rectangles as shown.

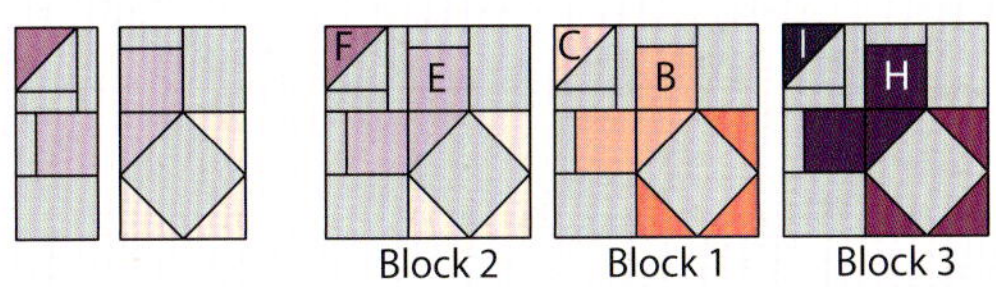

5. Sew the units created in Step 2 to the units created in Step 4 as shown, matching the Strip Unit fabric colors. If needed, trim to 10½" × 10½".

Quilt Assembly

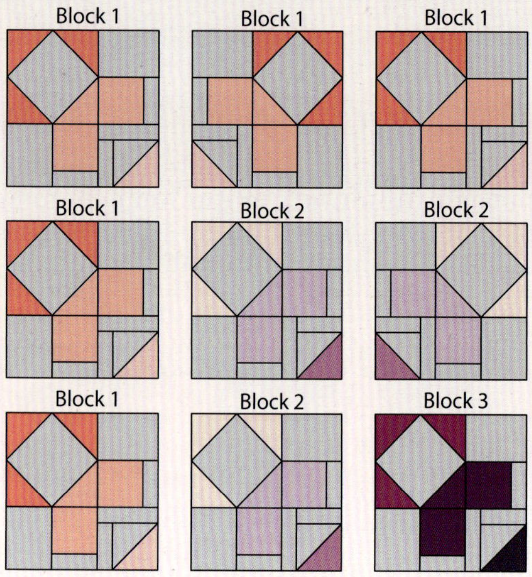

Quadrant Diagram

1. Assemble blocks as shown in the Quadrant Diagram to create 4 Quadrants. Sew the blocks first into rows of 3, then sew the rows together. Pay extra attention to the orientation and order of the blocks. Press the seams in alternating directions after sewing the blocks into rows so that the seams nest when you sew the rows together. The Quadrants should each measure 30½″ × 30½″.

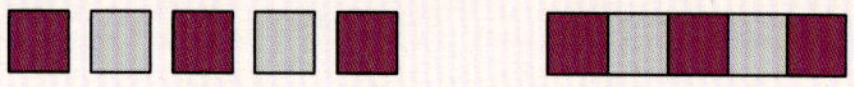

2. Sew together alternating J7 and G2 squares in sets of 5 as shown. Create 4 units that measure 2″ × 8″.

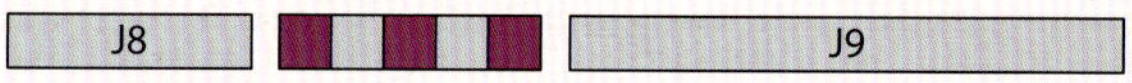

3. Sew a J8 strip and a J9 strip to each side of a unit from Step 2. If needed, trim to 30½″ × 2″. This unit is called Strip 1. Repeat to make a second Strip 1.

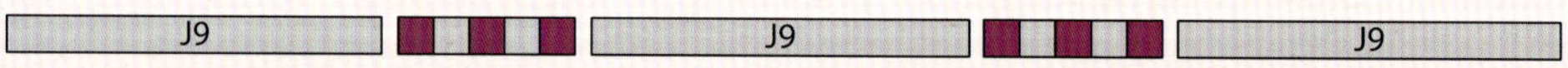

4. Sew together 3 J9 strips and the remaining 2 units from Step 2 as shown. If needed, trim to 62″ × 2″. This unit is called Strip 2.

5. Sew 2 Quadrants together with a Strip 1 in between, oriented as shown. Repeat with the other 2 Quadrants. Press the seams toward Strip 1.

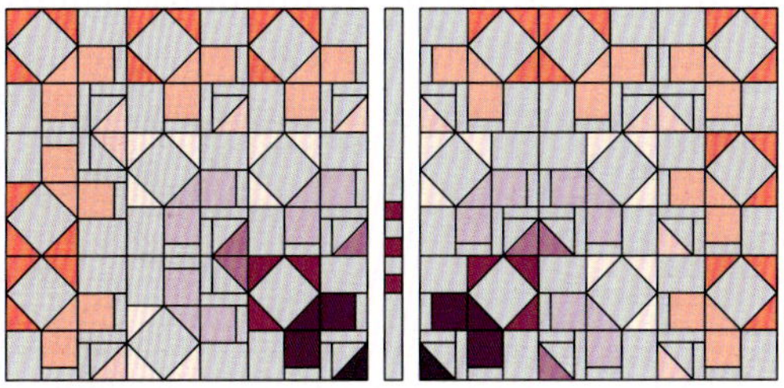

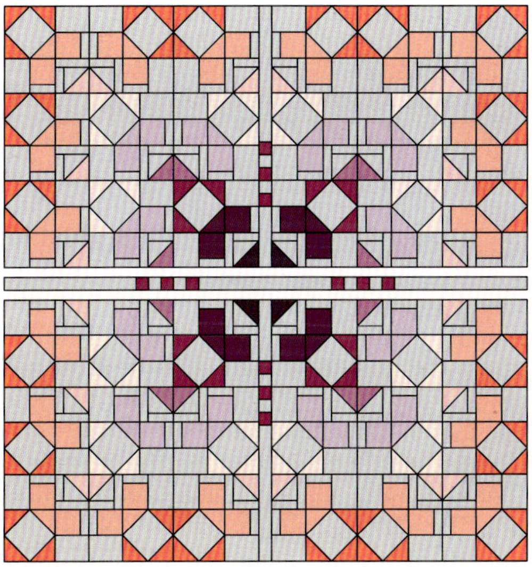

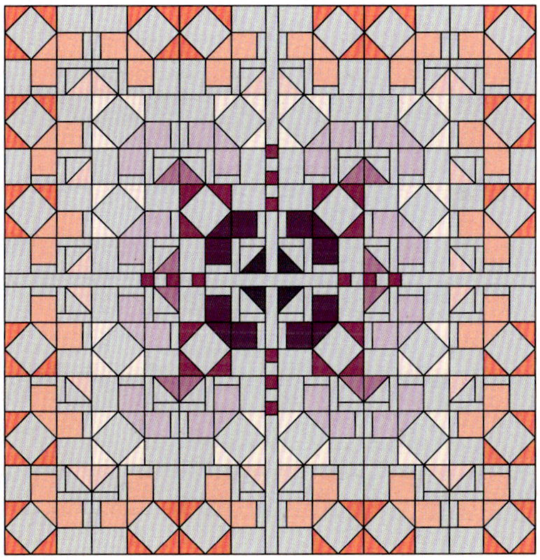

6. Sew together the units from Step 5 with a Strip 2 in between. Pin thoroughly to ensure the strip is centered. Press the seams toward Strip 2.

Portière Quilt

THROW 56" × 75"

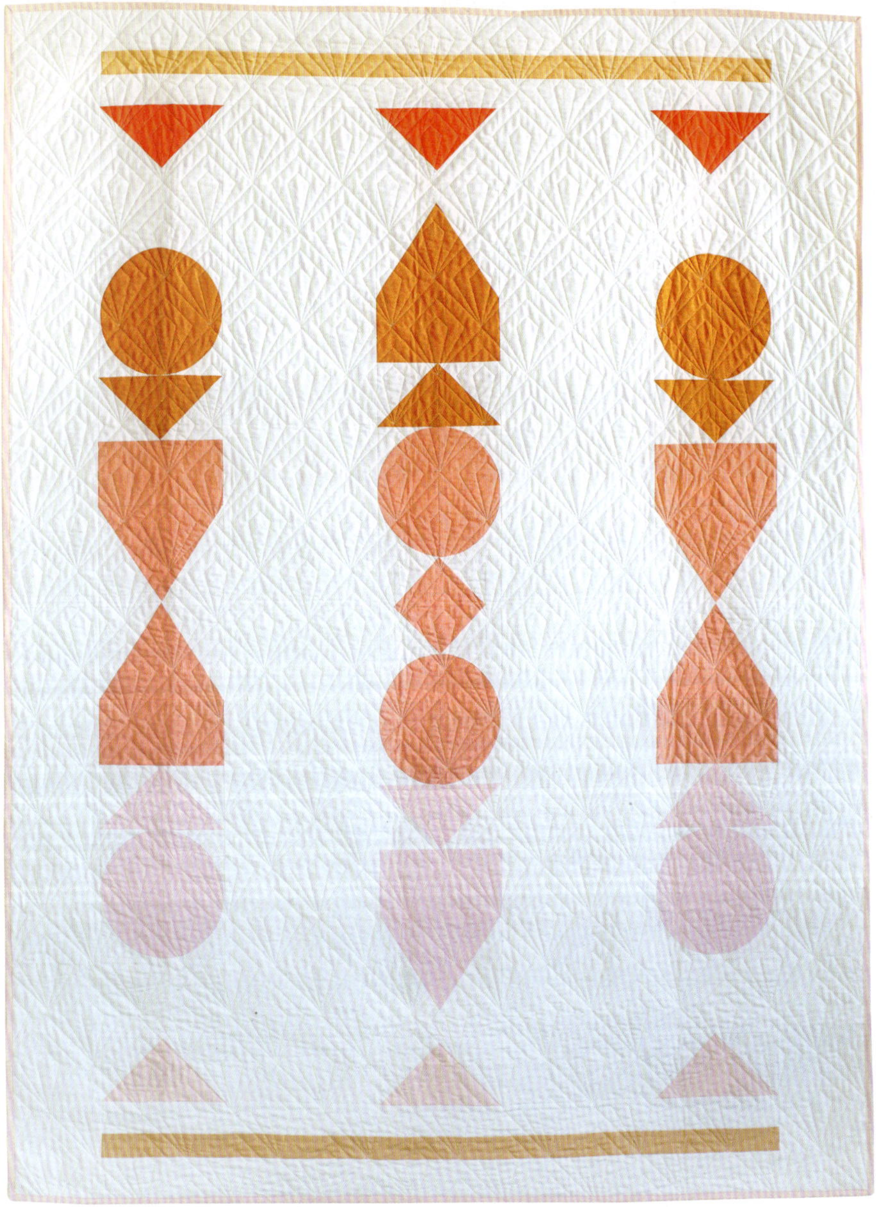

Portière was inspired by the bohemian beaded curtains that were so popular in the 1970s. Adding an ombré effect to the beaded shapes gives them so much visual interest! This pattern is a good opportunity to practice using templates. It's a skill builder that still comes together quickly. Using a mixed—color gradient on this quilt can be especially impactful, but it tends to look best when the color palette includes a linear value gradient. Prepare Templates 5–8 for this project (see Templates, page 126).

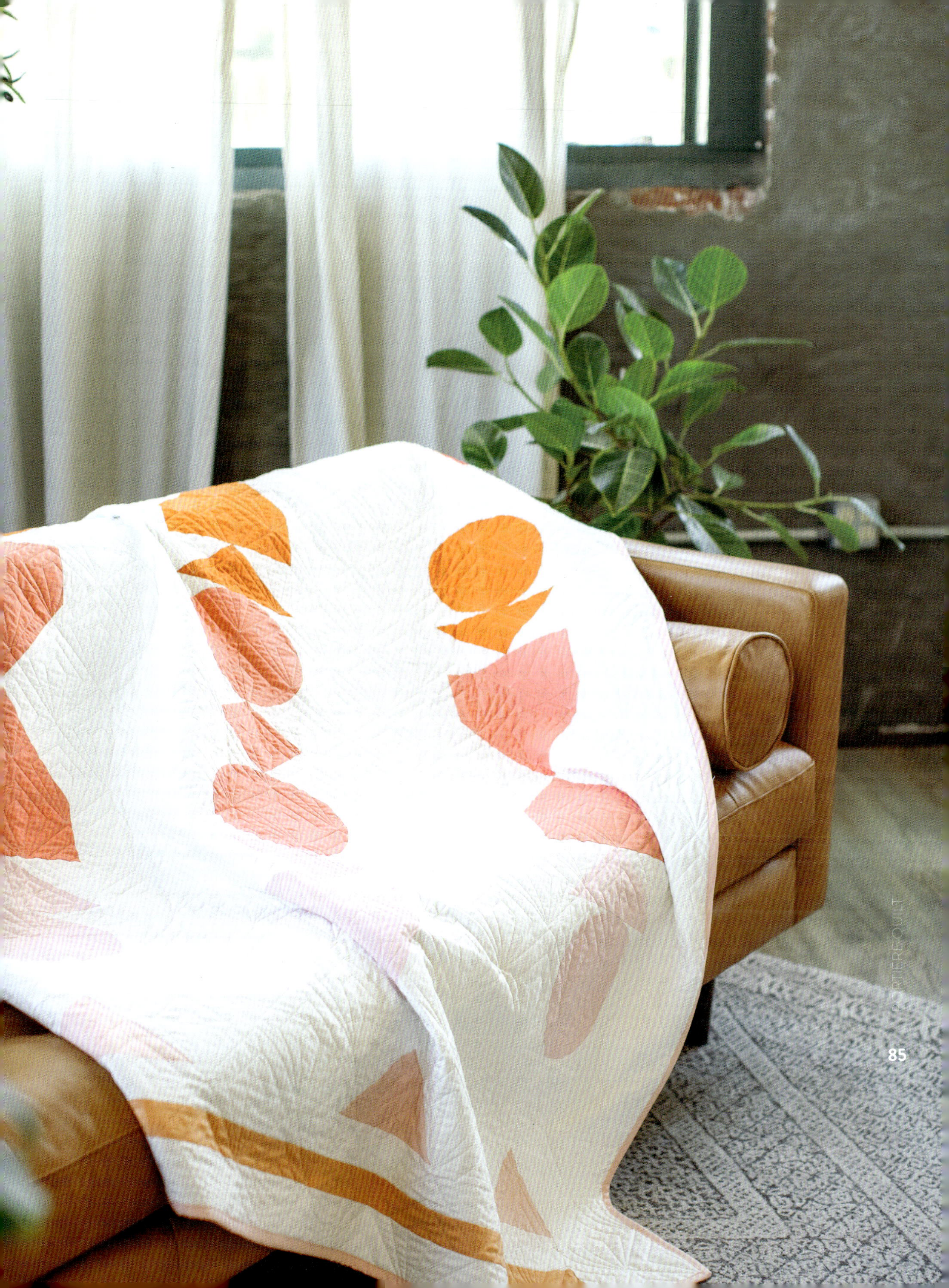

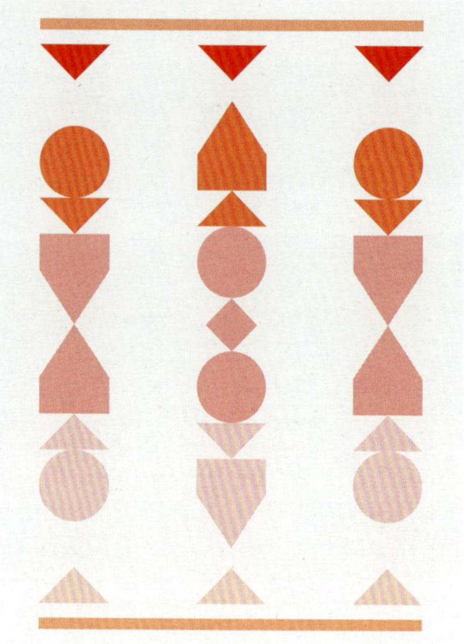

Analogous and value vertical linear gradient

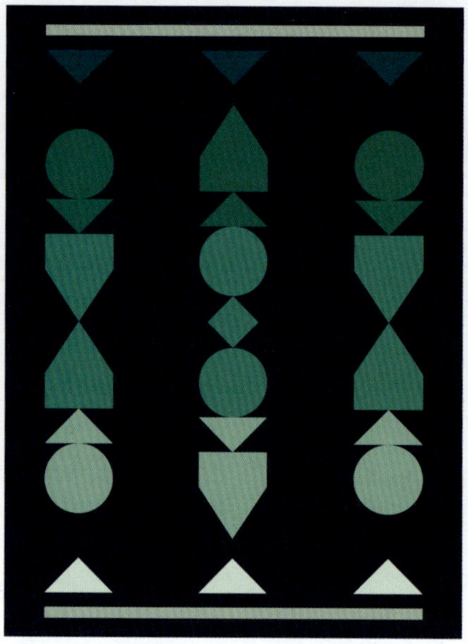

Monochromatic and value linear gradient, with an analogous color background

Fabric Requirements

Fabric *Riley Blake Confetti Cotton Solids*		Throw (56″ × 75″)
	Fabric A • *Sunset*	¼ yard
	Fabric B • *Pumpkin*	⅓ yard
	Fabric C • *Grapefruit*	⅔ yard
	Fabric D • *Frosting*	⅓ yard
	Fabric E • *Peaches N Cream*	¼ yard
	Fabric F • *Marmalade*	¼ yard
	Fabric G • *Off White*	3½ yards

Cutting Instructions

Fabric	Throw
A	*Cut 1 — 5″ × WOF strip; subcut into* 3 — 5″ × 5″ squares (**A1**)
B	*Cut 1 — 10″ × WOF strip; subcut into* 1 — Template 7 (**B3**) 4 — Template 5 (**B4**) 1 — 8½″ × 4½″ rectangle (**B2**) 3 — 5″ × 5″ squares (**B1**)
C	*Cut 1 — 9″ × WOF strip; subcut into* 4 — Template 7 (**C3**) 1 — 6½″ × 6½″ square (**C2**) *Cut 1 — 8¾″ × WOF strip; subcut into* 4 — Template 5 (**C4**) 4 — 4½″ × 8½″ rectangles (**C1**)
D	*Cut 1 — 10″ × WOF strip; subcut into* 1 — Template 7 (**D3**) 4 — Template 5 (**D4**) 1 — 8½″ × 4½ ″ rectangle (**D2**) 3 — 5″ × 5″ squares (**D1**)
E	*Cut 1 — 5″ × WOF strip; subcut into* 3 — 5″ × 5″ squares (**E1**)
F	*Cut 3 — 2″ × WOF strips, and sew them together; subcut into* 2 — 2″ × 44½″ (**F1**)
G	*Cut 3 — 10½″ × WOF strips, and sew together; subcut into* 2 — 10½″ × 62½″ strips (**G6**) *Cut 4 — 6½″ × WOF strips, and sew together; subcut into* 2 — 6½″ × 75½″ strips (**G9**) 2 — 6½″ × 1½″ rectangles (**G5**) *Cut 4 — 5½″ × WOF strips; subcut into* 12 — Template 6 (**G11**) 4 — 8½″ × 5½″ rectangles (**G2**) *Cut 3 — 5″ × WOF strips; subcut into* 6 — Template 8 (**G10**) 12 — 5″ × 5″ squares (**G1**) *Cut 3 — 3½″ × WOF strips, and sew together; subcut into* 2 — 3½″ × 44½″ strips (**G8**) 4 — 3½″ × 3½″ squares (**G4**) *Cut 3 — 2½″ × WOF strips, and sew together; subcut into* 2 — 2½″ × 44½″ strips (**G7**) 2 — 2½″ × 8½″ rectangles (**G3**)

Half-Square Triangle Unit Assembly

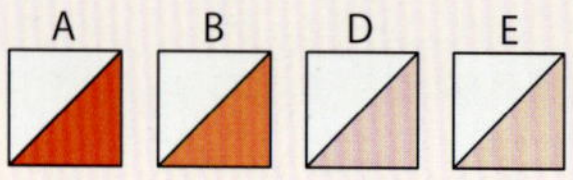

1. Match each A1, B1, D1, and E1 square with one G1 square. Make 6 Half-Square Triangles from each color by following the instructions in Two-at-a-Time (page 17). Trim the HSTs to 4½″ × 4½″.

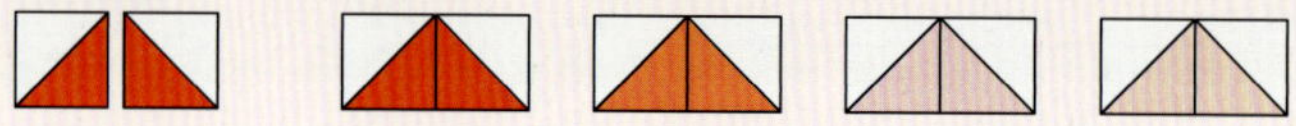

2. Sew pairs of HSTs together as shown to create 3 HST Units of each color. If needed, trim to 4½″ × 8½″. Press seams open.

Triangle Unit Assembly

1. Sew a G10 piece to 2 sides of each B3, C3, and D3 piece. Press the seams open. If needed, trim to 8½″ × 6½″. These are called Triangle Units.

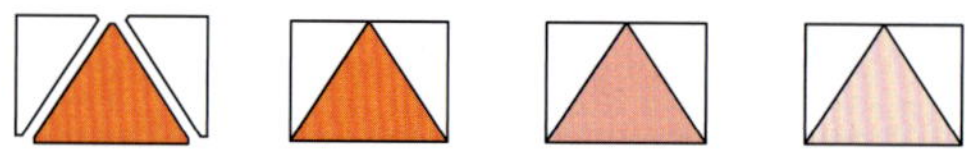

Square Unit Assembly

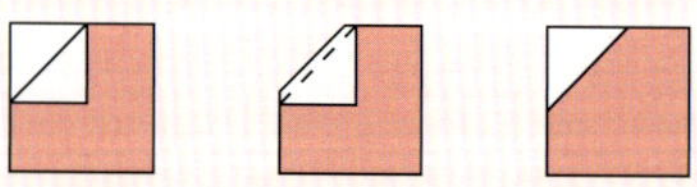

1. Draw a diagonal line on the wrong side of each G4 square. Place 1 G4 square on the top left corner of the C2 square. Sew along the line, then trim ¼″ away from the line. Press seam toward the C2 square.

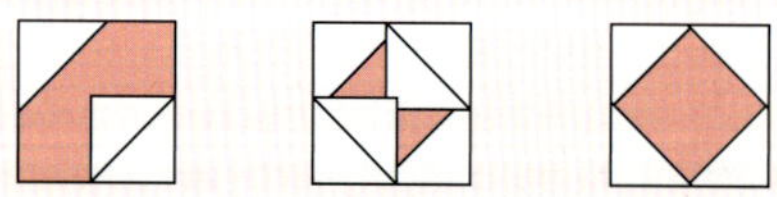

2. Repeat Step 1 to sew 3 G4 squares on the other 3 corners of the C2 square. If needed, trim to 6½″ × 6½″, taking care to preserve the seam allowance along the C2 points.

3. Sew G5 rectangles to each side of the square to finish the Square Unit. If needed, trim to 8½″ × 6½″.

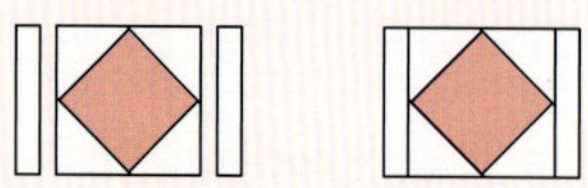

Circle Unit Assembly

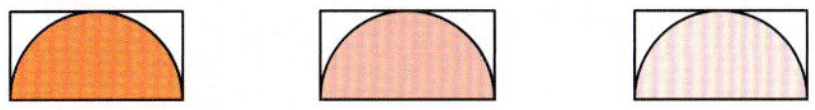

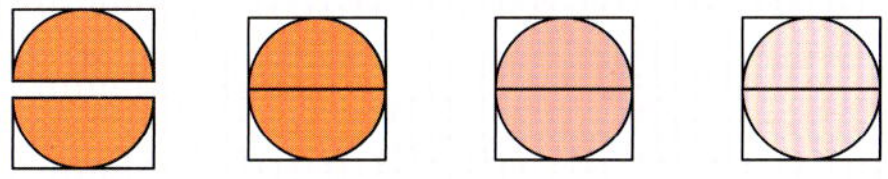

1. Match each B4, C4, and D4 with a G11 piece, then sew together into half circles (see Sewing Curves, page 15). Make 4 in each color. If needed, trim to 8½″ × 4½″.

2. Pair same—color half circles from Step 1. Sew together to create 2 Circle Units in each color. If needed, trim to 8½″ × 8½″. Press seams open.

Quilt Assembly

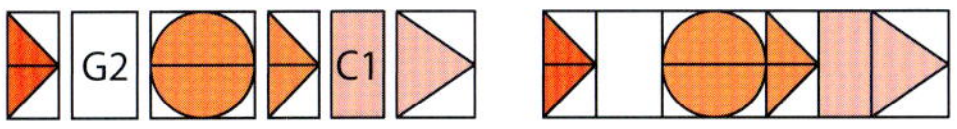

1. Sew together the following units and pieces as shown: HST Unit A, G2, Circle Unit B, HST Unit B, C1, and Triangle Unit C. Press all seams open. If needed, trim to 8½″ × 31½″. Repeat to make a second unit.

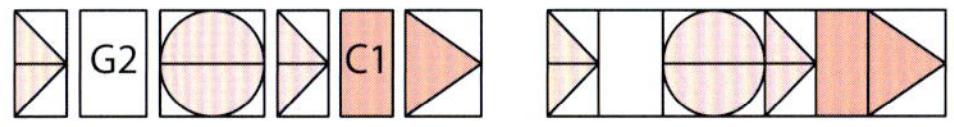

2. Sew together the following units and pieces as shown: HST Unit E, G2, Circle Unit D, HST Unit D, C1, and Triangle Unit C. Press all seams open. If needed, trim to 8½″ × 31½″. Repeat to make a second unit.

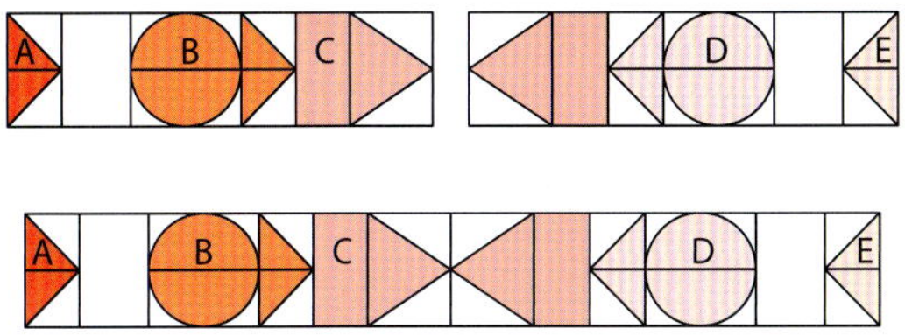

3. Sew the units from Steps 1–2 together as shown to create 2 Column 1 units. Press all seams open. If needed, trim to 8½″ × 62½″.

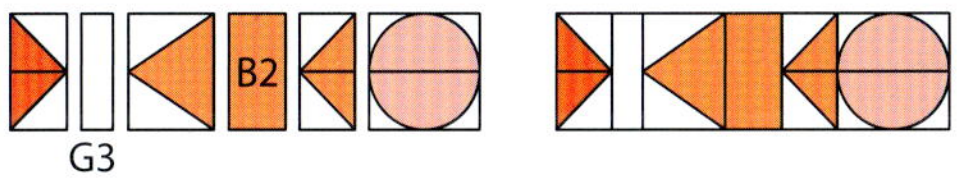

4. Sew together the following units and pieces as shown: HST Unit A, G3, Triangle Unit B, B2, HST Unit B, and Circle Unit C. Press all seams open. If needed, trim to 8½″ × 28½″.

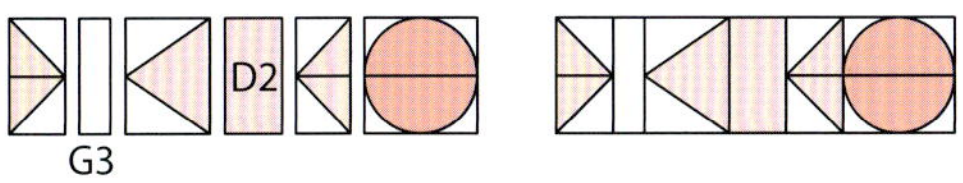

5. Sew together the following units and pieces as shown: HST Unit E, G3, Triangle Unit D, D2, HST Unit D, and Circle Unit C. Press all seams open. If needed, trim to 8½″ × 28½″.

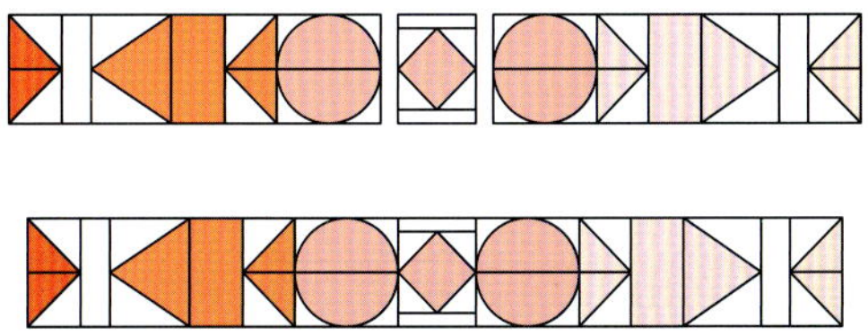

6. Sew the units from Steps 4–5 together as shown, with a Square Unit in the middle, to create 1 Column 2. Press all seams open. If needed, trim to 8½″ × 62½″.

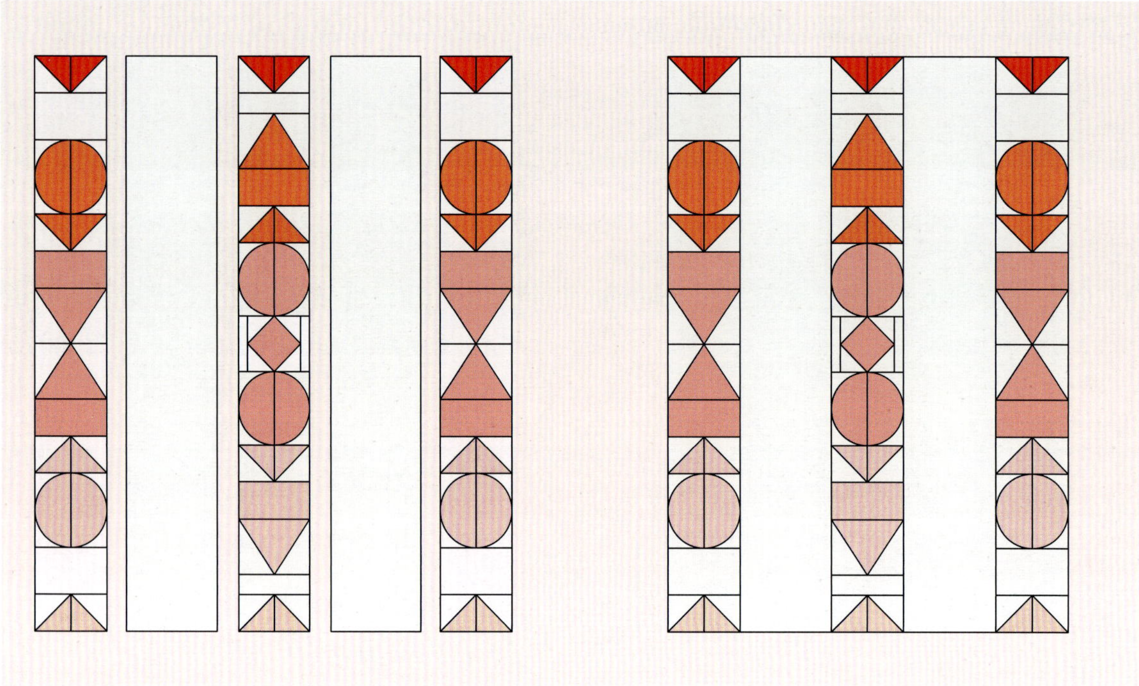

7. Using lots of pins, sew together the following units and pieces as shown: Column 1 unit, G6, Column 2 unit, G6, Column 1 unit. Press the seams toward the G6 pieces.

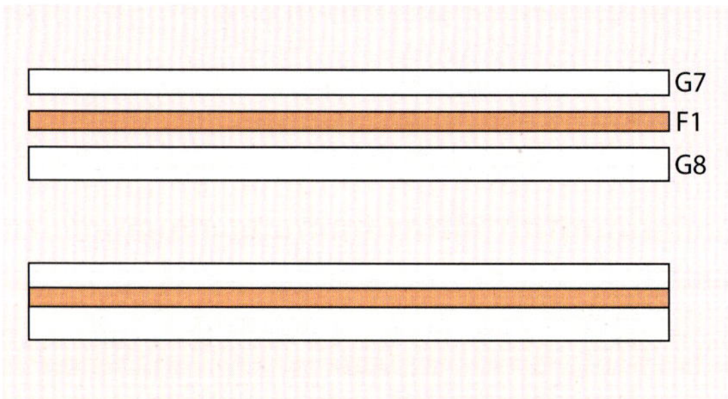

8. Sew together a G7, F1, and G8 piece, pressing seams toward the darker fabric. Repeat to create a second Border Unit.

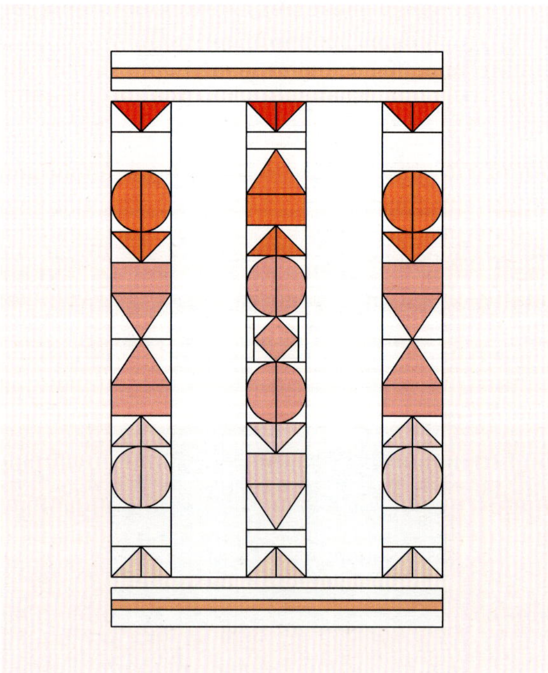

9. Sew the Border Units to the top and bottom of the quilt, orienting them so that G7 is attached to the quilt top.

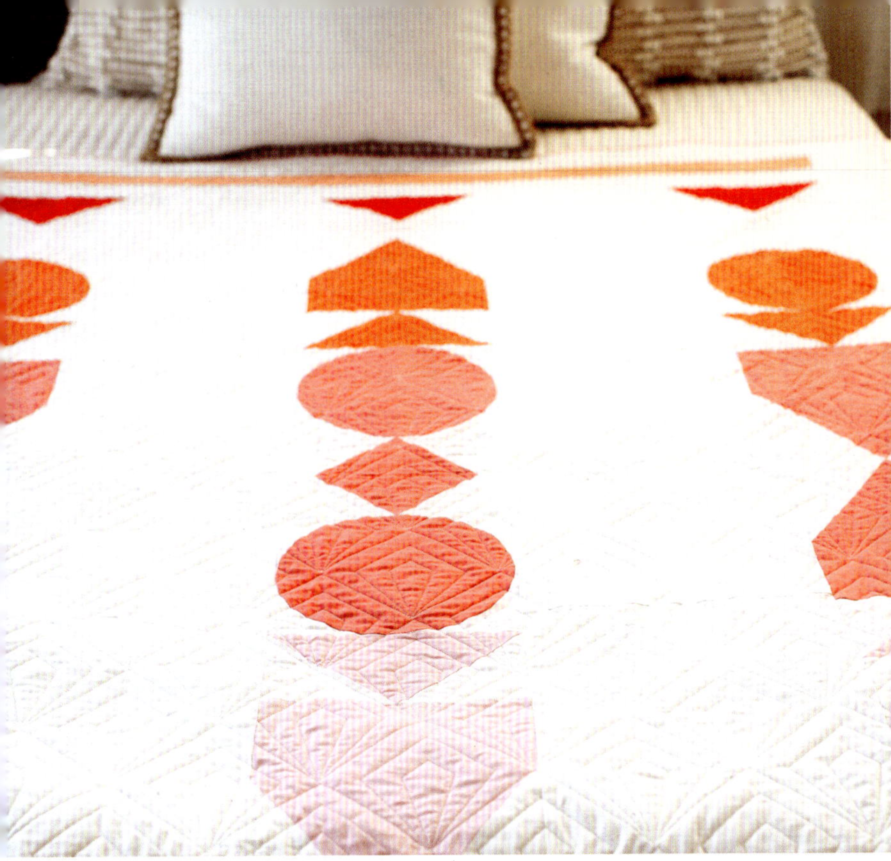
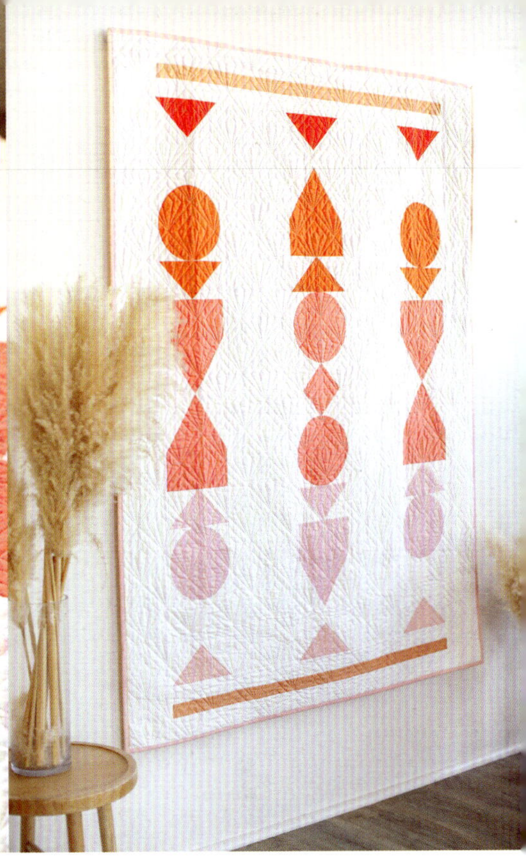

Sample quilt pieced by Heather Heck, longarm quilted by Jenn B Quilts.

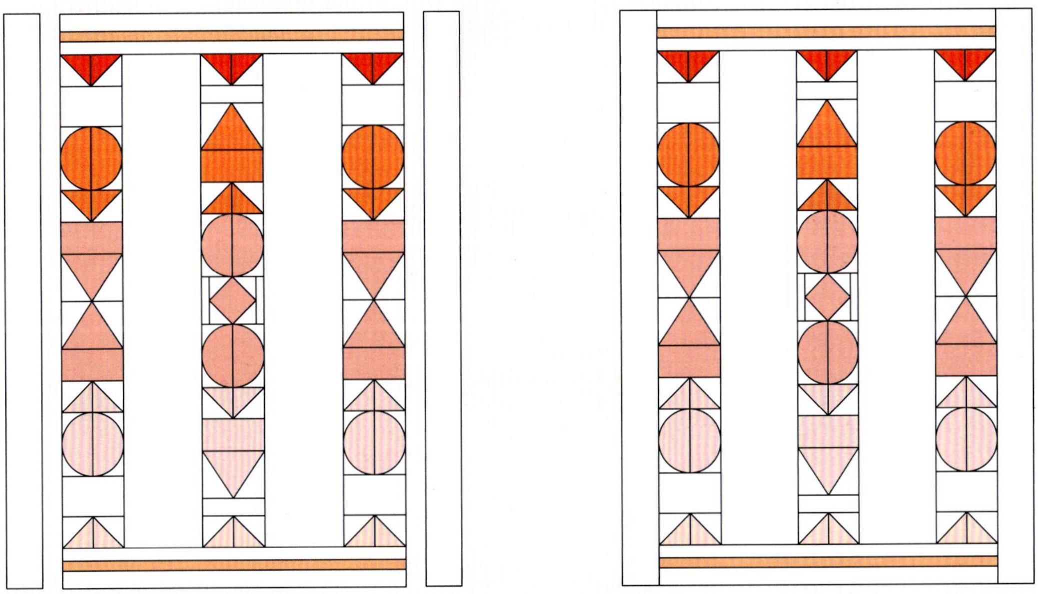

10. Sew a G9 strip to each side of the quilt top. Press the seams toward the G9 strips.

Primula Quilt

THROW SIZE 63″ × 63″

This pattern was inspired by four petalled primrose flowers. This quilt is unique, as it's the only design in this book that features a block gradient. Quilts with block gradients are often a bit more subtle when it comes to the overall ombré effect, but they can be just as striking! This quilt uses a limited selection of colors, so it is usually best to pick a monochromatic or analogous color scheme. This pattern has a few techniques that are a bit more challenging and require some precision, but the end result is so versatile depending on your color choices! Prepare Templates 9–11 (see Templates, page 126).

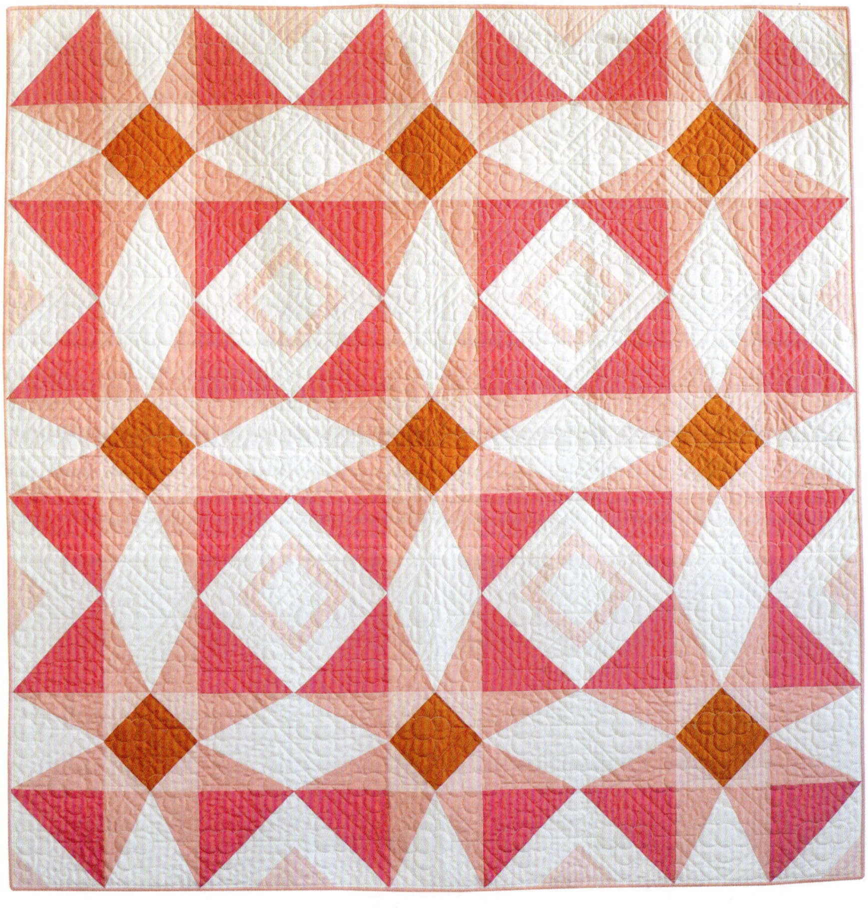

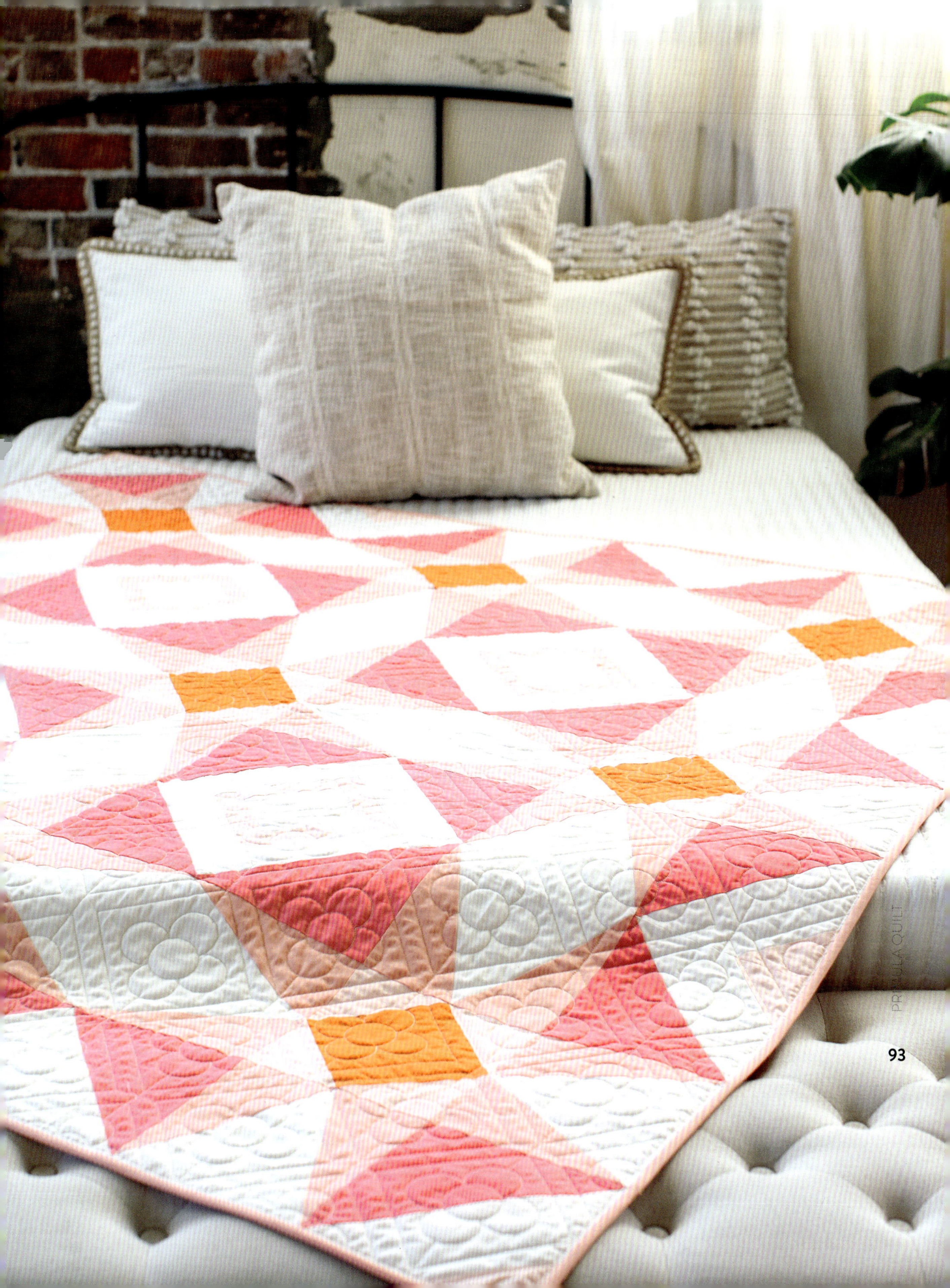

Fabric Requirements

Fabric *Riley Blake Confetti Cotton Solids*		Throw (56″ × 75″)
	Fabric A • *Sugar Pink*	1 yard
	Fabric B • *Grapefruit*	1¼ yard
	Fabric C • *Peaches N Cream*	¾ yard
	Fabric D • *Pumpkin*	⅜ yard
	Fabric E • *Cloud*	2¼ yards

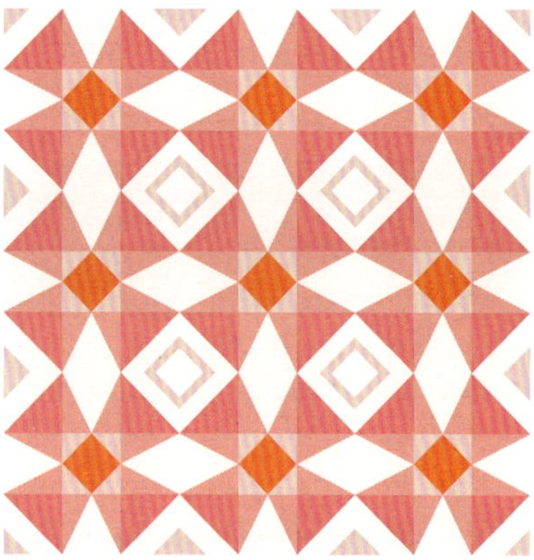

A monochromatic palette with a splash of an analogous color lets the block gradient effect shine.

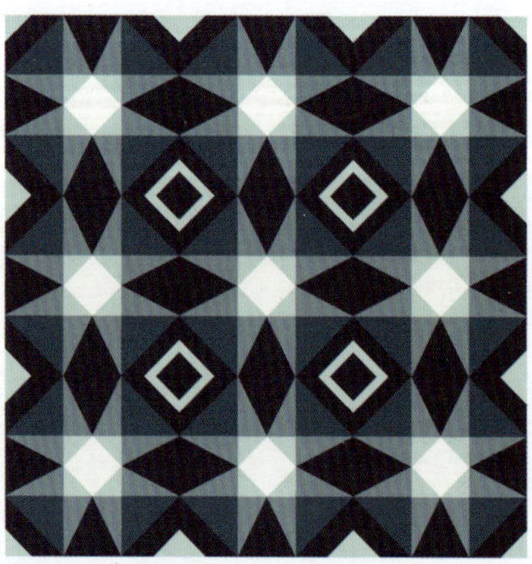

A dark background and monochromatic palette change the mood of this block gradient.

Cutting Instructions

Fabric	Throw
A	***Cut 4 – 8″ × WOF strips; subcut into*** 18 – 8″ × 8″ squares (**A1**)
B	***Cut 8 – 4½″ × WOF strips; subcut into*** 72 – Template 9* (**B1**)
C	***Cut 1 – 6½″ × WOF strip; subcut into*** 8 – 1½″ × 6½″ rectangles (**C2**) 8 – 1½″ × 4½″ rectangles (**C1**) ***Cut 2 – 4½″ × WOF strips; subcut into*** 18 – 4½″ × 4½″ squares (**C4**) ***Cut 2 – 3½″ × WOF strips; subcut into*** 20 – 3½″ × 3½″ squares (**C3**)
D	***Cut 2 – 5½″ × WOF strips; subcut into*** 9 – 5½″ × 5½″ squares (**D1**)
E	***Cut 3 – 15½″ × WOF strips; subcut into*** 12 – Template 11 (**E6**) 12 – Template 10 (**E5**) 4 – 4½″ × 4½″ squares (**E2**) ***Cut 2 – 8″ × WOF strips; subcut into*** 10 – 8″ × 8″ squares (**E1**) ***Cut 4 – 2½″ × WOF strips; subcut into*** 8 – 2½″ × 10½″ rectangles (**E4**) 8 – 2½″ × 6½″ rectangles (**E3**)

** Cut Template 9 as shown below for efficient fabric usage. If you are using a fabric with a right/wrong side, half of the template pieces should be cut with the template piece flipped so that the fabric pieces are mirrored.*

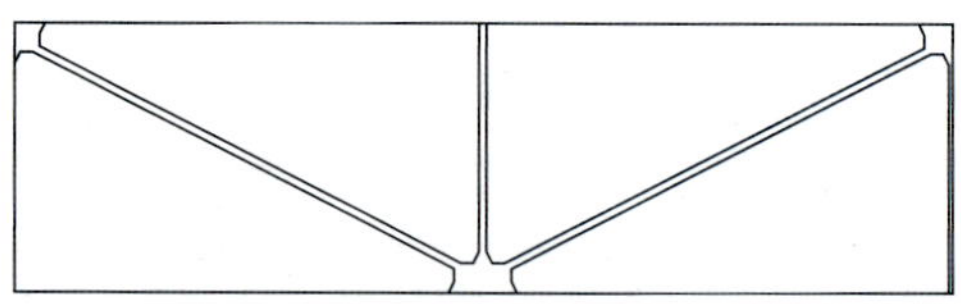

*** Nest templates as shown.*

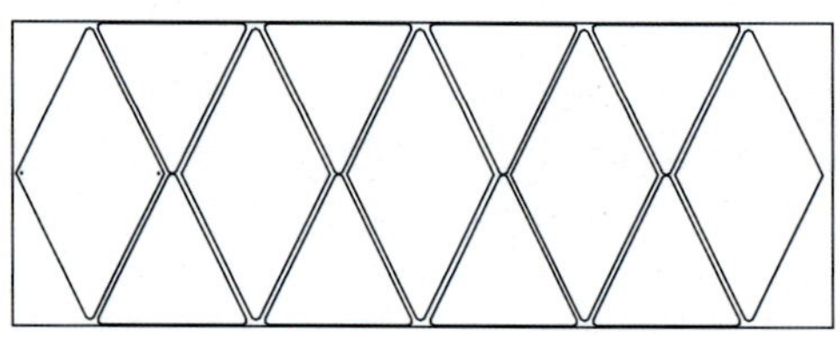

Half-Square Triangle Unit Assembly

1. Match each E1 with an A1 square, then follow the instructions in Half-Square Triangles using the two-at-a-time method (page 17) to create 20 HSTs. Trim the HST units to 7½″ × 7½″.

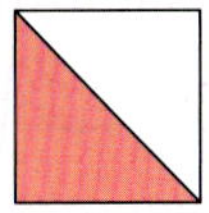

Block Assembly

BLOCK 1 ASSEMBLY

1. Cut each C4 square in half from corner to corner. Center a C4 triangle on the left side of each D1 square as shown. Sew. Repeat on the right side, and then on the top and the bottom of the D1 square. If needed, trim to 7½″ × 7½″, ensuring the seam allowance is preserved in each D1 corner. Repeat to make 9, and call this unit Block 1.

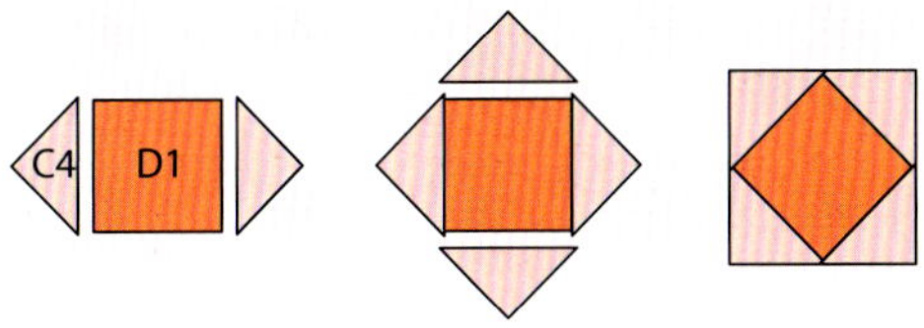

tip *Fold the C4 and D1 pieces in half in half, mark the centers, and then match them up to ensure the triangles are properly centered before sewing.*

BLOCK 2 ASSEMBLY

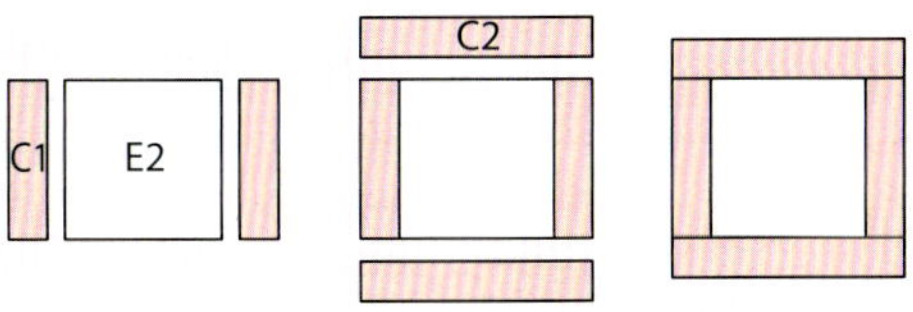

1. Sew a C1 piece to each side of each E2 square. Press the seams open. Then, sew a C2 piece to the top and bottom of the unit. If needed, trim to 6½″ × 6½″.

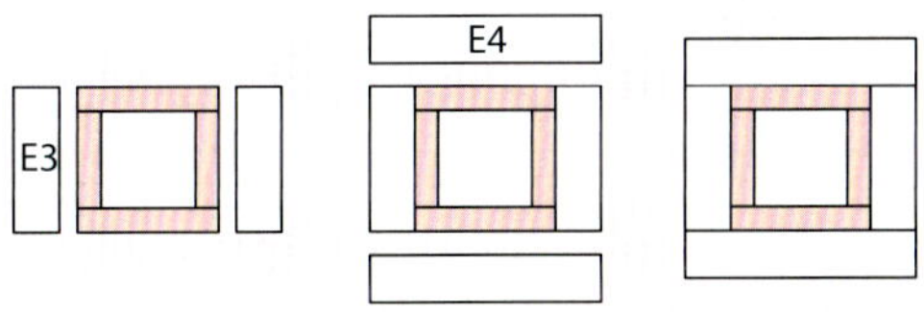

2. Repeat Step 1 to sew E3 and E4 rectangles around the unit from Step 1. If needed, trim to 10½″ × 10½″.

3. Cut each remaining A1 square in half from corner to corner. Center an A1 triangle on the left side of each unit from Step 2, and sew. Repeat on the right side, and then on the top and bottom. If needed, trim to 14½″ × 14½″, ensuring the seam allowance is preserved. Repeat to make 4, and call this unit Block 2.

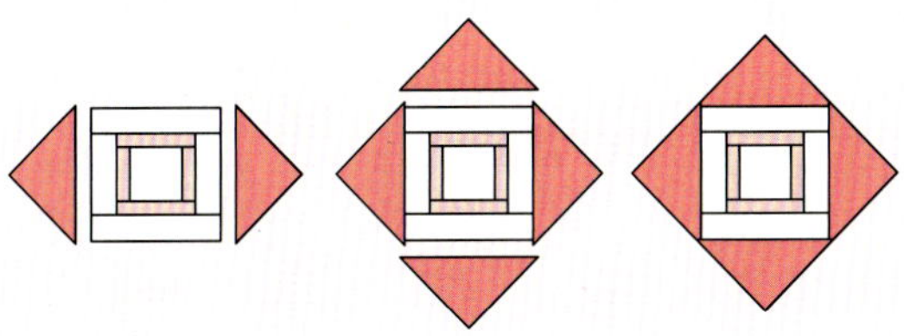

BLOCK 3 ASSEMBLY

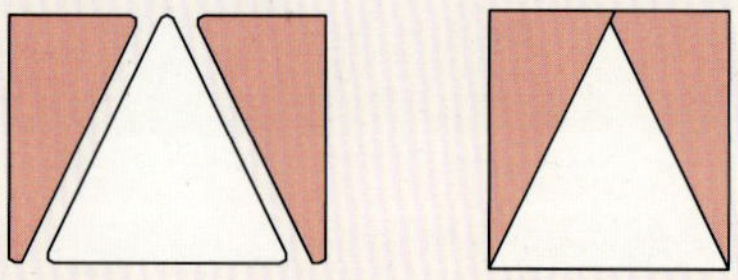

1. Sew a B1 piece to 2 sides of each E5 piece as shown. Press the seams towards the E5 piece after each seam. If needed, trim to 7½" × 7½". Repeat to make 12, and call this unit Block 3A.

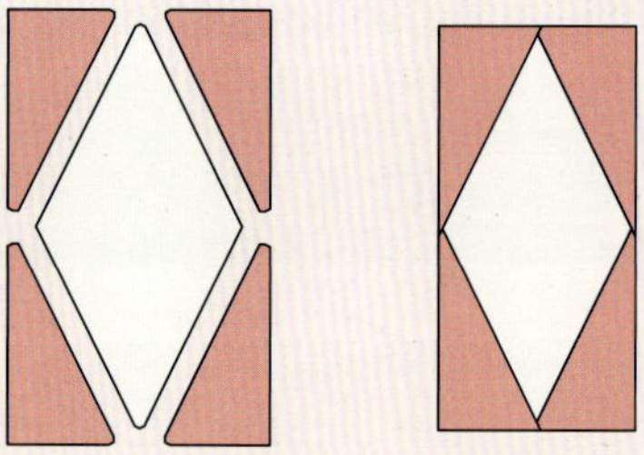

2. Sew a B1 piece to each side of each E6 piece, pressing open after each seam. If needed, trim to 7½" × 14½". Repeat to make 12, and call this unit Block 3B.

BLOCK 4 ASSEMBLY

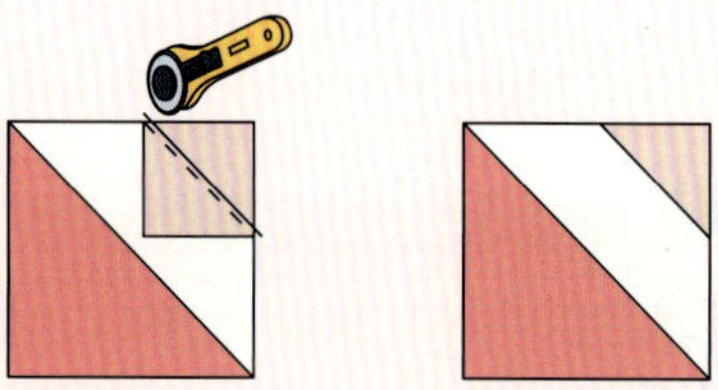

1. Draw a diagonal line across the wrong side of each C3 square. Place a square on the background section of each HST (from Half-Square Triangle Unit Assembly, page 95) as shown. Sew along the line, then cut ¼" from the line and press open. If needed, trim to 7½" × 7½". Repeat to make 20, and call this unit Block 4A.

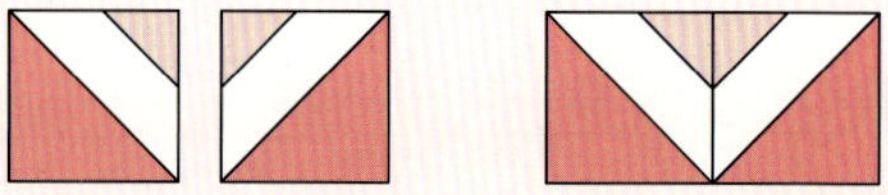

2. Pair and sew 16 Block 4As together as shown to make 8 units. Press the seams open. If needed, trim to 7½" × 14½". Call this unit Block 4B.

Column Assembly

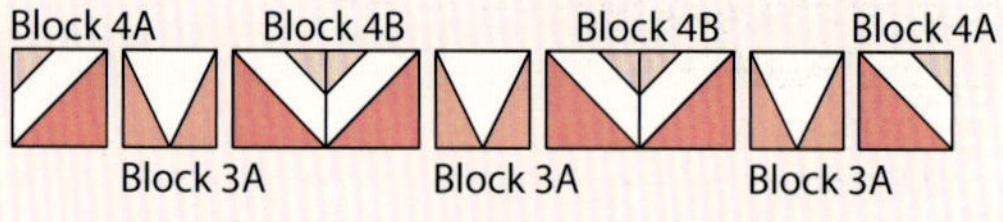

1. Sew together the following blocks in the order shown: Block 4A, Block 3A, and Block 4B. This is Column 1. Repeat to make a second Column 1. This column should measure 7½" × 63½".

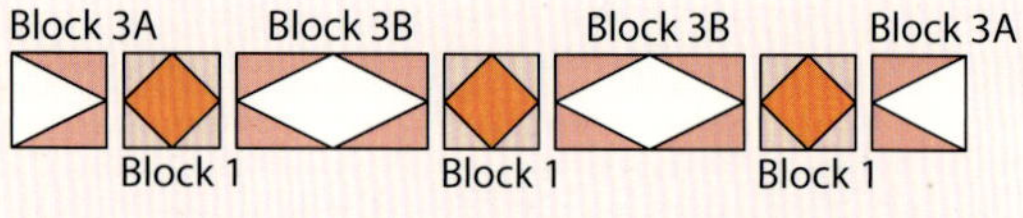

2. Sew together the following blocks in the order shown: Block 3A, Block 1, and Block 3B. This is Column 2. Repeat to make 2 more of Column 2. This column should measure 7½" × 63½".

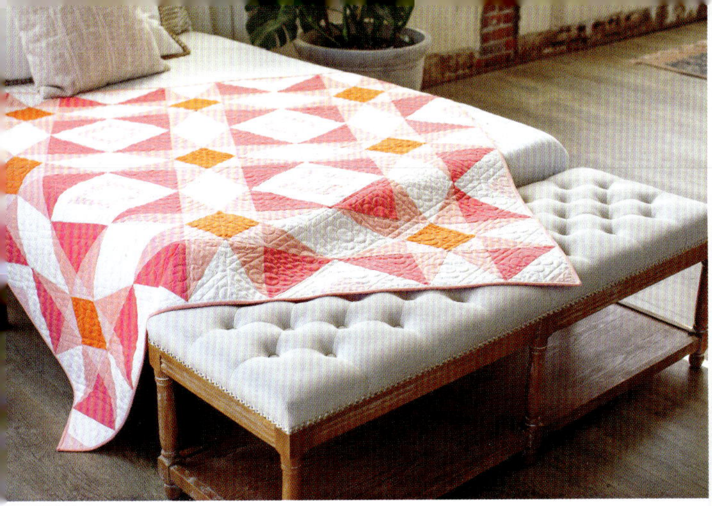

Sample quilt longarm quilted by Jenn B Quilts.

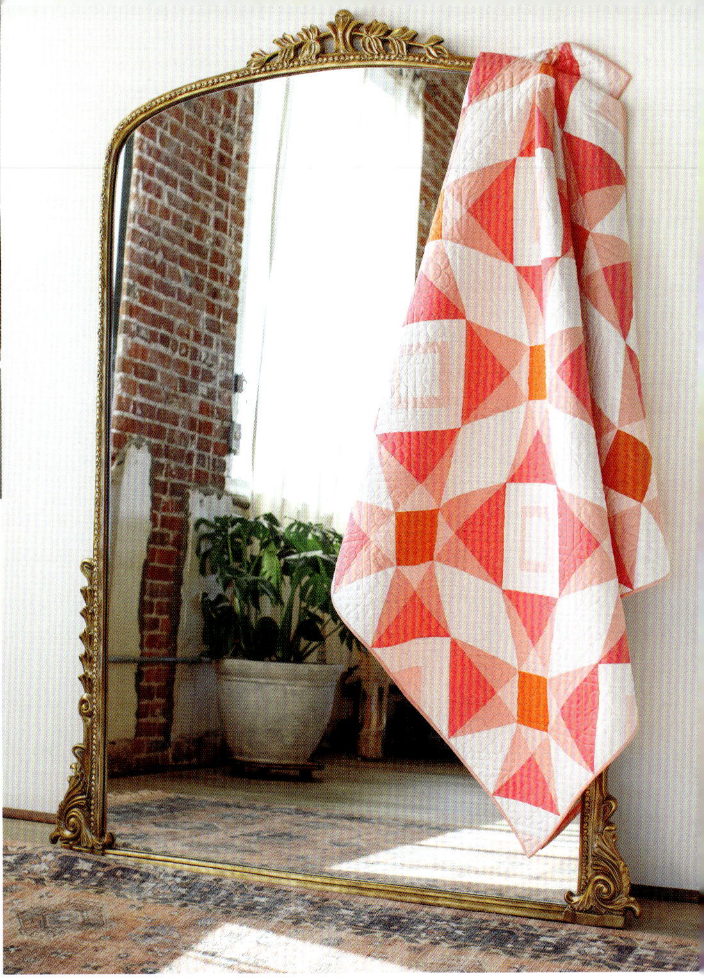

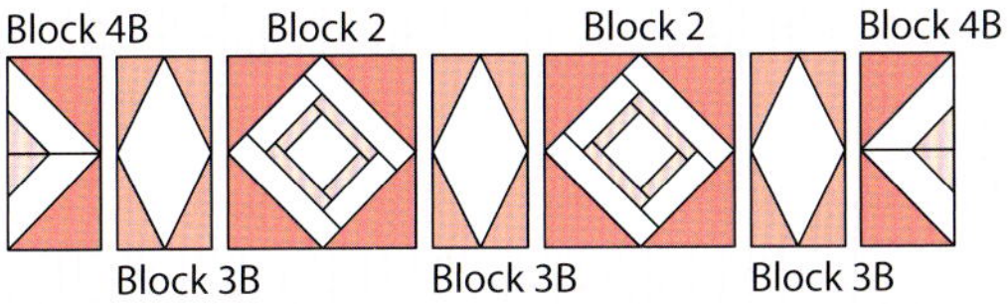

3. Sew together the following blocks in the order shown: Block 4B, Block 3B, and Block 2. This is Column 3. Repeat to make a second Column 3. If needed, trim to 14½″ × 63½″.

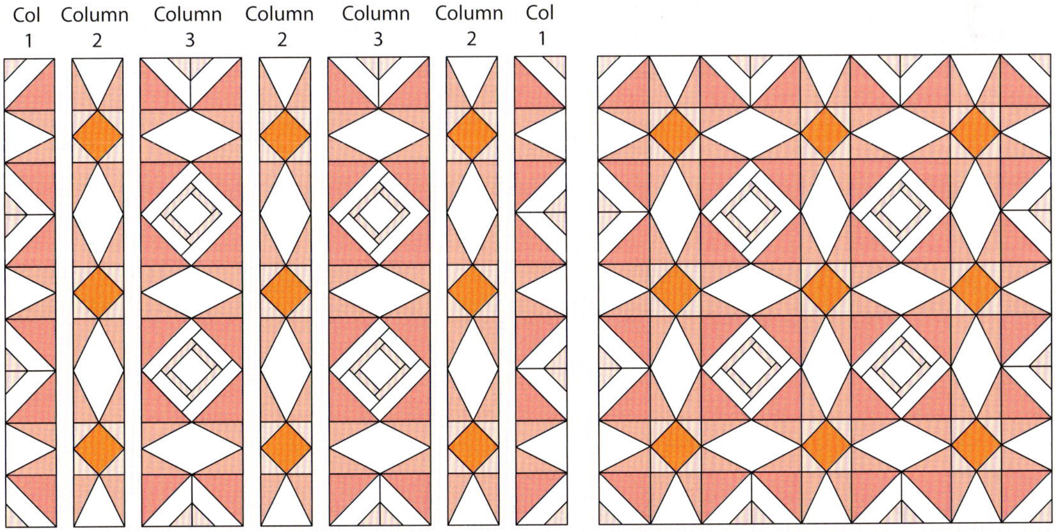

4. Sew the columns together in the order shown. Press all seams open.

Starfall Quilt

THROW SIZE 62″ × 76″

Starfall was inspired by a long exposure photo of the Perseid Meteor Shower. In the photo, the star streaks had an ombré quality, and I instantly imagined a quilt design with cascading stars in an ombré palette. This pattern works especially well with a combined hue and value shift, and I suggest trying a monochromatic or analogous color palette.

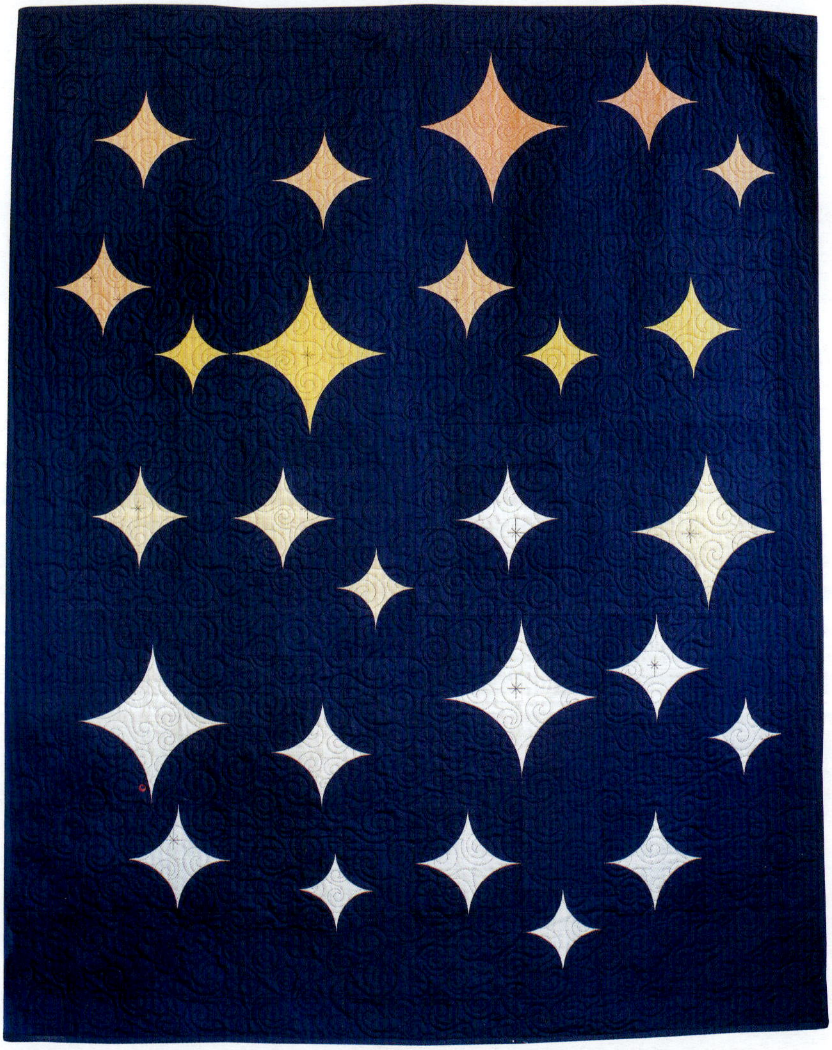

This pattern requires fairly precise curve sewing, but I've given extra trimming room in the templates; definitely don't skip the trimming on this one! If you're newer to curves, I'd recommend making a few test units and starting with the largest curved pieces first, since larger curves are easier to sew. Prepare Templates 12—17 (see Templates, page 126).

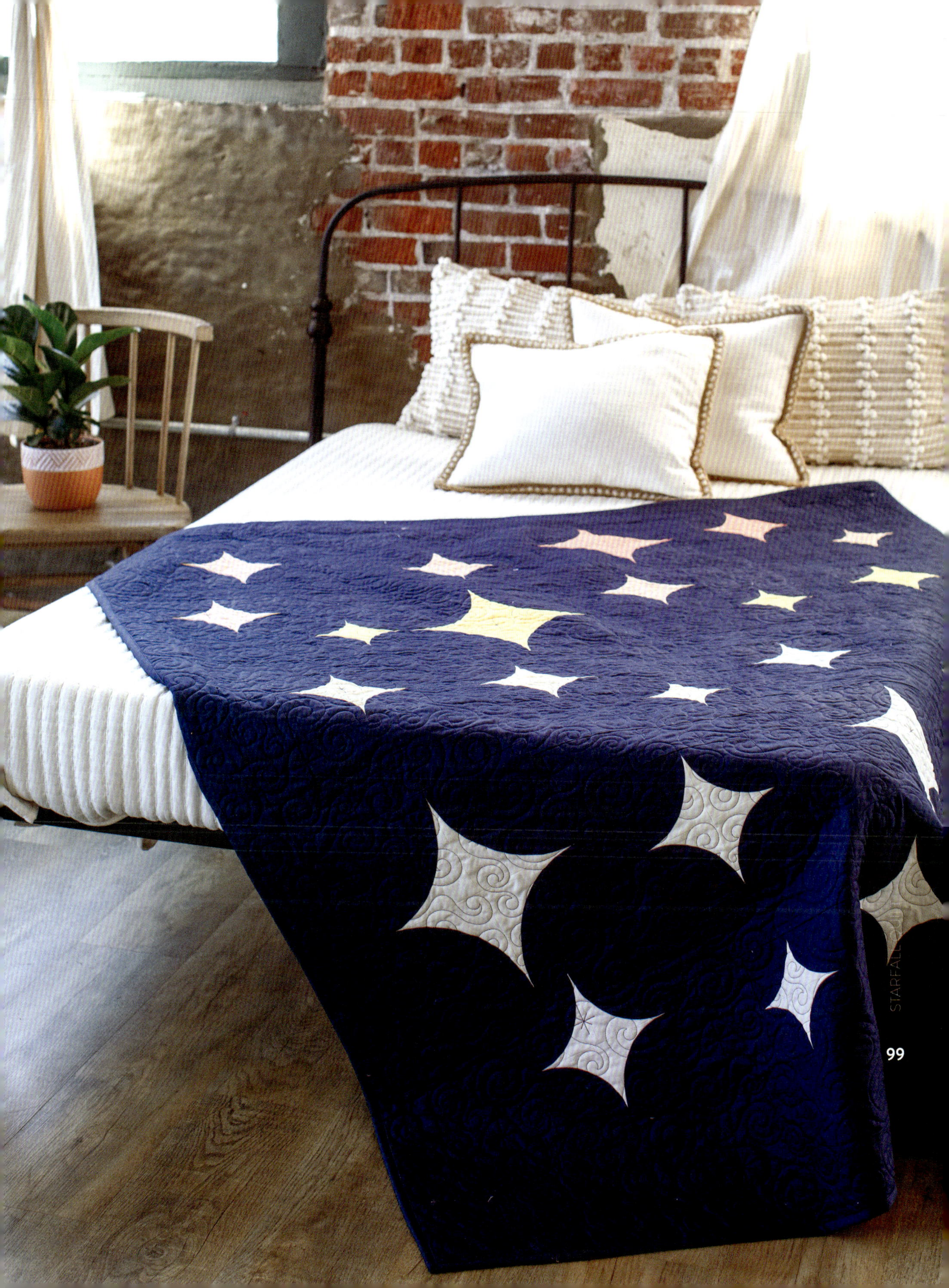

tip *These blocks have curves that extend to the edge of the finished unit, so you'll need to pay extra attention to the seam allowance. Make sure to trim precisely to allow exact ¼" seam allowances on each side of the curves.*

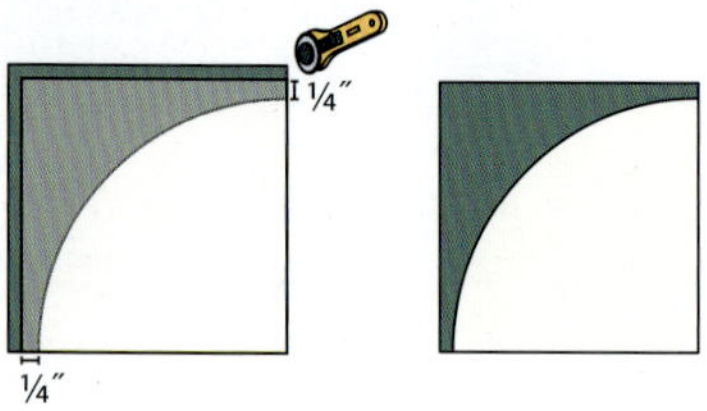

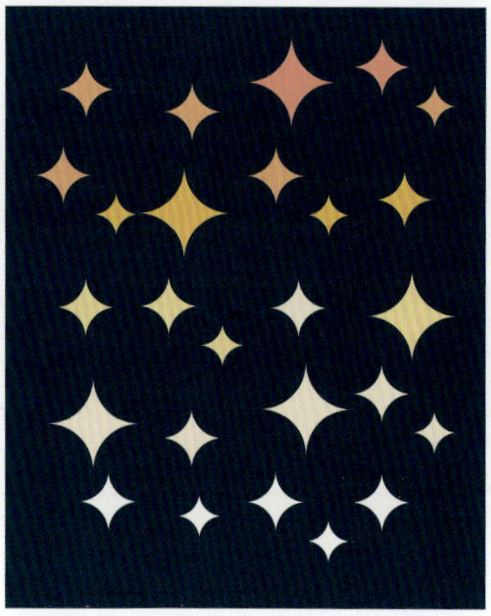

Analogous and value linear gradient with a dark background to simulate the night sky.

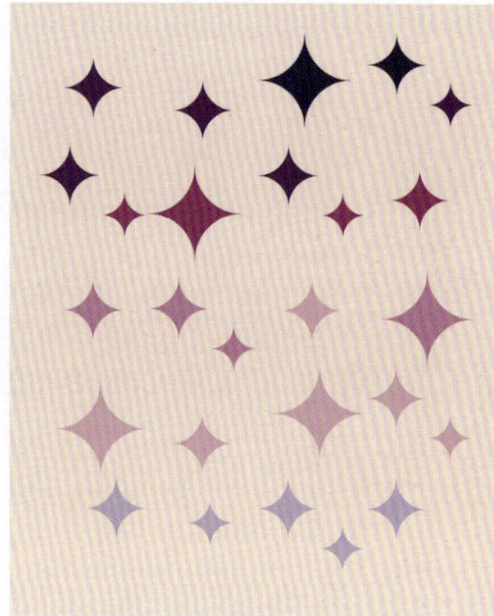

Monochromatic and value linear gradient with an analogous background.

Fabric Requirements

Fabric *Riley Blake Confetti Cotton Solids*		**Throw (62" × 76")**
	Fabric A • *Salmon*	¼ yard
	Fabric B • *Marmalade*	⅓ yard
	Fabric C • *Riley Yellow*	⅓ yard
	Fabric D • *Sunshine*	⅓ yard
	Fabric E • *Pearl*	½ yard
	Fabric F • *Off White*	⅓ yard
	Fabric G • *Riley Navy*	5 yards

Cutting Instructions

Note: Be sure to nest concave templates for efficient cutting.

Fabric	Throw	
A	*Cut 1 — 6¾″ × WOF strip; subcut into* 4 — Template 15 (**A1**) 4 — Template 16 (**A2**)	
B	*Cut 2 — 4¾″ × WOF strips; subcut into* 16 — Template 16 (**B2**) 4 — Template 17 (**B3**)	
C	*Cut 1 — 6¾″ × WOF strip; subcut into* 4 — Template 15 (**C1**) 4 — Template 16 (**C2**) *Cut 1 — 3¾″ × WOF strip; subcut into* 8 — Template 17 (**C3**)	
D	*Cut 1 — 6¾″ × WOF strip; subcut into* 4 — Template 15 (**D1**) 8 — Template 16 (**D2**) *Cut 1 — 3¾″ × WOF strip; subcut into* 4 — Template 17 (**D3**)	
E	*Cut 1 — 6¾″ × WOF strip; subcut into* 8 — Template 15 (**E1**) *Cut 1 — 4¾″ × WOF strip; subcut into* 12 — Template 16 (**E2**)	
F	*Cut 1 — 4¾″ × WOF strip; subcut into* 12 — Template 16 (**F2**) *Cut 1 — 3¾″ × WOF strip; subcut into* 12 — Template 17 (**F3**)	
G	*Cut 3 — 14½″ × WOF strips; subcut into* 2 — 6½″ × 14½″ rectangles (**G11**) 1 — 5½″ × 14½″ rectangle (**G14**) 13 — 3½″ × 14½″ rectangles (**G7**) 5 — 2½″ × 14½″ rectangles (**G5**) 5 — 2½″ × 12½″ rectangles (**G4**) *Cut 1 — 8½″ × WOF strip; subcut into* 12 — 3½″ × 8½″ rectangles (**G6**) *Cut 7 — 6½″ × WOF strips; subcut into* 20 — Template 12 (**G1**) 8 — 6½″ × 8½″ rectangles (**G8**) 6 — 6½″ × 2½″ rectangles (**G10**) 6 — 6½″ × 6½″ squares (**G9**) 1 — 6½″ × 5½″ rectangle (**G13**) 1 — 6½″ × 3½″ rectangle (**G12**)	*Cut 7 — 4½″ × WOF strips; subcut into* 56 — Template 13 (**G2**) *Cut 10 — 3½″ × WOF strips; subcut into* 28 — Template 14 (**G3**) *Sew remaining 7 strips together; subcut into* 2 — 3½″ × 70½″ strips (**G15**) 2 — 3½″ × 62½″ strips (**G16**)

Star Unit Assembly

1. Following the instructions in Sewing Curves (page 15), make Quarter Circle Units, pairing the fabrics as indicated by Table 1. Refer to Table 1 to make the total number of each Quarter Circle Unit (QCU), and the trim size for the QCUs.

2. Sew matching sets of 4 Quarter Circle Units together to create Star Units. Refer to Table 1 for the name and number of each Star Unit to make. Press the seams open.

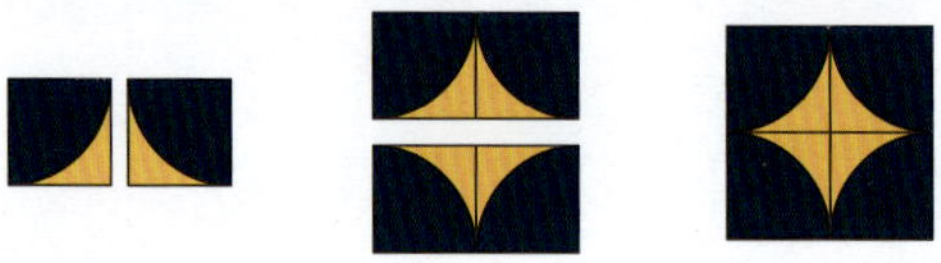

tip *Labeling the Star Units and sorting them by size will help with the next section of block assembly!*

Table 1

Pieces	# of QCU	QCU Trim Size	Star Unit Name	# of Star Units
A1/G1	4	6½″ × 6½″	Star 1A	1
A2/G2	4	4½″ × 4½″	Star 2A	1
B2/G2	16	4½″ × 4½″	Star 2B	4
B3/G3	4	3½″ × 3½″	Star 3B	1
C1/G1	4	6½″ × 6½″	Star 1C	1
C2/G2	4	4½″ × 4½″	Star 2C	1
C3/G3	8	3½″ × 3½″	Star 3C	2
D1/G1	4	6½″ × 6½″	Star 1D	1
D2/G2	8	4½″ × 4½″	Star 2D	2
D3/G3	4	3½″ × 3½″	Star 3D	1
E1/G1	8	6½″ × 6½″	Star 1E	2
E2/G2	12	4½″ × 4½″	Star 2E	3
F2/G2	12	4½″ × 4½″	Star 2F	3
F3/G3	12	3½″ × 3½″	Star 3F	3

Block Assembly

BLOCK 1

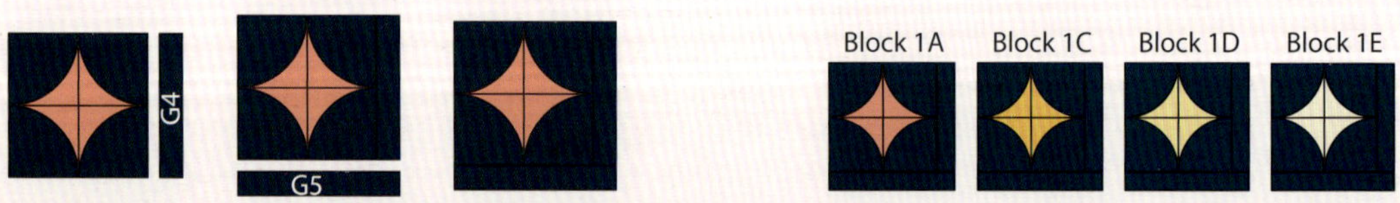

1. Sew a G4 piece to the right side of each Star 1A, Star 1C, Star 1D, and Star 1E units. Then, sew a G5 piece to the bottom of each block. If needed, trim to 14½″ × 14½″.

BLOCK 2

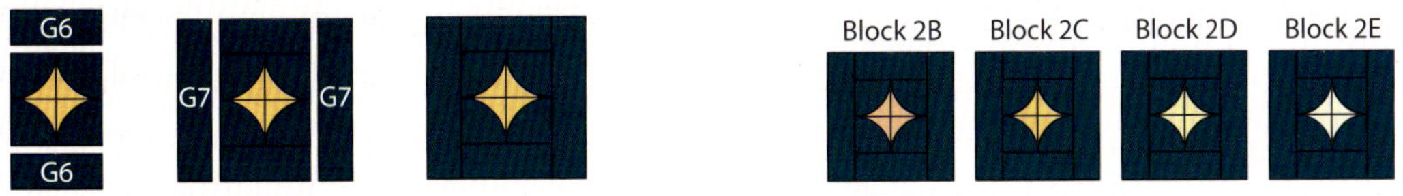

1. Sew a G6 piece to the top and bottom of 2 Star 2B, 2 Star 2E, 1 Star 2C, and 1 Star 2D. Then, sew a G7 piece to the left and right side of each block. If needed, trim to 14½″ × 14½″.

BLOCK 3

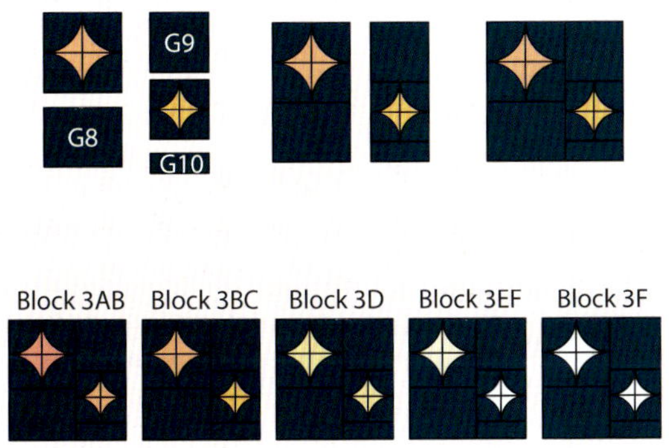

Table 2

Star Unit 2	Star Unit 3	# of Block 3
Star 2A	Star 3B	1
Star 2B	Star 3C	2
Star 2D	Star 3D	1
Star 2E	Star 3F	1
Star 2F	Star 3F	1

1. Pair the star units shown in Table 2. For each pair of units, sew a Star Unit 2 to a G8 piece, pressing the seam away from the star unit. Then, sew a G9 piece, a Star Unit 3, and a G10 piece, pressing the seams away from the star unit. Sew these two columns together and press the seam open. If needed, trim to 14½″ × 14½″.

BLOCK 4

1. Sew a G8 piece to the bottom of each remaining Star 2F unit. Press the seam toward the G8 piece. Sew a G11 piece to the left side of the unit. Press the seam toward the G11 piece. If needed, trim to 14½" × 14½".

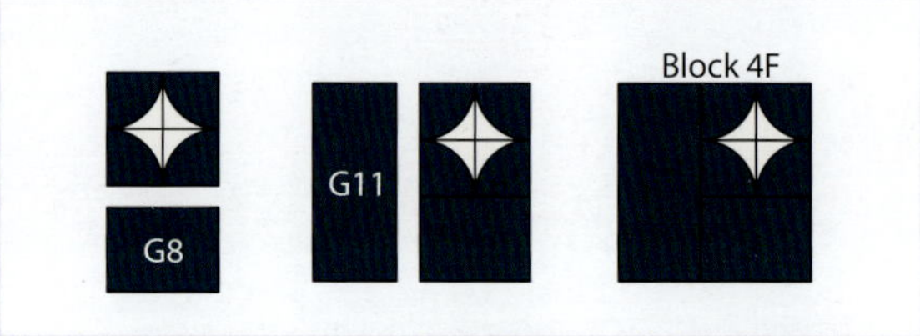

BLOCK 5

1. Sew a G13 piece to the left side of a Star 3F unit and a G12 piece to the right side. Press the seams away from the star unit. Sew a G14 piece to the bottom of the unit. If needed, trim to 14½" × 11½".

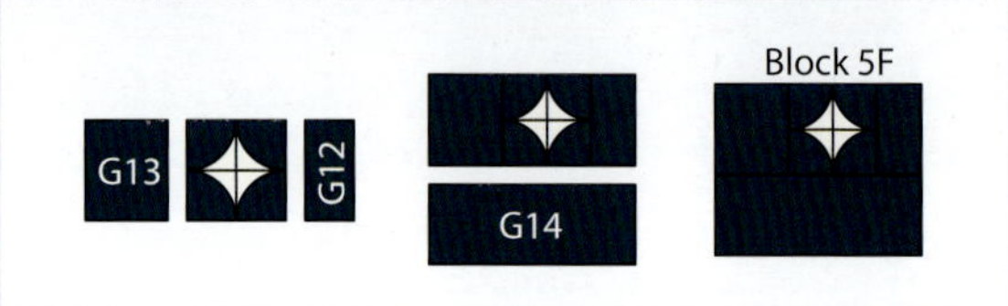

Quilt Assembly

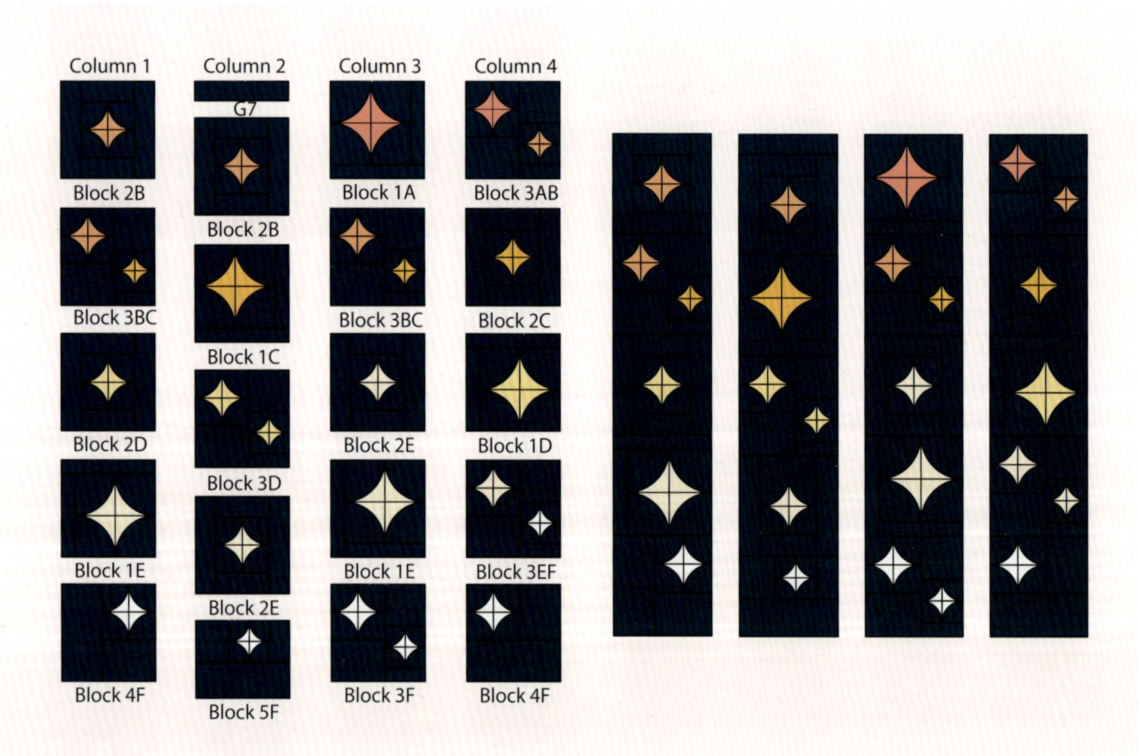

1. Sew together the following blocks and pieces to create four columns. Press seams open. Note the orientation of Blocks 1 and 4.

Column 1: Block 2B, Block 3BC, Block 2D, Block 1E, Block 4F

Column 2: G7, Block 2B, Block 1C, Block 3D, Block 2E, Block 5F

Column 3: Block 1A, Block 3BC, Block 2E, Block 1E, Block 3F

Column 4: Block 3AB, Block 2C, Block 1D, Block 3EF, Block 4F

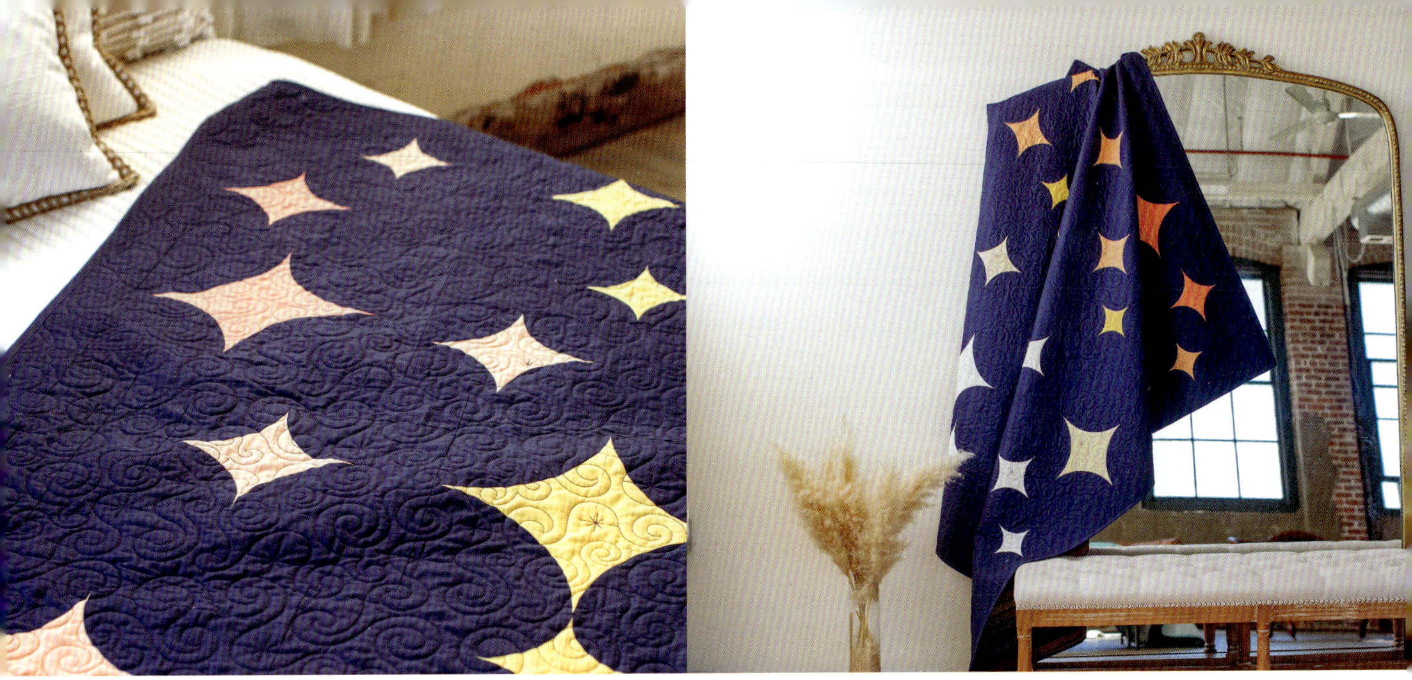

Sample quilt pieced by Katie Dean and longarm quilted by Trace Creek Quilting.

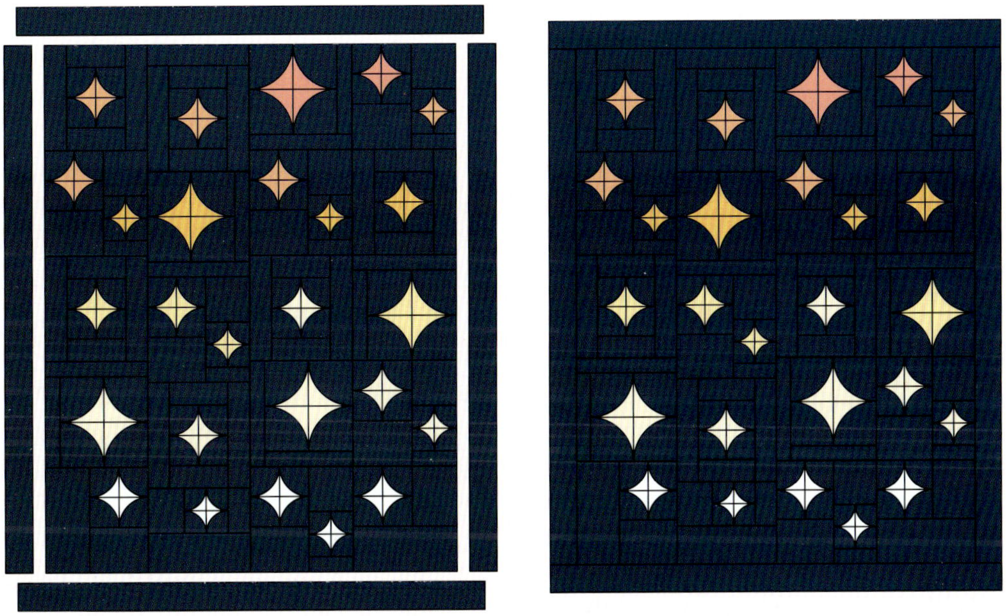

2. Sew the columns together to create the quilt top. Press seams open.

3. Sew the G15 strips to the left and right sides of the quilt. Press the seams toward the G15 strips. Sew the G16 strips to the top and bottom of the quilt. Press the seams toward the G16 strips.

tip *If you want a shorter quilt, trim the top and bottom borders to whatever size you'd prefer (or leave them off entirely!).*

MINI PROJECTS

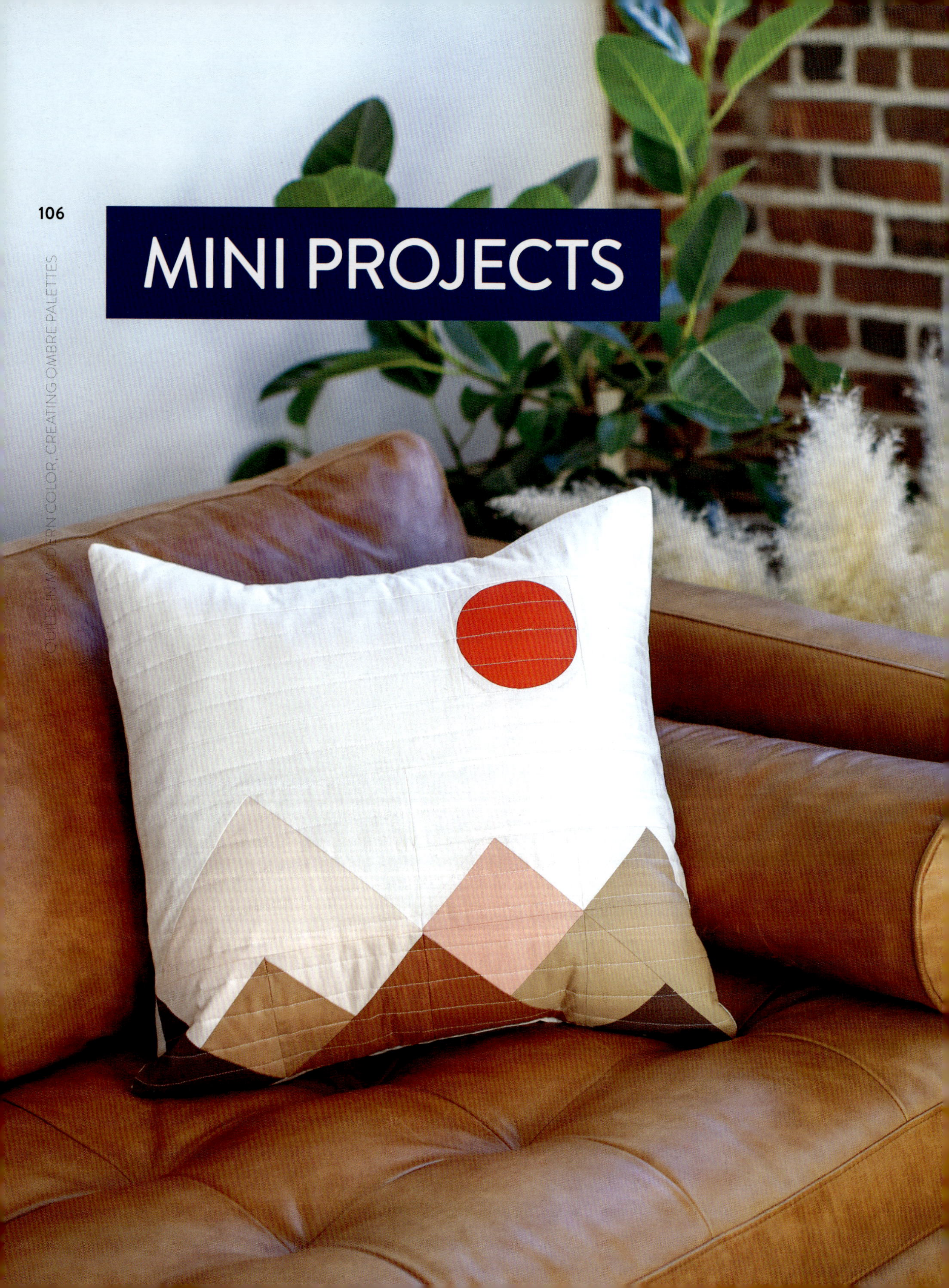

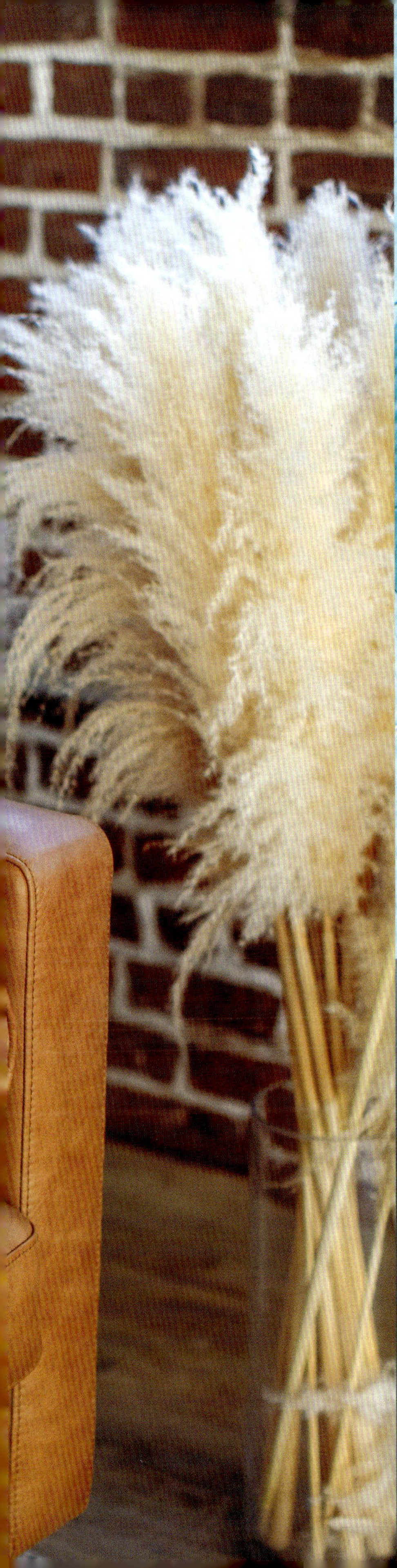
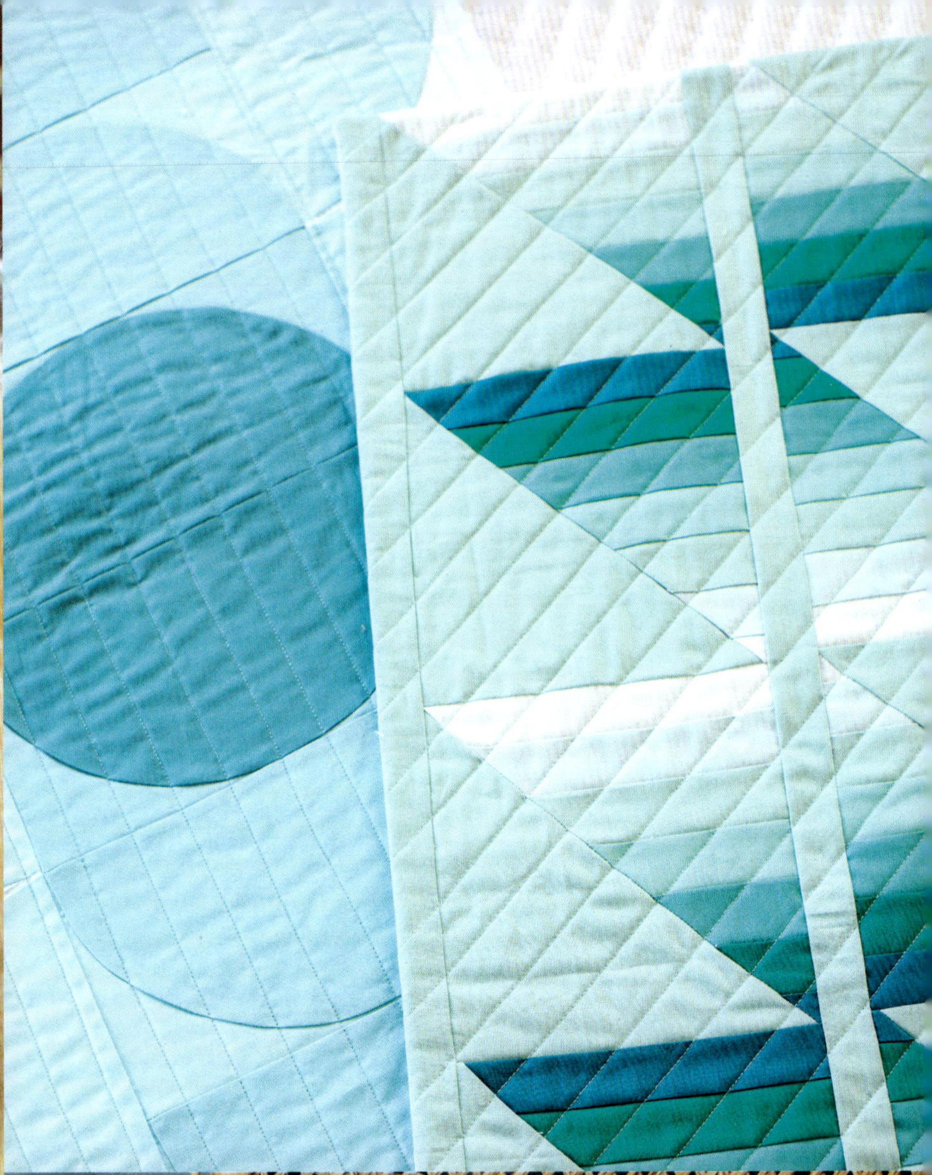
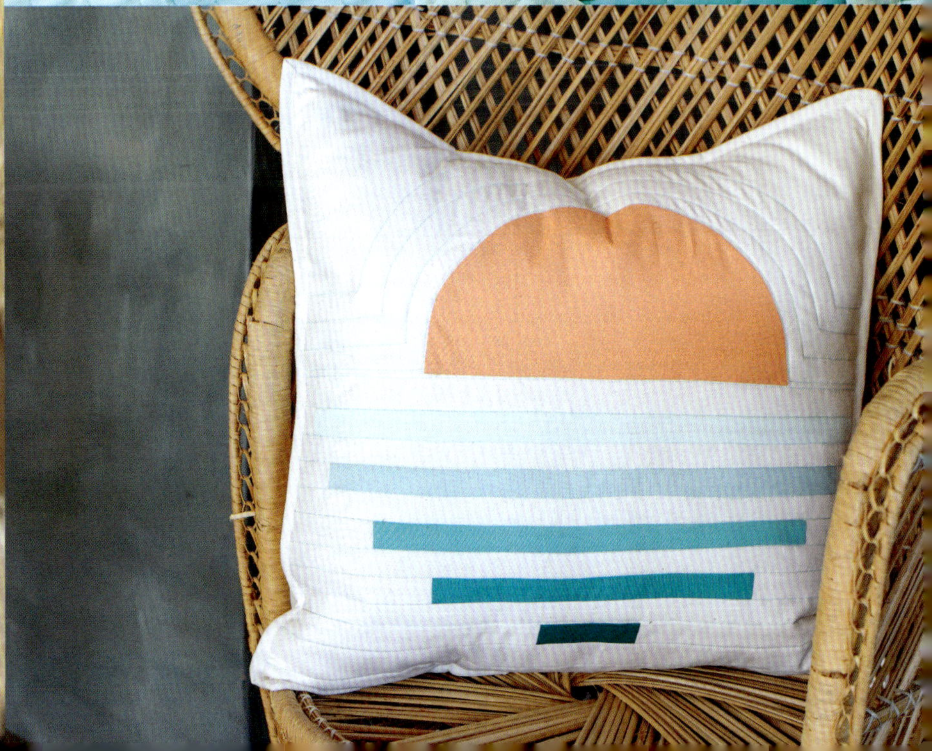

Bloom Wall Hanging

WALL HANGING SIZE 20″ × 30″

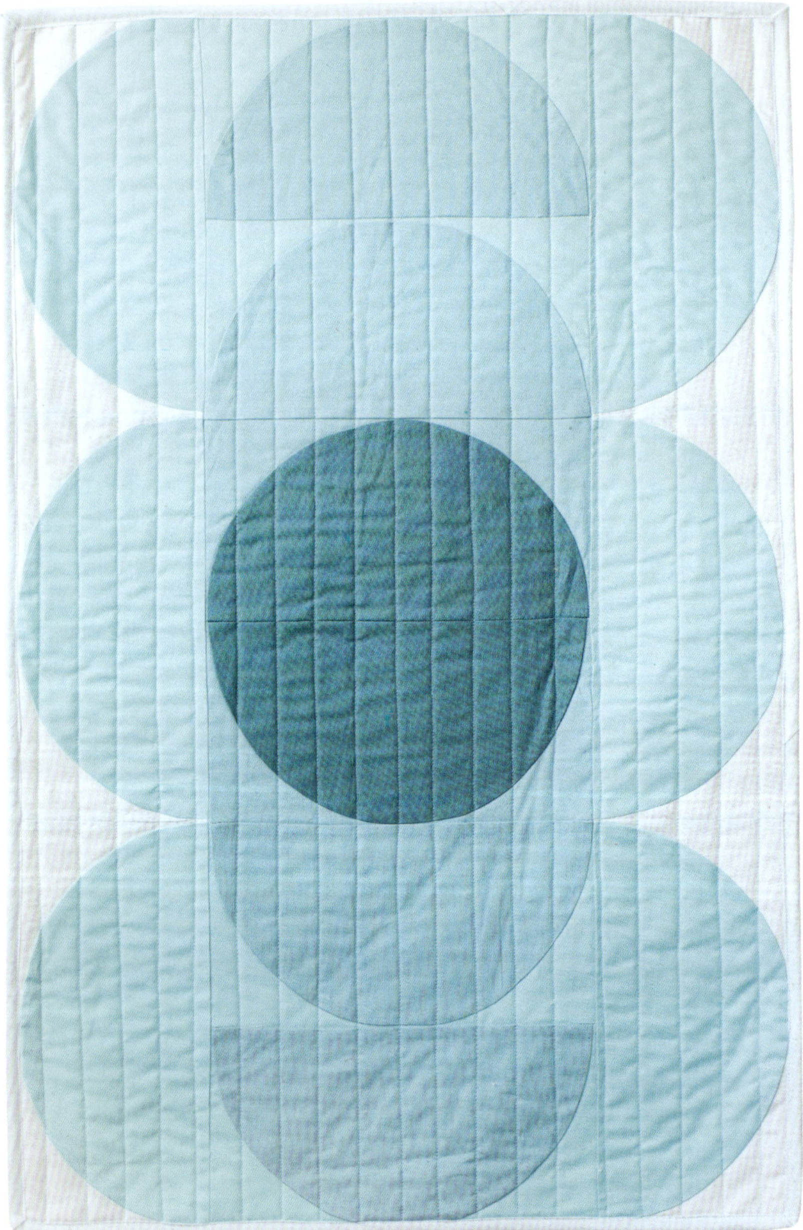

Bloom is an excellent pattern if you're new to curves and want some practice. Made entirely of large curves, it's a quick finish if you're experienced with this technique and a great skill builder if you aren't! Sticking to an analogous or monochromatic color palette is best with this pattern, since it only has four colors. Prepare Templates 18 and 19 (see Templates, page 126).

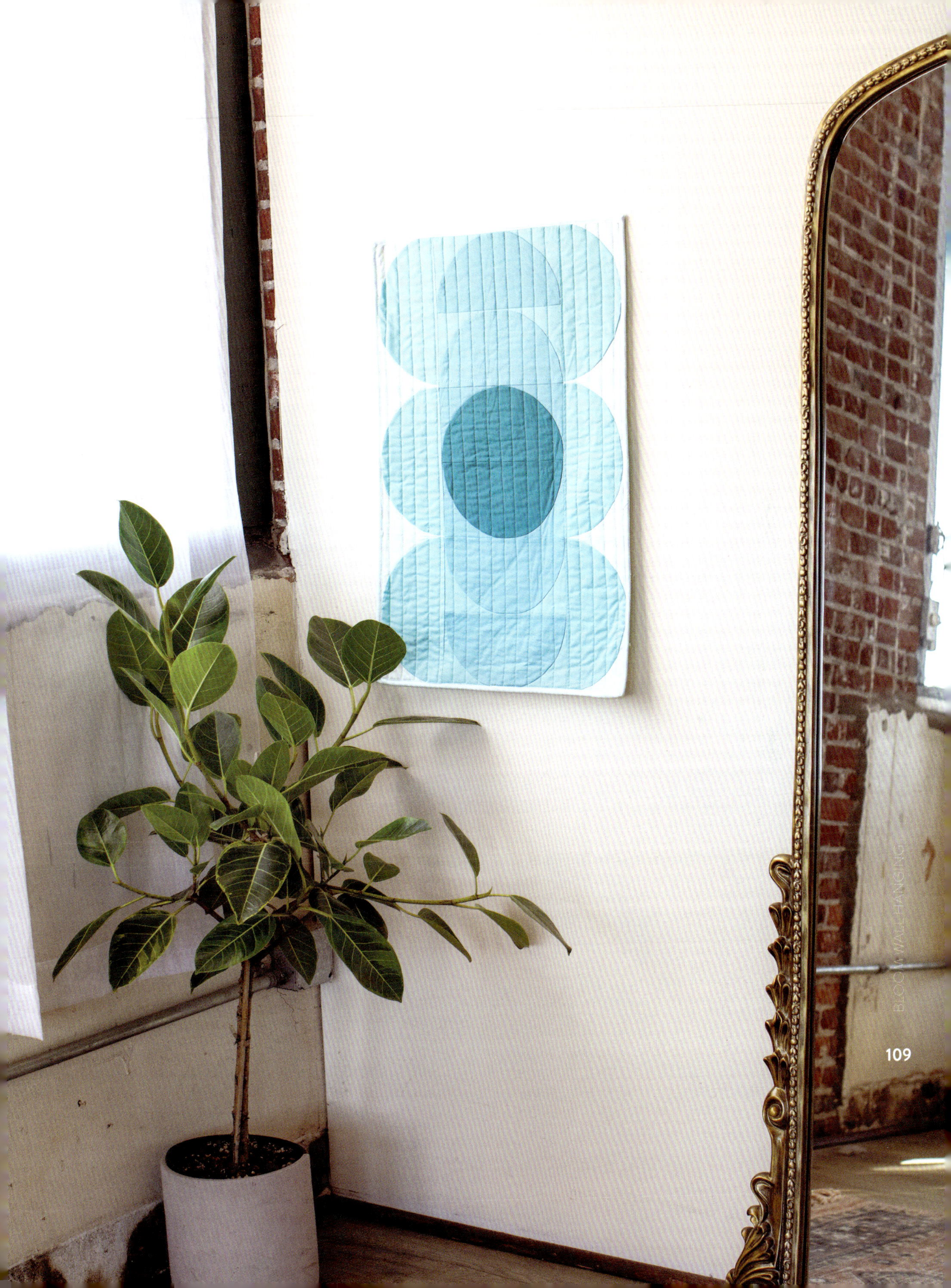

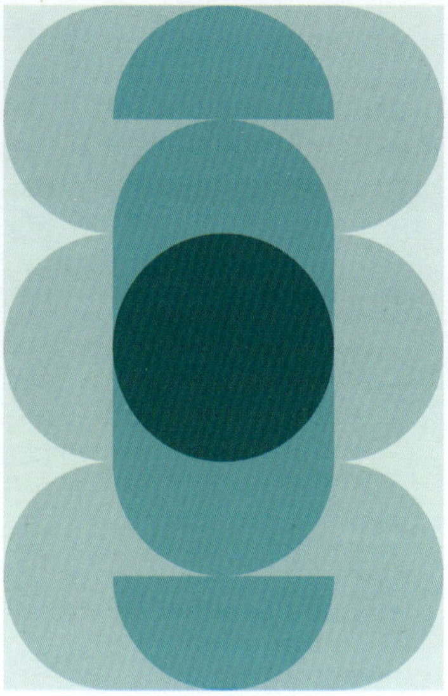

Monochromatic palette with the darkest color in the center.

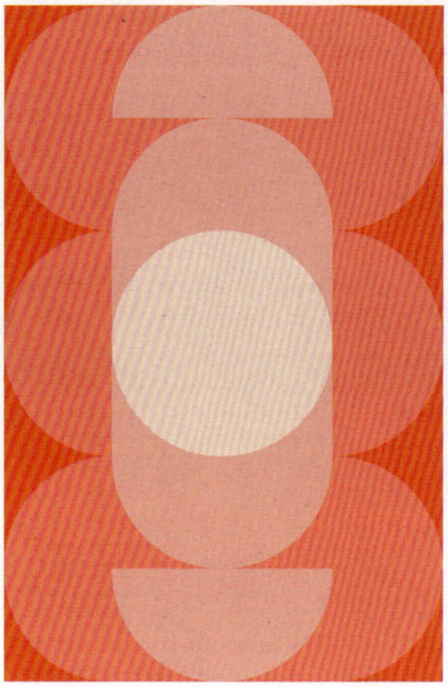

Monochromatic palette with the darkest color in the background.

Fabric Requirements

Fabric *Riley Blake Confetti Cotton Solids*		Mini (20″ × 30″)
	Fabric A • *Riley Teal*	¼ yard
	Fabric B • *Cottage*	½ yard
	Fabric C • *Scuba*	⅔ yard
	Fabric D • *Bleached Denim*	¼ yard

Cutting Instructions

Fabric	Mini
A	*Cut 1 – 5½″ × WOF strip; subcut into* 2 – Template 18 (**A1**)
B	*Cut 1 – 5½″ × WOF strip; subcut into* 4 – Template 18 (**B1**) *Cut 1 – 5¾″ × WOF strip; subcut into* 2 – Template 19 (**B2**)
C	*Cut 1 – 6½″ × WOF strip; subcut into* 4 – Template 19 (**C2**)* *Cut 1 – 10½″ × WOF strip; subcut into* 6 – Template 18 (**C1**)
D	*Cut 1 – 6½″ × WOF strip; subcut into* 6 – Template 19 (**D2**)*

** Nest templates as shown*

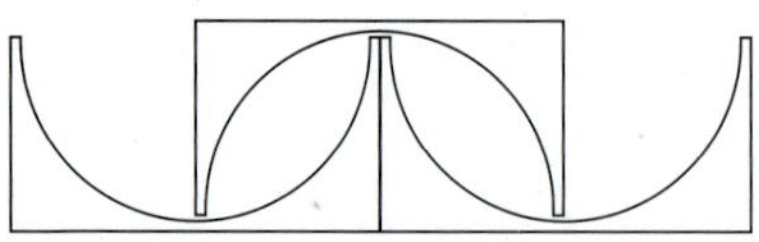

Half Circle Units

1. Match each A1 piece with a B2 piece, each B1 piece with a C2 piece, and each C1 piece with a D2 piece. Follow the instructions in Sewing Curves (page 15) to create the number of A/B Half Circle Units, B/C Half Circle Units, and C/D Half Circle Units shown in Diagram 1. Press the seams towards the convex pieces. If needed, trim to 5½″ × 10½″.

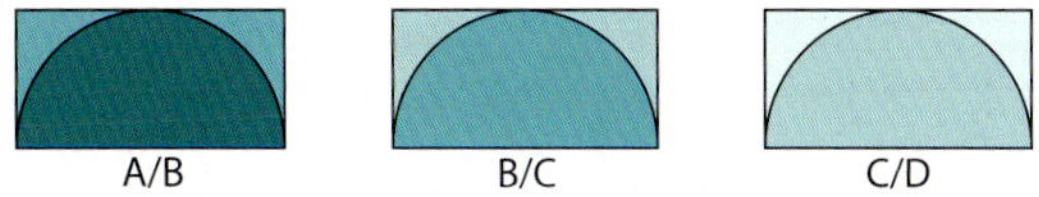

Diagram 1

Assembly

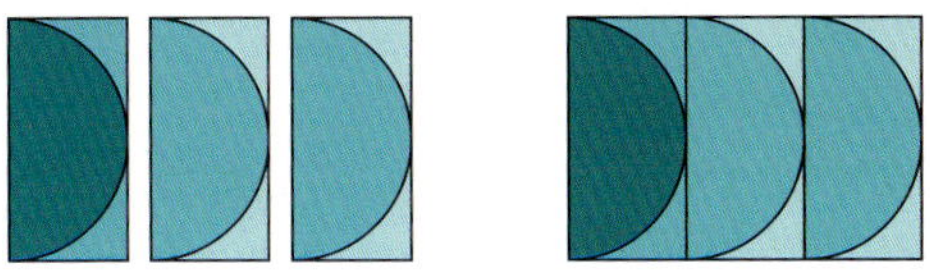

1. Sew together an A/B Half Circle Unit and 2 B/C Half Circle Units. Repeat to create a second unit. Press seams towards the Template 2 pieces. If needed, trim to 15½″ × 10½″.

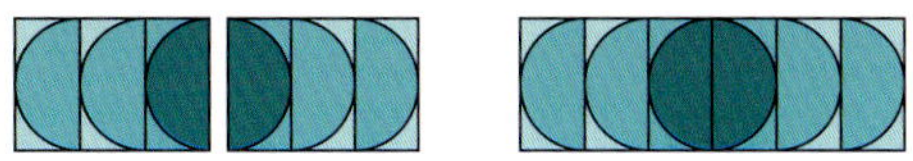

2. Sew together the units from Step 1 as shown to create 1 Middle Column. Press seams open. If needed, trim to 30½″ × 10½″.

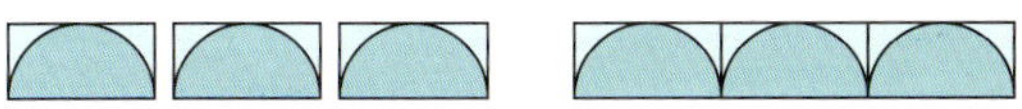

3. Sew together 3 C/D Half Circle Units. Press the seams open. Repeat to create a second unit. If needed, trim to 5½″ × 30½″. These are Edge Columns.

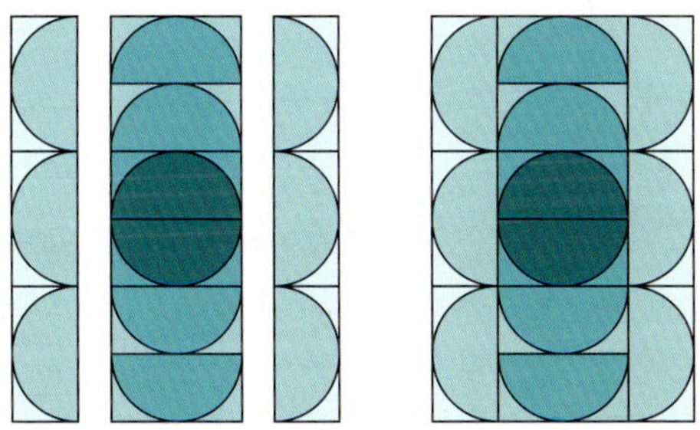

4. Sew together the Edge Columns and the Middle Column as shown. Press the seams toward the Edge Columns.

Horizon Pillow Cover

PILLOW COVER SIZE 20″ × 20″

This pattern was inspired by the sunset at our favorite beach house on the Oregon coast. This quick project is a good example of the impact that even small doses of ombré color palettes can have! Prepare Templates 20 and 21 (see Templates, page 126).

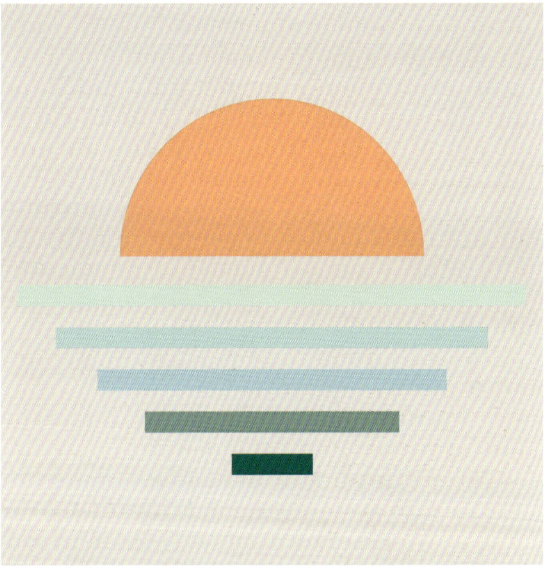

A monochromatic linear ombré with a pop of complementary color for the sun.

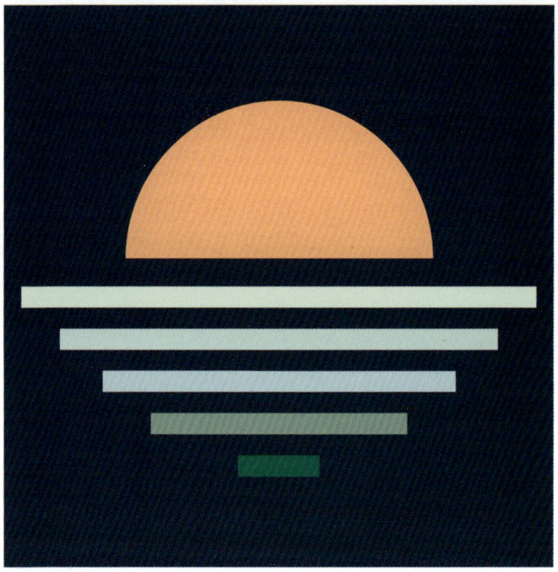

The same palette with a dark background.

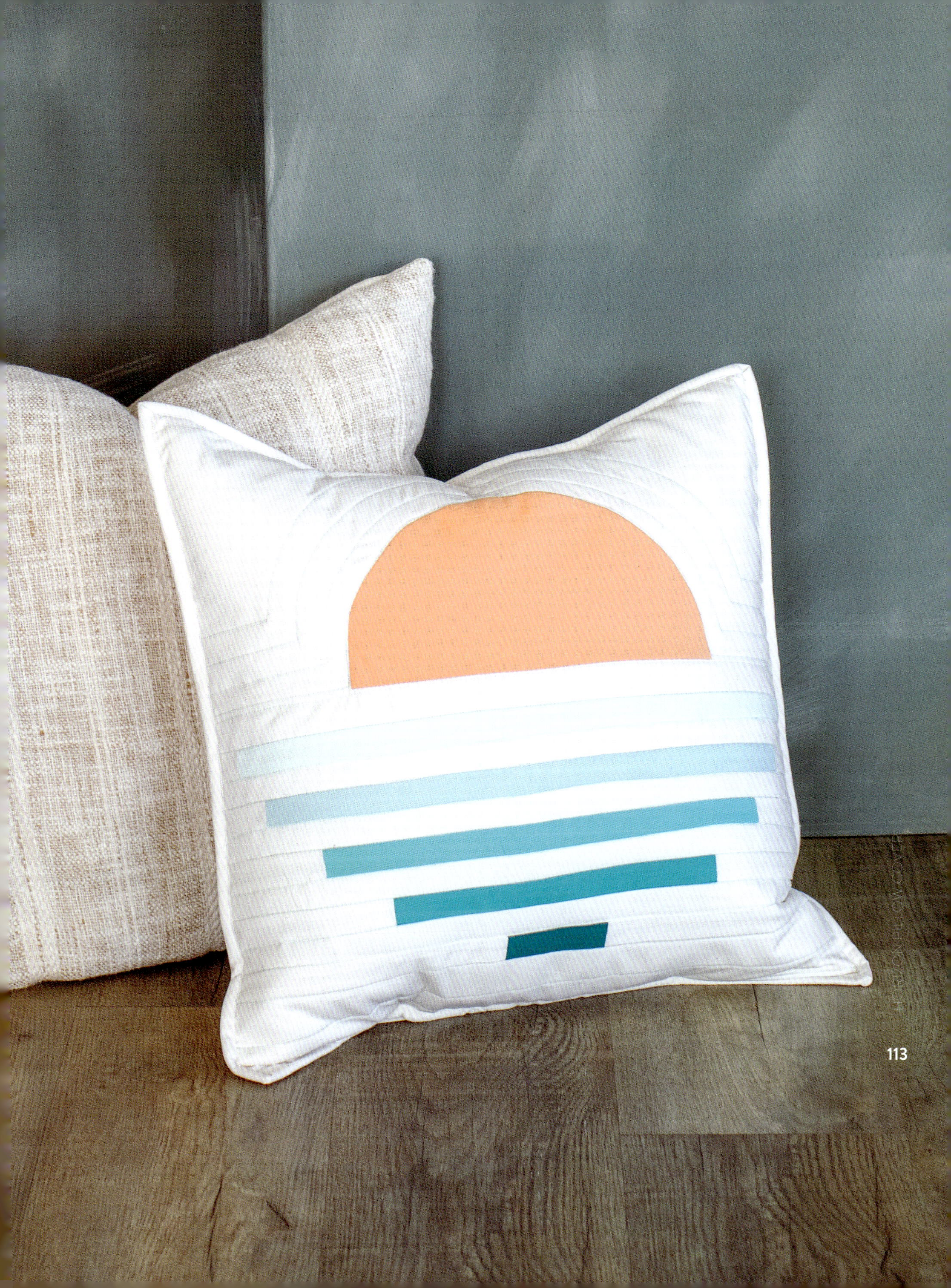

Fabric Requirements

Fabric *Riley Blake Confetti Cotton Solids*		Pillow Cover (20″ × 20″)
	Fabric A • *Misty*	⅛ yard
	Fabric B • *Songbird*	⅛ yard
	Fabric C • *Seaglass*	⅛ yard
	Fabric D • *Vivid*	⅛ yard
	Fabric E • *Jade*	⅛ yard
	Fabric F • *Marmalade*	¼ yard or 1 FE
	Fabric G • *Ivory*	½ yard

Cutting Instructions

Fabric	Pillow Cover
A	*Cut 1 – 1¼″ × 18½″ rectangle* (**A1**)
B	*Cut 1 – 1¼″ × 16½″ rectangle* (**B1**)
C	*Cut 1 – 1¼″ × 13½″ rectangle* (**C1**)
D	*Cut 1 – 1¼″ × 10″ rectangle* (**D1**)
E	*Cut 1 – 1¼″ × 3½″ rectangle* (**E1**)
F	*Cut 1 – Template 20* (**F1**)
G	*Cut 1 – 9¾″ × WOF strip; subcut into* 1 – 9¾″ × 20¾″ rectangle (**G9**) 1 – 3¾″ × 20½″ rectangle (**G8**) 1 – 1½″ × 20½″ rectangle (**G7**) *Cut 4 – 1¼″ × WOF strips; subcut into* 4 – 1¼″ × 20½″ rectangles (**G6**) 2 – 1¼″ × 9″ rectangles (**G5**) 2 – 1¼″ × 5¾″ rectangles (**G4**) 2 – 1¼″ × 4″ rectangles (**G3**) 2 – 1¼″ × 2½″ rectangles (**G2**) 2 – 1¼″ × 1½″ rectangles (**G1**)

Half Circle Unit

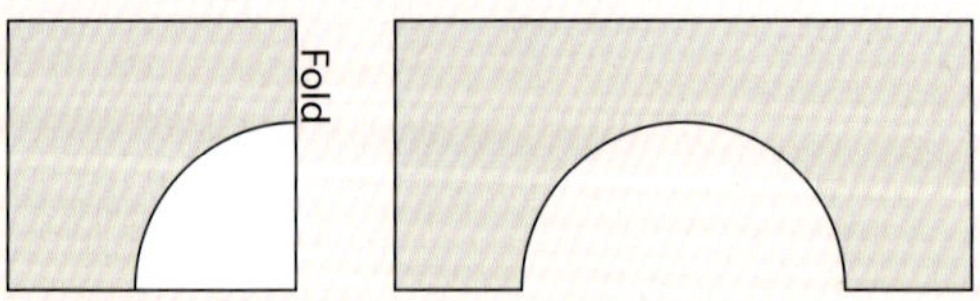

1. Fold the G9 piece in half widthwise. Line up Template 21 with the fold, then cut out the curved shape.

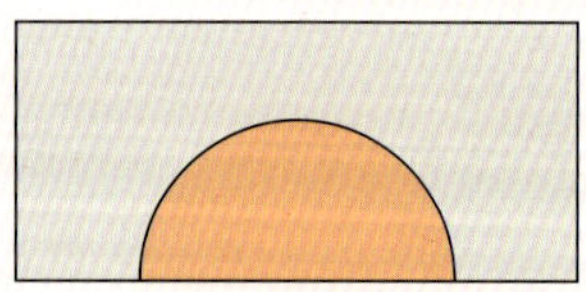

2. Pair the F1 piece with the G9 piece, then follow the instructions in Sewing Curves (page 15) to create a Half Circle Unit. Trim this unit to 20½″ × 9½″.

Block Assembly

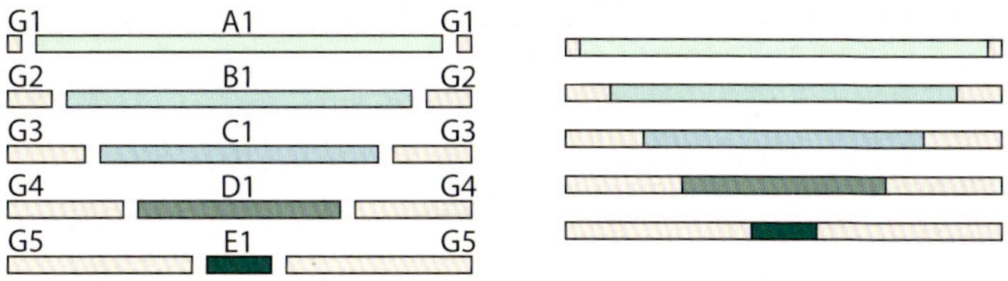

Diagram 1

1. Sew together the pieces listed in Table 1, referencing Diagram 1 for the correct order of pieces. Press toward the dark side. For each color piece, use 2 background pieces.

Table 1

Background Pieces	Color Piece
G1	A1
G2	B1
G3	C1
G4	D1
G5	E1

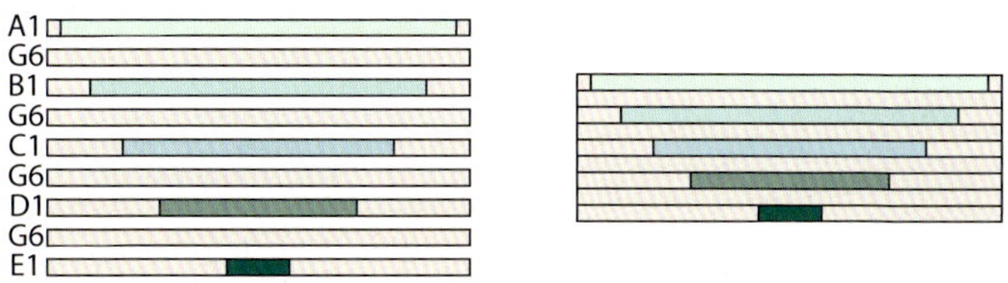

2. Arrange the units from Step 1 as shown with a G6 piece between. Sew together, and press the seams open. If needed, trim to 20½″ × 8¼″.

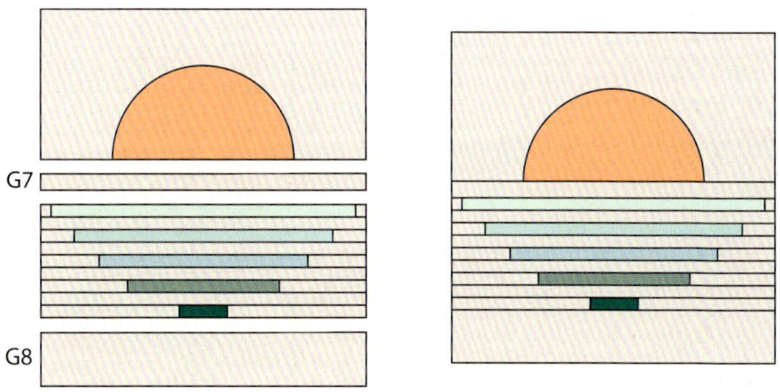

3. Sew together the Half Circle Unit, the G7 piece, the unit from Step 2, and the G8 piece, as shown. Press the seams open.

4. To finish the pillow, see Pillow Covers (page 19).

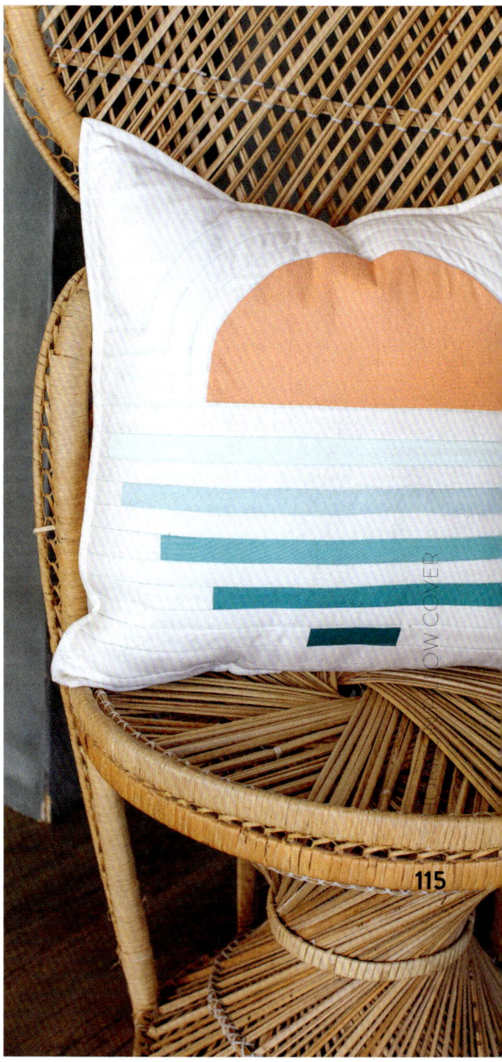

Aventurine Wall Hanging

WALL HANGING SIZE 16″ × 26″

Aventurine is named after a gorgeous green quartz. This pattern features a fun half—square triangle technique that gives you a lot of ombré possibilities. Once you've finished the strip pieced HSTs, it comes together quickly. I like to use one of the featured fabric colors as the background fabric too, but this pattern is written so that you have the flexibility to use a different background color if you'd prefer.

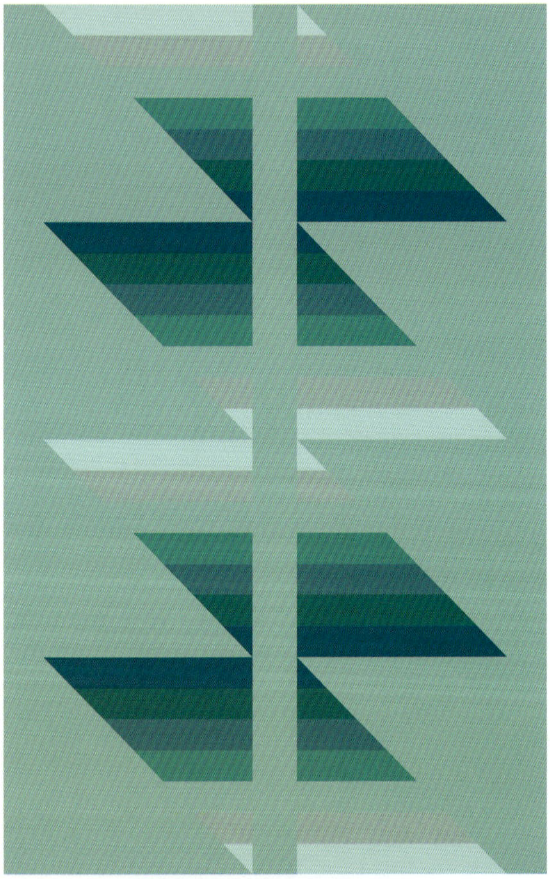

Monochromatic color palette

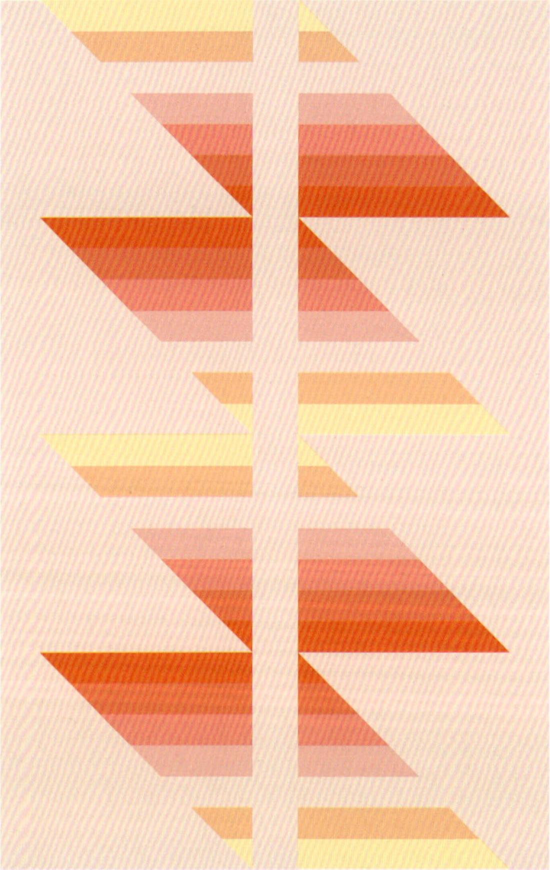

Analogous color palette

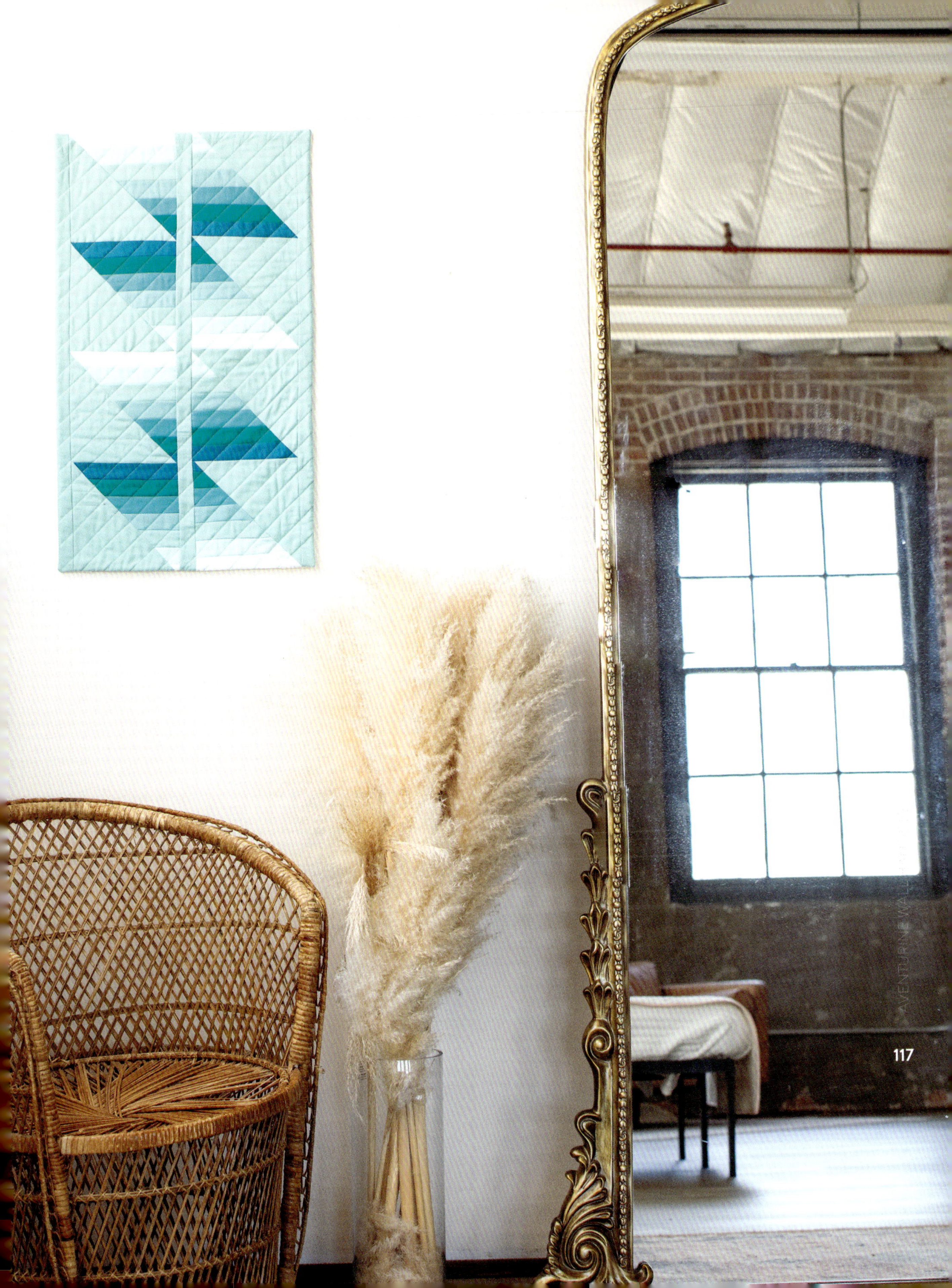

Fabric Requirements

	Fabric *Riley Blake Confetti Cotton Solids*	Mini (16″ × 26″)
	Fabric A • *Oceanside*	⅛ yard
	Fabric B • *Poseidon*	⅛ yard
	Fabric C • *Rainforest*	⅛ yard
	Fabric D • *Seaglass*	⅛ yard
	Fabric E • *Seafoam*	⅛ yard
	Fabric F • *Songbird*	⅛ yard
	Fabric G • *Misty*	⅛ yard
	Fabric H • *Seafoam*	½ yard

Cutting Instructions

Fabric	Mini
A–G	1 – 1½″ × WOF strip (**A1 – G1**)
H	*Cut 1 – 7½″ × WOF strip; subcut into* 4 – 7½″ × 7½″ squares (**H1**) *Cut 3 – 1½″ × WOF strips; subcut into* 3 – 1½″ × 26½″ rectangles (**H2**)

Half-Square Triangle Units

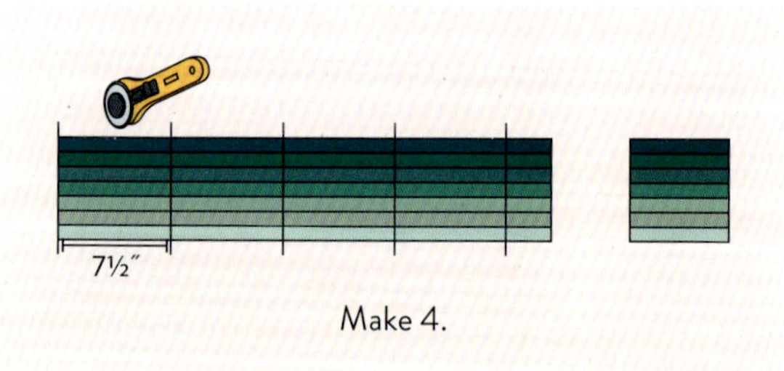

1. Sew together strips A1-G1 using a scant ¼″ seam allowance in the desired gradient order. Press the seams toward the darker fabric. Subcut into 4 Strip Squares 7½″ × 7½″.

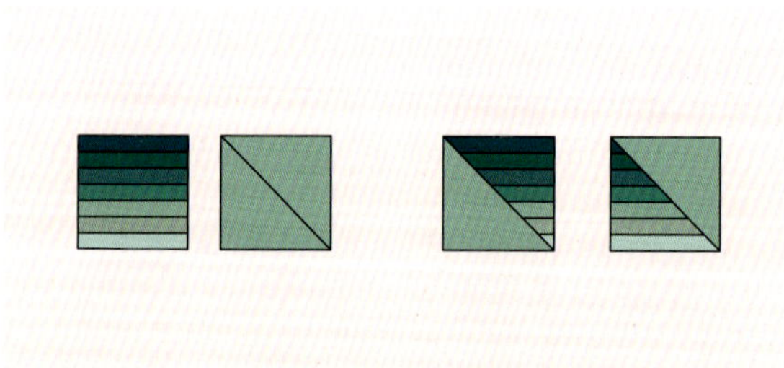

2. Draw a diagonal line across the wrong side of each H1 square, then pair each H1 square with a Strip Square from Step 1. Following the instructions for making two-at-a-time Half Square Triangles (page 17) create 8 Strip HSTs. Press the seams towards the Strip Square. Trim to 7″ × 7″. Note that this will create two different orientations of HSTs.

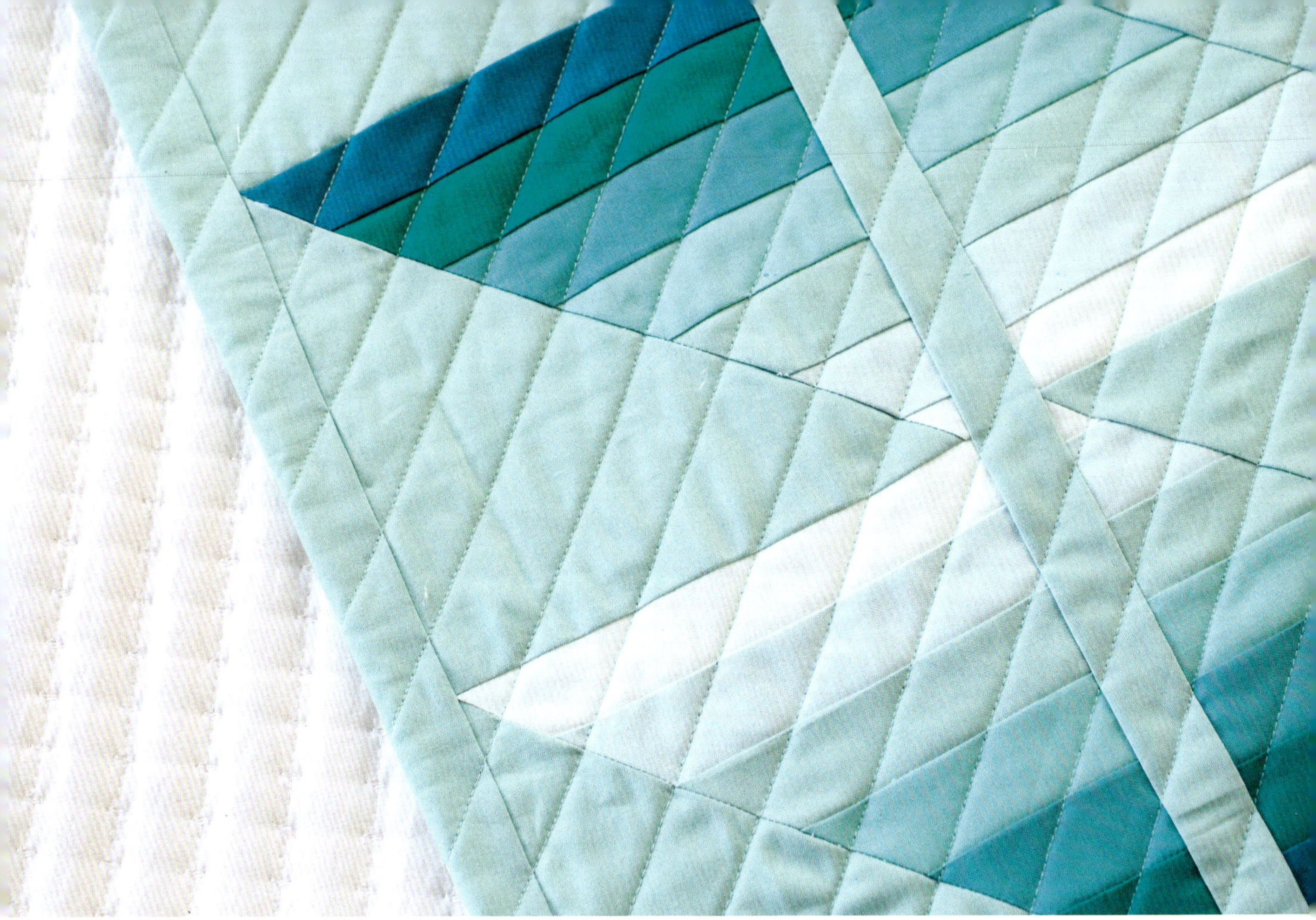

Block Assembly

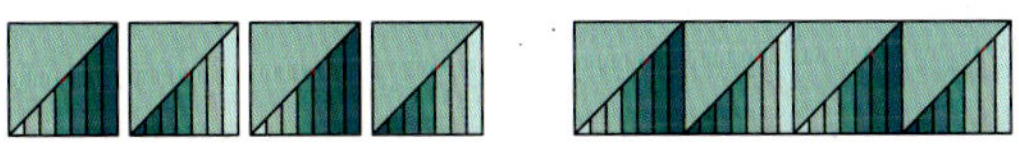

1. Sew together 2 sets of 4 Strip HSTs as shown, alternating the HST orientations. If needed, trim to 7″ × 26½″.

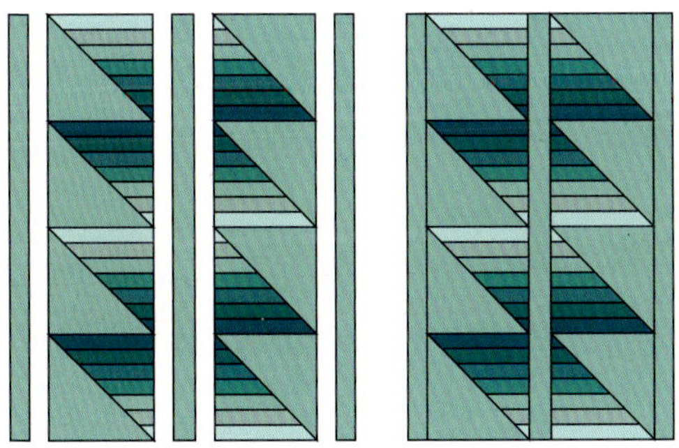

2. Arrange the units from Step 1 with alternating H3 pieces, orienting as shown. Sew together, and press the seams toward the H3 pieces.

Teton Pillow

PILLOW SIZE 20″ × 20″

This pattern was inspired by the gorgeous mountains of Grand Teton National Park. Mountain patterns are always some of my favorites to design, and I love the natural ombré effect we see as mountains move further into the distance. This pattern is very versatile and works for a wide range of color palettes; it is also very scrap friendly! I don't often use brown in my quilts, but a brown to pink analogous gradient gives an earthy feel to a landscape pattern. Prepare Templates 22 and 23 (see Templates, page 126).

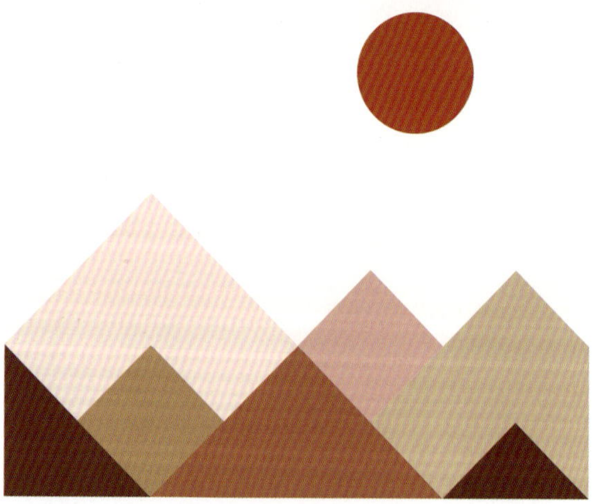

Analogous gradient

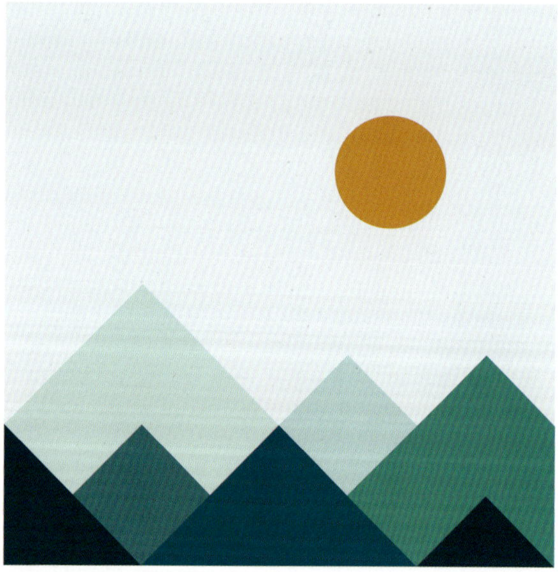

Monochromatic gradient

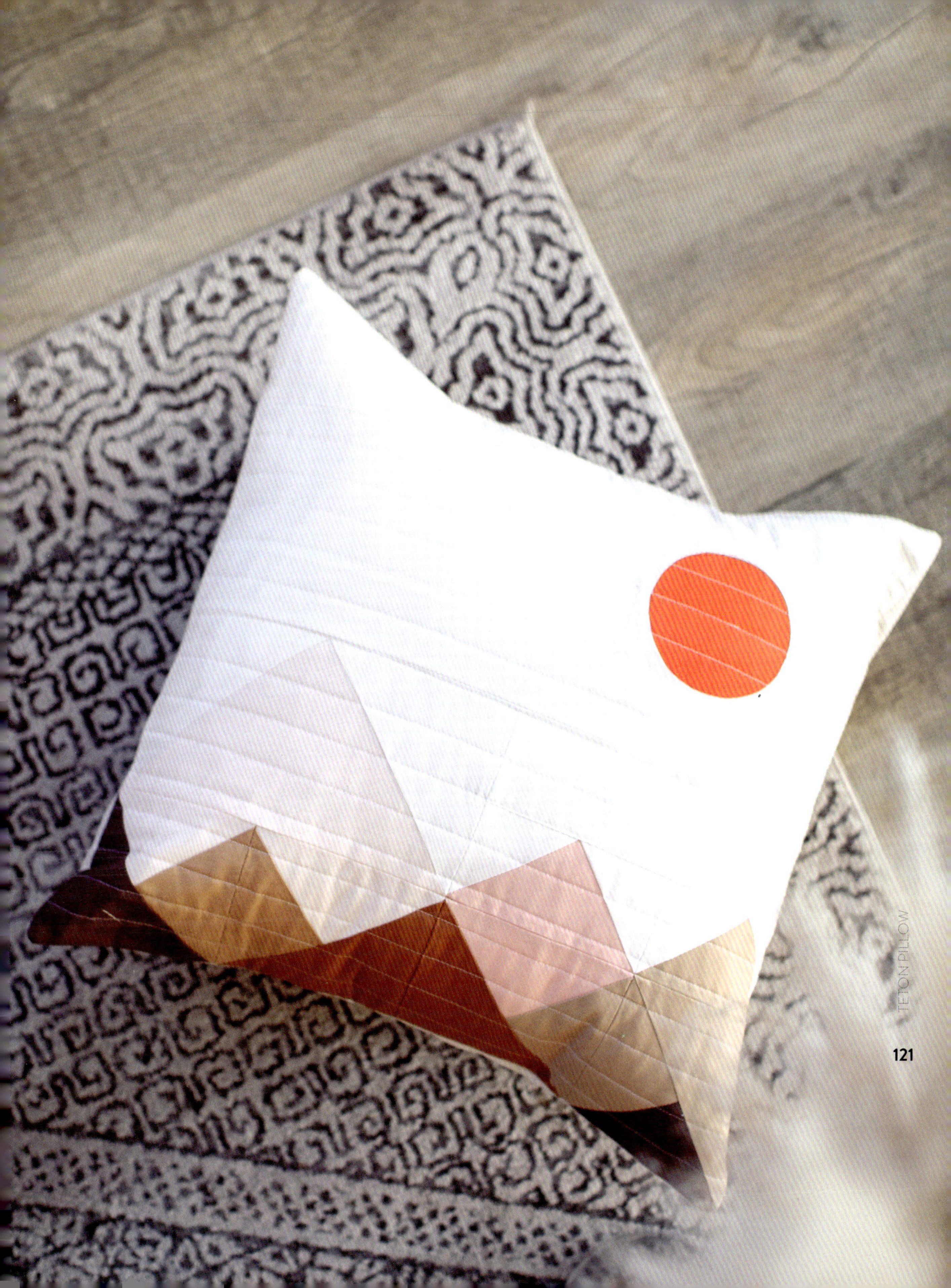

Fabric Requirements

Fabric *Riley Blake Confetti Cotton Solids*	Pillow (20″ × 20″)
Fabric A • *Riley Brown*	¼ yard or 1 FE
Fabric B • *Cinnamon*	¼ yard or 1 FE
Fabric C • *Nutmeg*	¼ yard or 1 FE
Fabric D • *Tea Dye*	¼ yard or 1 FE
Fabric E • *Mellow Rose*	¼ yard or 1 FE
Fabric F • *Ballerina*	¼ yard or 1 FE
Fabric G • *Burnt Orange*	¼ yard or 1 FE
Fabric H • *Cloud*	½ yard

Cutting Instructions

Fabric	Pillow
A	*Cut 1 – 6½″ × WOF strip; subcut into* 1 – 6½″ × 6½″ square (**A1**) 1 – 6″ × 6″ square (**A2**)
B	*Cut 1 – 6″ × WOF strip; subcut into* 1 – 6″ × 6″ square (**B1**)
C	*Cut 1 – 6½″ × WOF strip; subcut into* 1 – 6½″ × 6½″ square (**C1**)
D	*Cut 1 – 6½″ × WOF strip; subcut into* 2 – 6½″ × 6½″ squares (**D1**) 1 – 6″ × 6″ square (**D2**) 1 – 3″ × 5½″ rectangle (**D3**)
E	*Cut 1 – 6½″ × WOF strip; subcut into* 1 – 6½″ × 6½″ square (**E1**) 1 – 6″ × 6″ square (**E2**) 1 – 3″ × 5½″ rectangle (**E3**)
F	*Cut 1 – 6½″ × WOF strip; subcut into* 1 – 6½″ × 6½″ square (**F1**) 1 – 5½″ × 10½″ rectangle (**F2**)
G	*Cut 1 – 4½″ × WOF strip; subcut into* 2 – Template 22 (**G1**)
H	*Cut 1 – 4½″ × WOF strip; subcut into* 1 – 4½″ × 20½″ rectangle (**H7**) 1 – 4½″ × 12½″ rectangle (**H5**) 1 – 4½″ × 4½″ rectangle (**H6**) *Cut 1 – 5½″ × WOF strip; subcut into* 2 – 5½″ × 5½″ squares (**H3**) 2 – Template 23 (**H1**) 1 – 2½″ × 20½″ rectangle (**H8**) *Cut 1 – 3″ × WOF strip; subcut into* 1 – 3″ × 10½″ rectangle (**H4**) 4 – 3″ × 3″ squares (**H2**)

Half Circle Units

1. Pair a G1 piece with a H1 piece, then follow the instructions in Sewing Curves (page 15) to create 2 Half Circle Units. Trim each unit to 2½" × 4½". Then, sew these units together to create a single Sun Unit. Press the seam open.

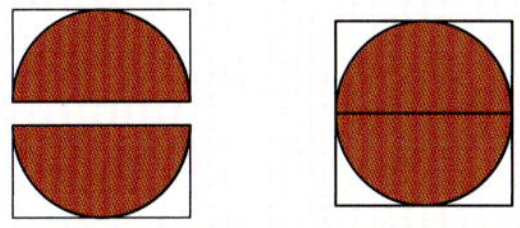

Flying Geese Units

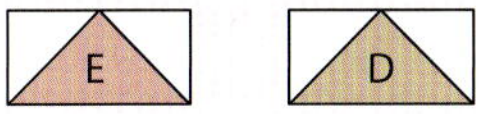

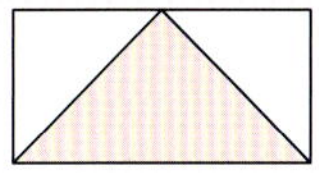

1. Using the D3, E3, and H2 pieces, create 2 Flying Geese units following the instructions in One-at-a-Time (page 18). These units will be called Flying Geese D and Flying Geese E. Trim these units to 3" × 5½".

2. Using the F2 and H3 pieces, repeat Step 1 to create another unit, this time called Flying Geese F. Trim to 5½" × 10½".

Quarter-Square Triangle Units

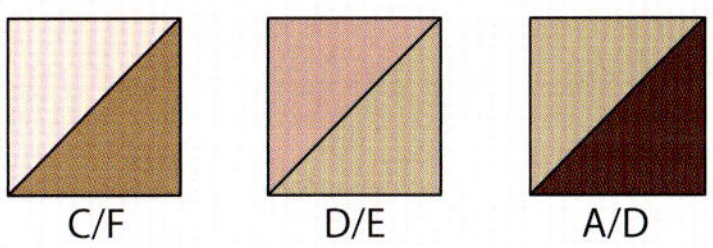

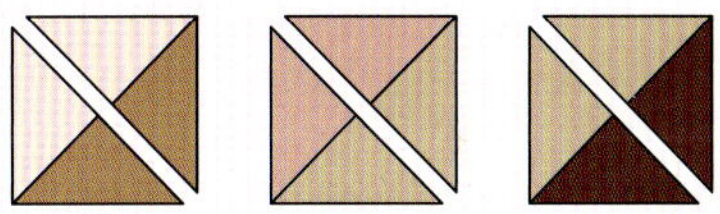

1. Pair together: C1/F1, D1/E1, and A1/D1. Follow the instructions in Two-at-a-Time (page 17) to create Half Square triangles from each pair. Trim the HST units to 6" × 6". Only one each of the D/E and A/D HSTs will be used.

2. Cut each HST in half along the diagonal as shown.

3. Cut each A2, B1, and D2 piece along the diagonal from corner to corner. Then, refer to Diagram 1 and sew these triangles to the units from Step 2 to create one of each unit shown. Press the seams open, and trim each of these units to 5½" × 5½".

Note: There will be some triangles and cut HSTs leftover that will not be used.

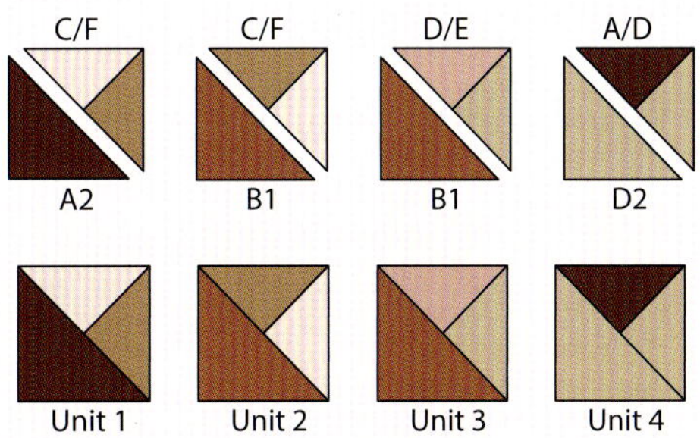

Diagram 1

Quilt Assembly

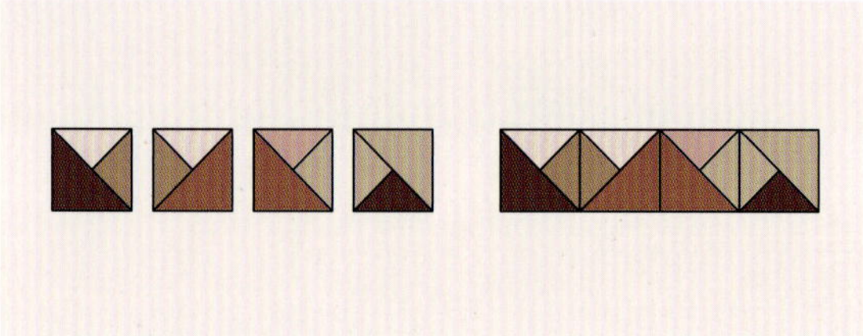

1. Sew together the units from the previous section as shown, in order, paying close attention to the orientation. Press the seams open. If needed, trim to 20½″ × 5½″. Call this Row 1.

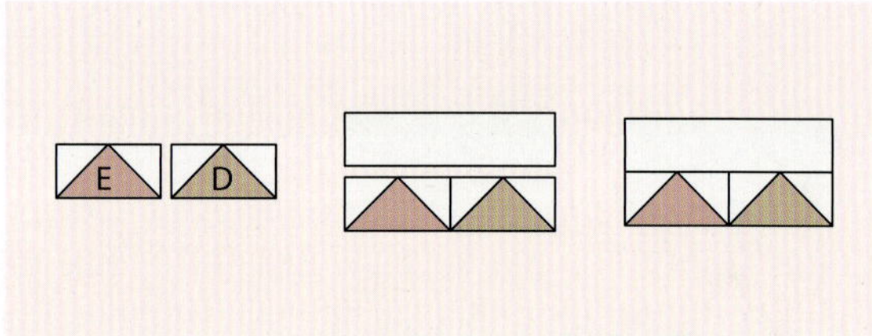

2. Sew together Flying Geese D and Flying Geese E. Press the seams open. Sew an H4 piece to the top. Press the seam toward the H4 piece. If needed, trim to 10½″ × 5½″.

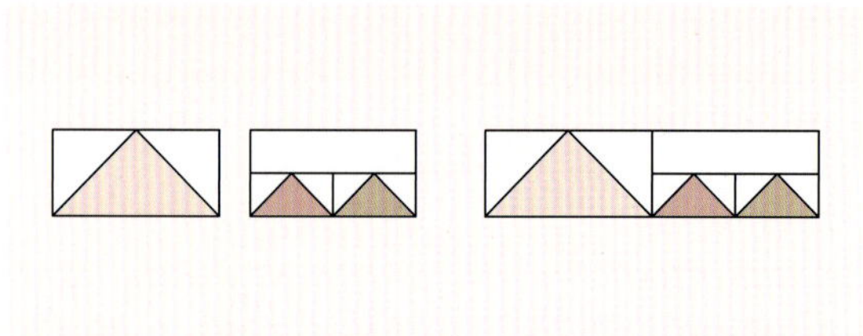

3. Sew the Flying Geese F to the left side of the unit from Step 2. Press the seam open. If needed, trim to 20½″ × 5½″. Call this Row 2.

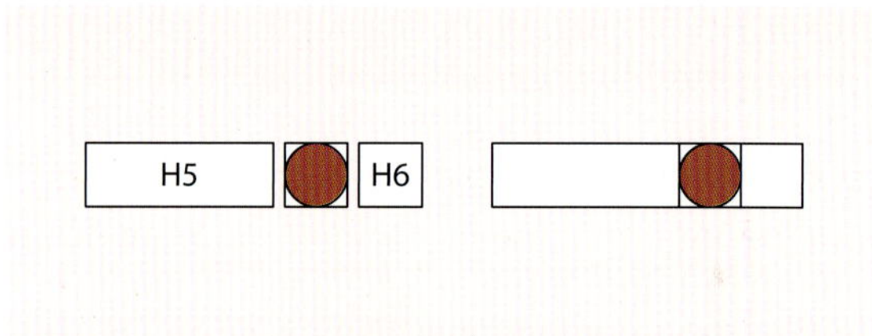

4. Sew together the H5 piece, the Sun Unit, and the H6 piece. Press the seams away from the Sun Unit. If needed, trim to 20½″ × 4½″. Call this Row 3.

5. Sew together H7, Row 3, H8, Row 2, and Row 1 as shown. Press all seams open.

6. To finish the pillow, see Pillow Covers (page 19).

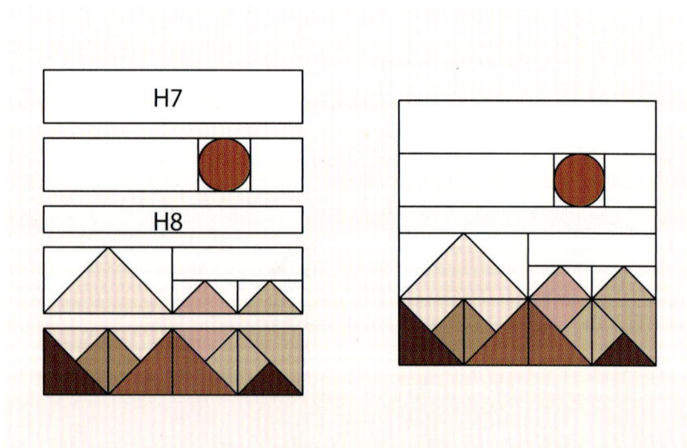

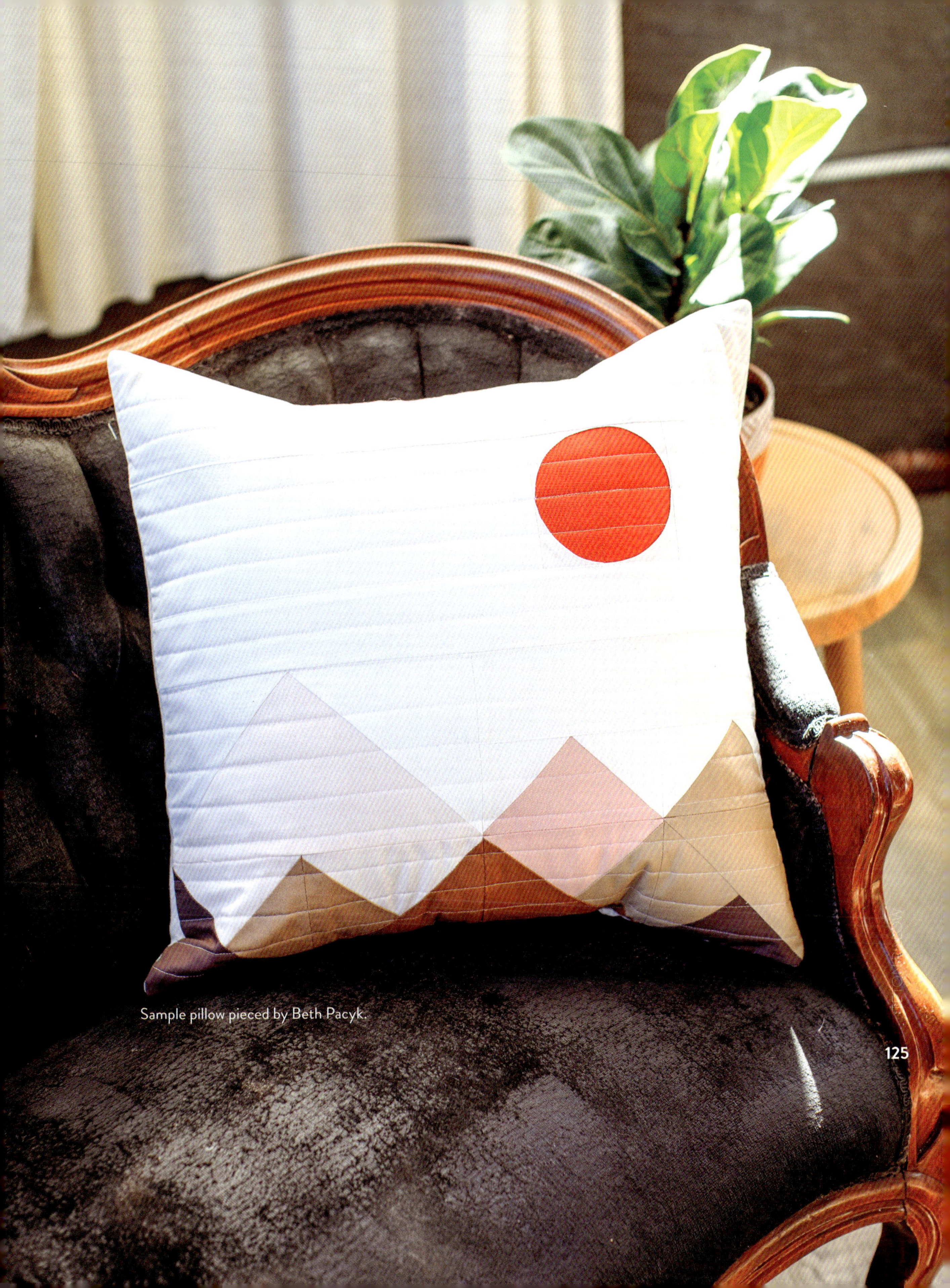

Sample pillow pieced by Beth Pacyk.

Templates

For more on working with the templates, see Using Templates (page 14). To download all full-sized templates used in this book, scan this QR code or go to tinyurl.com/11599-patterns-download.

Enlarge the templates 400%.

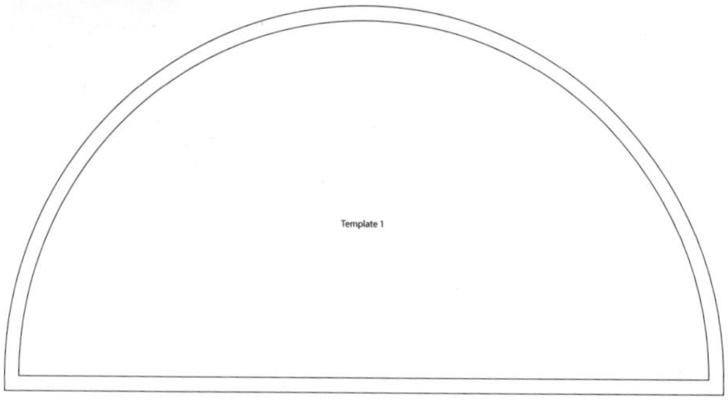

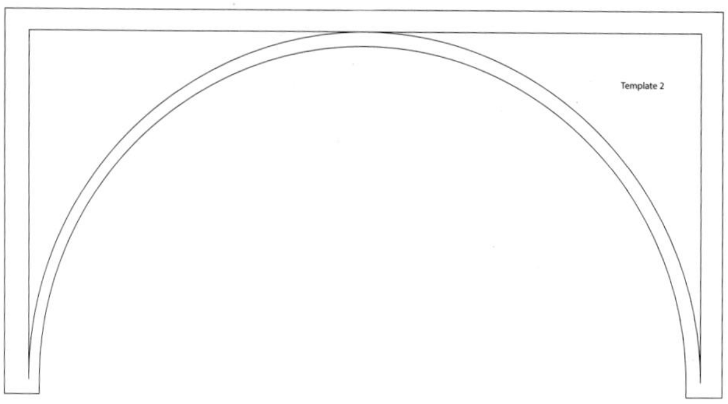

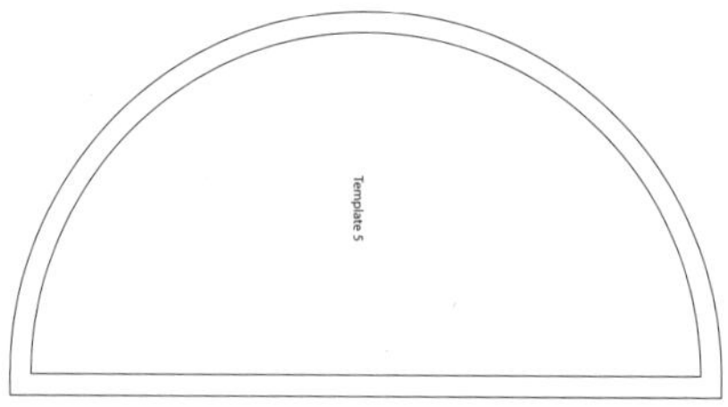

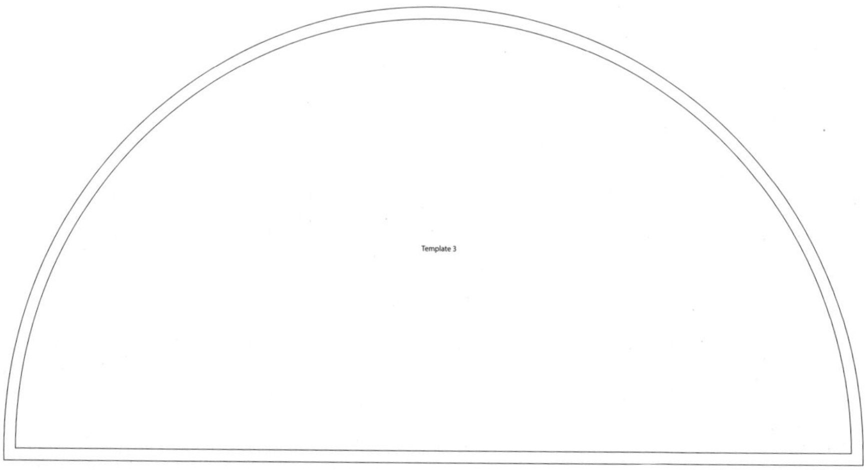

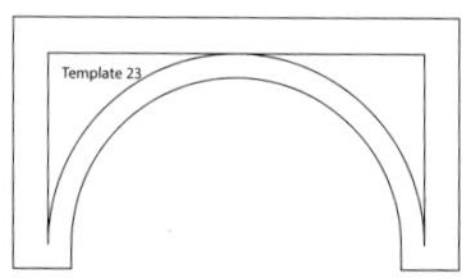

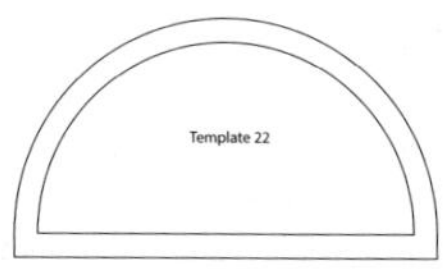

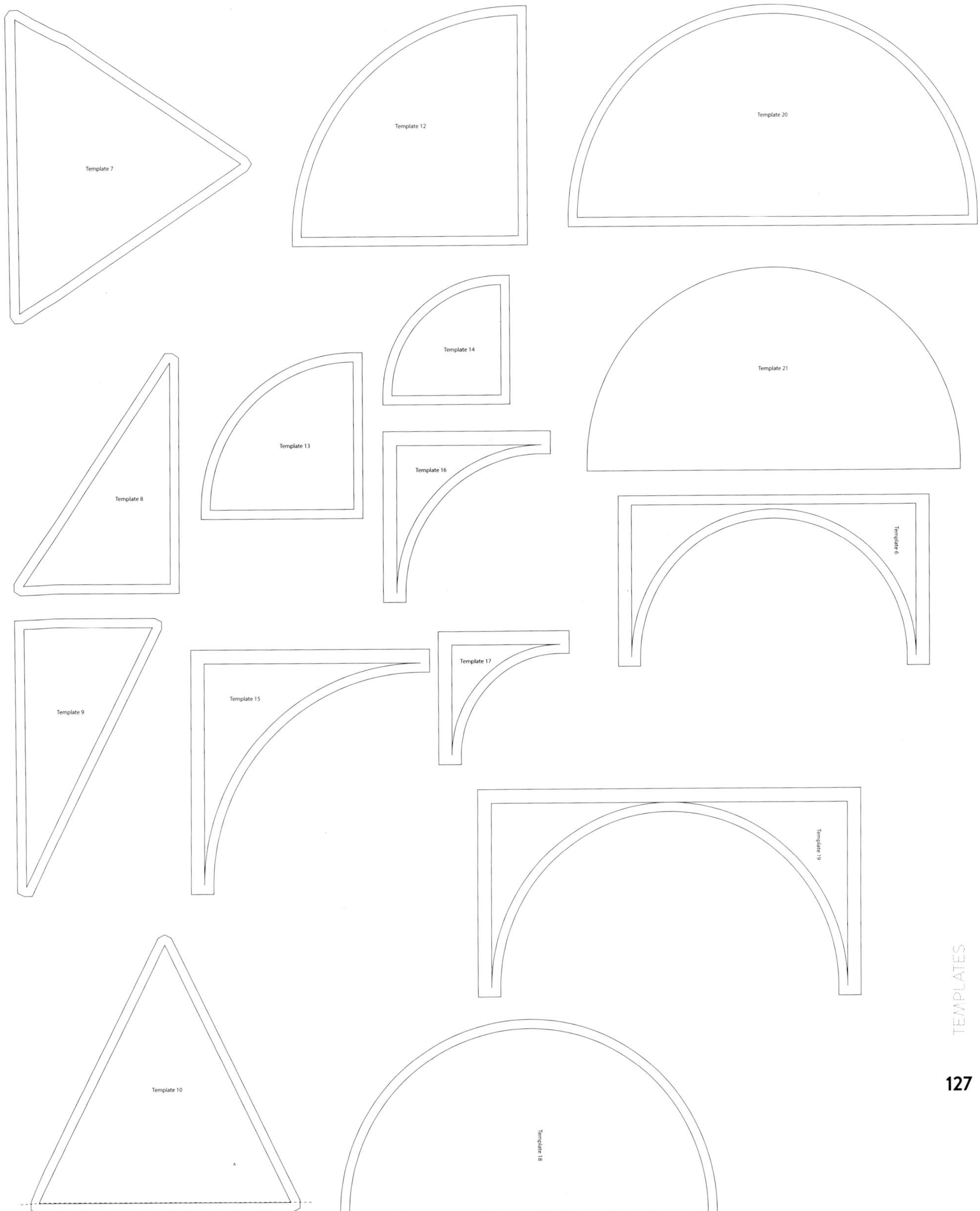

Cut two Template 10 and glue together on the dotted line to create Template 11.

About the Author

Amber Elliot is a modern quilter, pattern designer, and educator. She runs the *Modern Makes Membership*, teaches technique courses and pattern writing, and releases unique modern patterns under the Alderwood Studio brand.

She has been sewing since she was old enough to hold a needle, and quilting for two decades. She currently resides in Portland, Oregon with her family and enjoys finding creative inspiration in the beautiful Pacific Northwest. In her free time she enjoys gardening, knitting, painting, and enjoying her two young children.

Visit Amber online and follow on social media!
Website: alderwood-studio.com   Instagram: @alderwoodstudio   Facebook: /alderwoodstudio
Pinterest: /alderwoodstudio   YouTube: /alderwoodstudio

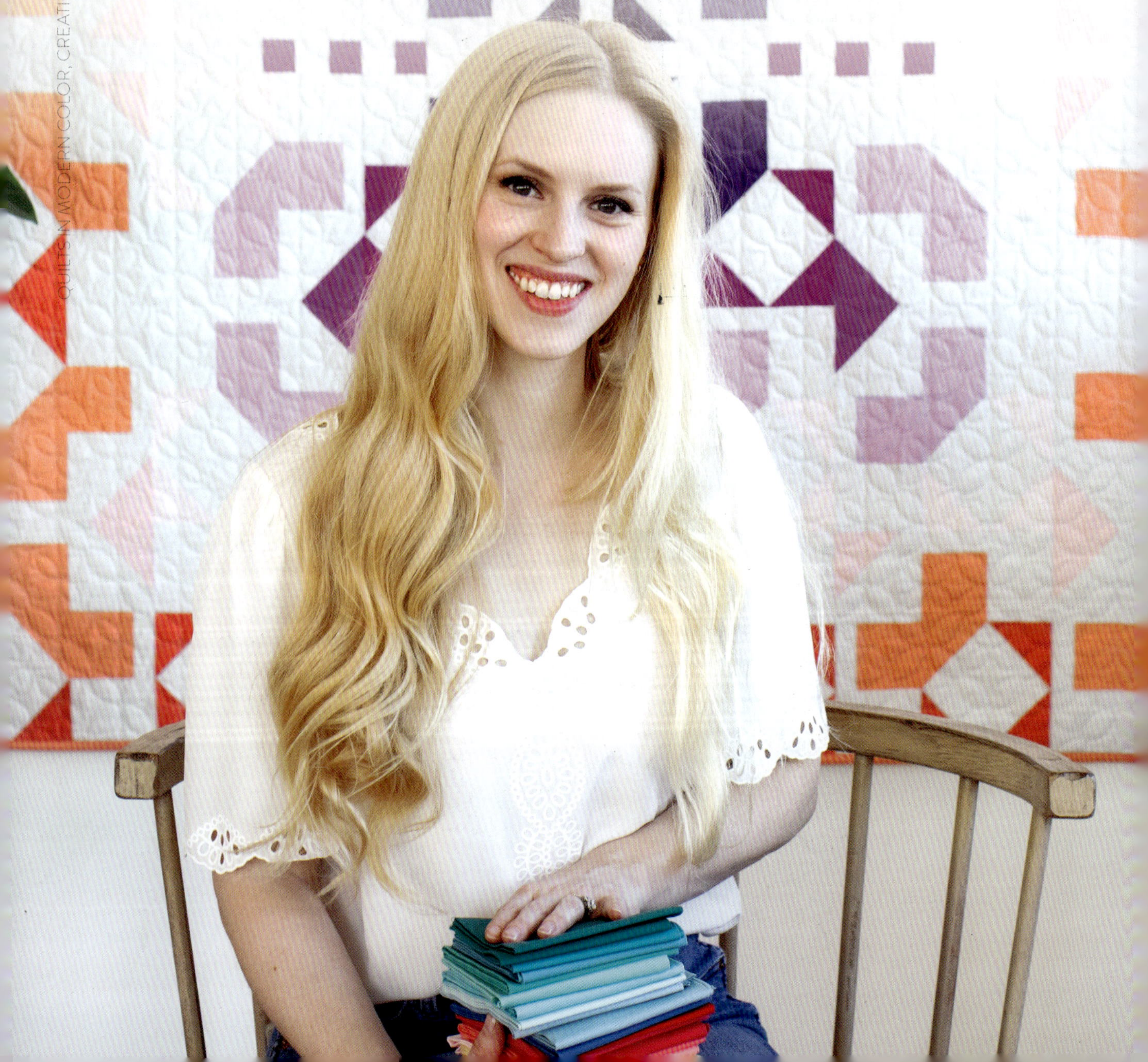